HEIDELBERG
TRANSCULTURAL STUDIES

Edited by

SUSANNE ENDERWITZ

MELANIE TREDE

STEFAN WEINFURTER

Volume 1

Historicizing the “Beyond”

The Mongolian Invasion as a New Dimension of Violence?

Edited by
FRANK KRÄMER
KATHARINA SCHMIDT
JULIKA SINGER

Universitätsverlag
WINTER
Heidelberg

Bibliografische Information der Deutschen Nationalbibliothek

Die Deutsche Nationalbibliothek verzeichnet diese Publikation in der Deutschen Nationalbibliografie; detaillierte bibliografische Daten sind im Internet über *http://dnb.d-nb.de* abrufbar.

UMSCHLAGBILD

Yada Isshô (1858–1913):
Môko shûrai ezu 'Tsushima no sanjô' (The terror of Tsushima), 1909
Oil on canvas, 88 x 131 cm,
Honbutsuji Tempel in Ukiha.

ISBN 978-3-8253-5746-7

Imprimé en Allemagne · Printed in Germany
Druck: Memminger MedienCentrum, 87700 Memmingen

Gedruckt auf umweltfreundlichem, chlorfrei gebleichtem und alterungsbeständigem Papier

Den Verlag erreichen Sie im Internet unter:
www.winter-verlag-hd.de

Contents

STEFAN WEINFURTER

Preface to the Series

One human race – one history? Historical research has begun to pay great attention to this thought during the past years. In the 1990's, questions of methodology with respect to this approach were subjected to intensifying discussions and reflections. At the Historians' Conference in Munich in 1996, Roman Herzog, who was Germany's President at the time, emphatically encouraged his listeners to pursue this approach in his opening address.

From the outset, there was agreement that the history of mankind cannot be coterminous with „world history". A mere stringing together of national or regional studies is not, and cannot be, the aim of writing the history of mankind. Rather, it is the interaction between peoples and their cultures, whether direct or indirect, conscious or subconscious, in all their variations with which we are concerned here. Underlying this framework is the conviction that the flow of the wide-ranging entanglements of ways of human life and configurations of order – understood as a "transcultural flow" in all directions – never comes to an end. For some time, the concept of "global history" has stood for such a perspective.

A question to be asked along these lines would be the following: Must a global history unfold in world-encompassing systems? If so, this approach would only be relevant to a brief period of our history. Hence, it has long been agreed that what concerns us, rather, is the consciousness of the principle of mutual exchange processes as such. In this understanding, attention can also be directed to bounded spaces (as, for instance, the Mediterranean region) or regional fields of research. A stringent delimitation would continue to be problematic, however: According to which criteria should spaces be differentiated from one another? And how is the time frame of investigation to be established? If everything constantly "flows" in history, as it were, methodical comparisons could become questionable, since all boundaries – with respect to space as well as time – would seem arbitrary. How can cultural transfers, then, be identified? Must we direct our attention to extreme cases, i.e. historical situations in which cultures approach and interpenetrate one another, more or less violently or as a result of political decisions? Is it the processes of migration, for instance, that would be of help to us here? Or the storming of the western European world by the Mongols? Here, too, we would hesitate, for it would be necessary to ask to what extent the bearers of such cultures ought to be seen as being homogenous and unchanging. Such a uniformity would contradict the axiom of the constant hybridity of cultures themselves.

Such questions, and many others as well, have been intensely discussed for years, and at Heidelberg University, an especially intensive debate on this approach has been developing around the cluster "Asia and Europe" as well as the program for young scholars, "Transcultural Studies". In numerous projects, the approach of transculturality and of global history is being tried out in cross-disciplinary frameworks. It is wholly in this sense that we consider the series which begins with this volume – as a forum for scholarly discussions on this topic. We hope that a wealth of sound and helpful studies will emerge that can contribute to the advancement of this exceedingly fascinating approach through scholarly debates and criticism.

Frank Krämer, Katharina Schmidt, Julika Singer (Heidelberg)

Introduction

In 1817, the Czech historian Vaclav Hanka published a medieval manuscript that he dated to the 13th century, apparently the oldest document in the Czech language. Overnight, he became the new star of the Czech intellectual elite and a hero in the struggle for the awakening Czech national identity. His stunning medieval discovery consisted, in part, of an interesting piece of poetry about an alleged battle between Czechs and Mongols near the city Olmütz, where the brave general Jaroslaw supposedly defeated the barbarian hordes from the East.[1] Hitherto completely unknown, the battle of Olmütz and the brave hero Jaroslaw became an inherent part of Czech historiography and even of the Czechs` collective memory. As a matter of fact, during their horrible raids in Eastern Europe, the Mongols did also reach Olmütz; unfortunately for the modern Czech patriots, however, they were never beaten by a mysterious Jaroslaw, nor has any other victory against them been recorded. In the end, it became obvious – though not without an enormous amount of research having been necessary – that Hanka had faked the whole manuscript, line by line.[2] His scholarly reputation was ruined, but the myth of the brave citiziens of Olmütz and their general remained alive. How was it possible for an experience of extreme violence to be rediscovered after more than 500 years, albeit in the context of a thorough transformation and reinvention?

During the last decade, an increasing number of historians has thrown a spotlight on the topic of violence. They have chosen a variety of approaches, often using historical anthropology to explain the phenomenon of violence and its impact on human life.[3] Despite its advantages, this approach involves the risk of overgeneralization. For, not only was society in the Middle Ages char-

1 Hanka himself edited the manuscript and published it together with a German translation: *Königinhofer Handschrift. Sammlung altböhmischer lyrisch-epischer Gesaenge nebst andern altböhmischen Gedichten*, ed. Václav Hanka/Václav Alois Svoboda, (Prag 1829).

2 A detailed discussion of the controversy in historic research of the late 19th century is provided by Berthold Bretholz, "Die Tataren in Mähren und die moderne mährische Urkundenfälschung", in *Zeitschrift des Vereins für die Geschichte Mährens und Schlesiens*, 1 (1897), 1-65.

3 A good review of the main research accounts was given by Manuel Braun/Cornelia Herberichs, Gewalt im Mittelalter: Überlegungen zu ihrer Erforschung, in *Gewalt im Mittelalter. Realitäten – Imaginationen*, ed. Manuel Braun/Cornelia Herberichs, (München 2005), 7-38.

acterized by an increasing diversity of the living environment of the various social groups such as citizens, peasants or the nobility; the written sources that allow us to gain an insight into experiences of violence in the first place, particularly their mental dimension, are anything but balanced. Nevertheless, though numbers of victims indicated in the sources often differ and medieval sources tend to exaggeration, medieval Hungary probably lost a large part of its population during the brief occupation by the Mongols in 1241.[4] Eyewitness Rogerius of Torre Maggiore tells us of massacres of unimaginable dimensions in which countless people were slain within a few hours, with the result that huge heaps of corpses polluted water and air for several weeks, as it was impossible to burn them all. Even after a long time, people found half-decayed bodies by the wayside which continued to remind them of the horrible invasion.[5] However, the marks of trauma that these impressions left on the collective consciousness as well as on the individual memory are difficult to identify on the basis of the available sources, which are not only few in number but also greatly colored by topical and stylistic traditions. The picture is further complicated by controversies over the actual significance of violence in the Middle Ages. Recent research on the social meaning of violence within medieval European societies has contradicted the older notions of the unlimited violence of the Middle Ages and of the limitation of violence as a product of modern state formation. Ethnologically oriented studies on topics such as the medieval feud have shown that, already during medieval times, violence was often subjected to a strict system of rules and sequences.[6] At the same time, however, it seems that medieval studies research sometimes consciously tries to prove medieval "progressiveness" and "modernity" in order to be able to disprove the prejudices about the "dark Middle Ages". Thus, at least in the field of violence research, it sometimes happens that the real suffering of individuals becomes less and less visible behind the image of a totally regulated and ritualized use of violence. Even though violence, especially in the court life and within the community of social elites in the High Middle Ages, was extremely limited, certain parts of the medieval society as well as regions at the occidental periphery were left untouched by this system of regulation. During the formatitive phase of their empire, the Mongols attacked in particular the so-called "frontier societies" at the edges of cultural communities, such as

4 A carefully considered estimation is given by Peter Jackson, *The Mongols and the West. 1221-1410*, (Harlow 2005), 68-70.

5 Cf. Rogerius of Torre Maggiore, Carme Miserabile, ed. Ladislaus Juhász, in SRH II, (Budapest 1938), 543-588, here § 30.

6 Cf. Gerd Althoff, Regeln der Gewaltanwendung im Mittelalter, in *Kulturen der Gewalt. Ritualisierung und Symbolisierung von Gewalt in der Geschichte*, ed. Rolf Peter Sieferle, (Frankfurt 1998), 154-170.

the Hungarian kingdom or the Chinese Tangut empire, that were used to transcultural violence as was often committed by nomadic or semi-nomadic societies.[7] Whether this fact may have given rise to a different mentality towards external violence, through a kind of inurement that made the Mongolian invasion appear to be only one of many similar experiences of violence, is a question of central importance. In general, to be sure, many sources from various cultures emphasize the peculiarity of the Mongolian invasion and the dimension of the collective suffering caused by the nomadic invaders. And in the process of its historicization, the experience of the Mongols` attacks became extremely important for national identity formation, as can also be shown in a comparative or transcultural perspective. In view of these circumstances, it is indeed important to ask whether the Mongols' violence reached new dimensions that left even in these "frontier societies" marks of trauma with a long-term impact on their collective consciousness. In Russia, even today, the term "Tatar yoke" has highly emotional undertones that always connote experiences of extreme violence. Historians have often focused more on the material or economic effects of the Mongol destruction than on its mental influence. A combination of sociocultural and individual-psychological viewpoints could offer a fruitful possibility of a new way of understanding. Dealing with the experience of violence is, above all, a psychological process which can be of importance for individuals or whole nations even a long time after the healing of the physical wounds.

For Japan, the Mongolian invasions of 1274 and 1281 were not nearly as cataclysmic as for the affected regions in Eastern Europe and the Middle East since the outcome of the battles was a victorious one for the Japanese. Of the countries that are treated in this conference volume, Japan is the only one that was not conquered by the Mongols, and this led to differences in the ways in which the experience of foreign violence was received and interpreted in later times. Still, the short but violent encounters with the foreign invaders were devastating for the inhabitants as well as the warriors of Northern Kyūshū and was engraved in their memory in the form of legends about frightening demons from abroad and their miraculous defeat.

In a way reminiscent of the example of the Czech historian above, it can be observed that the Japanese remembrance of the Mongolian invasions of 1274 and 1281 was rediscovered and transformed after hundreds of years. And likewise, the cultural memory of the medieval raids had a strong impact on the

7 For a better understanding of such societies and their specific „frontier ideology" in the middle ages, cf. Nora Berend`s case study of 13th century Hungary: *At the gate of Christendom. Jews, Muslims, and "pagans" in medieval Hungary. c.1000- c.1301*, (Cambridge et al. 2001), 163-171.

consolidation of the national consciousness especially at the beginning of the nation-building process in 19th century – a period of great socio-political changes and instability that were accompanied by a loss of traditional moral values. The vast number of visual materials representing the Mongolian invasions that were produced during this turbulent period of Japan's modernization[8] testifies to the enormous interest in national myths that enabled citizens to identify with a strong community and its heroes. Following Michael Jeismann, constructing the image of an enemy could be regarded as constitutive of a national feeling.[9] Hence, representations of the Mongolian invasion were virtually predestined to contribute to the shaping and defining of a collective consciousness of community that distinguishes itself from the violent and evil 'other'.

This pattern also applies, for example, to the picture chosen for the cover illustration of this volume – an oil painting which was part of a narrative series on the Mongolian invasions by the Japanese painter Yada Isshō (1858-1913) dating from 1896.[10] It shows the massacre of Japanese civilians on the island of Tsushima in 1274 rendered in Western oil painting technique that made it possible to convey an almost unbearable realism and a terrifying immediacy. The scene evokes a whole panorama of violence and horror: Mongol warriors act with casual cruelty, slaughtering men, eating their hearts, and piercing the palms of a Japanese woman who still holds her baby; other women are already being dragged along by their hair to the Mongol fleet to be hung up by their hands as living shields while the corpse of another woman lies beneath a fettered and crying toddler.

Such an explicit display of violence and the very asymmetric constellation of power follow a calculated psychological strategy of inflaming the viewer through a kind of *David-versus-Goliath* effect, bringing about a moral appraisal that leads to radically taking sides with the weaker party.[11] The stress

8 A number of examples can be found in the exhibition catalogue *Egakareta rekishi: Kindai Nihon bijutsu ni miru densetsu to shinwa – The Images of History in Japanese Modern Art*, ed. Prefectural Museum of Modern Art, Hyōgo; Prefectural Museum of Modern Art, Kanagawa (Tōkyō: Inshōsha, 1993).

9 Michael Jeismann, *Das Vaterland der Feinde. Studien zum nationalen Feindbegriff und Selbstverständnis in Deutschland und Frankreich 1792-1918* (Stuttgart: Klett-Cotta, 1992).

10 C.f. Judith Fröhlich, "Vom Krieger zu den Kriegerwerten. Die Mongoleneinfälle des 13. Jahrhunderts und deren Umdeutung im 19. Jahrhundert in Japan", in *Zeitschrift der Deutschen Morgenländischen Gesellschaft*, 159/1 (2009): 81-104. And Masanobu Nishimoto, *Yomigaeru Meiji kaiga: Shūfuku sareta Yada Isshō ‚Mōko shūrai ezu'* (Fukuoka: Fukuoka kenritsu bijutsukan, 2005).

11 More on the pictorial strategies of violent conflicts c.f. Godehard Janzing, "Bildstrategien asymmetrischer Gewaltkonflikte", in *Kritische Berichte*, 33/1: Ikonographie der Gewalt (2005), 21-35.

on gender aspects, evident in the image of a barbarous mistreatment of defenceless women, intensifies the hierarchical and bipolar structure.[12] Hence, it is not possible to remain neutral when looking at the image – emotions are whipped up, and the Mongol warriors, stylized as an embodiment of foreign terror and violence, become the symbolic, archetypical object of xenophobia.

Interestingly, and almost paradoxically, not only the naturalistic rendering and the technical methods of oil painting applied in the picture but also its socio-psychological strategies draw their inspirations from a western tradition of painting, namely history painting. Western history painting of the same period gave expression to a historical understanding in which past and present were linked by cyclical dynamics. It did not simply give an account of past events but was also a means of providing useful instruction for the contemporaries and was meant to reveal supposedly timeless truths and values. [13] In the case of Yada Isshō's painting, the reductive representation of the violent acts was meant to create meaning out of violence – it is a monumental warning of a foreign menace that was meant to uphold its validity throughout history.

When Chingiz Khan, probably the best known Mongol, died in 1227 during a retaliation campaign against the Chinese kingdom of the Tanguts, the boundaries of his empire surpassed all dimensions that a Nomadic realm has ever achieved. Suddenly, many Asian and European societies saw themselves confronted with a new and extremely violent enemy that was to have a far-reaching influence on the collective memory of the affected nations in East and West. In the process of its historicizing, the Mongolian invasion became extremely important for national identity formation and for the definition of social affiliation, something which expecially becomes evident in a comparative or transcultural perspective.

In the Middle East, other questions arise from a totally different situation, as the Mongols stayed there for several centuries and established their own dynasty: Does Mongol violence as depicted in the local sources show a quality different from that which is reflected in the historicizing of the invasions in other affected countries? Is there a recognizable 'master narrative' characteriz-

[12] This kind of stress on an assumed natural difference between the sexes, the vulnerable and suffering female as a counterbalance to the fighting male, is an inherent part of traditional traditional Western visual memory. C. f. Silke Wenk: "Sichtbarkeitsverhältnisse: Assymmetrische Kriege and (a)symmetrische Geschlechterbilder", in *Bilderpolitik in Zeiten von Krieg und Terror. Medien, Macht und Geschlechterverhältnisse,* ed. *Linda Hentschel (Berlin: bbooks, 2008), 29-49.*

[13] A very versatile study on the representation of national myths in history painting is given in Stefan Germer, "Retrovision: Die rückblickende Erfindung der Nationen durch die Kunst", in *Mythen der Nationen: Ein europäisches Panorama*, ed. Monika Flacke (München/Berlin: Koehler & Amelang Verlagsgesellschaft mbH/Deutsches Historisches Museum, 1998), 33-52.

ing the various texts, or do their interpretations of the invasion fundamentally diverge from one another? Was the perception of this violent encounter influenced by the invaders themselves?

Ibn al-Athir, one of the most important historians and known for his detailed reports about the crusades, had to surrender and to follow the advice of his friends. From that moment on, he had to report about the catastrophe that was about to be brought in from the East by warriors from the East Asian steppe: the Mongols. In his book *al-kamil fi al-tarikh*[14] Ibn al-Athir states that even he, as an experienced historian, was too horrified and overwhelmed by the incoming news to mention the impending disaster. Thus, he was unwilling to recount the terrifying events. The Muslims' shock must have been especially immense after years of fighting against the crusaders who had threatened the Islam from the West. Now, all of a sudden, a new calamity from the East started to menace the Islam from the opposite direction. Within a few years, the Mongols with their leader Chingiz Khan had become a serious threat to all the regions around the steppes that constituted their realm. To the Muslim community, whose religious center was located in Baghdad, a city that was to be conquered and destroyed later – in 1258 –, the danger appeared to be rather diffuse and far away in the early phases. This might help explain why it took historiographers some time to report on this new and dangerous empire that was in the process of gaining more and more territory and invading one realm after another. In the year 617/1220, Ibn al-Athir could not help breaking his silence to tell about the Tartars, as he calls the Mongols throughout his work. He explicitly informs the reader that his friends had insisted that the time has now come to make the Mongol disaster known in his chronicle.

To Ibn al-Athir, the danger must have appeared dreadful since he wished himself dead or unborn rather than having to be present at this event. He was convinced that no history book that had ever been written contained anything similar. He had never had direct contact with the Mongols, but he was provided with second- and third-hand information about the violent acts in the East. What he reveals in his chronicle is terrifying, especially for a thirteenth-century Muslim who did not know anything about the steppe traditions of the Mongols. He reports that the Mongols not only killed everybody who stood in their way but were also faster than Alexander the Great in conquering the world. Moreover, he adds that they did not know any religion and that they ate animals of all kinds, including dogs and pigs. The most shocking fact for the Muslims must have been that the Mongols did not know the concept of mar-

[14] For an excellent translation of the original Arabic text read: Ibn al-Athir, The years 589-629, 1193-1231. the Ayyubidds after Saladin and the Mongol menace, translated by Donald S. Richards (Aldershot: Ashgate, 2008).

riage, which meant that no father knew who his sons were.[15] These facts lent the new enemies the aura of Gog and Magog, signaling to the readers, in turn, that the end of the world was near. What else could this be but a divine punishment?

After Ibn al-Athir started to speak of the the dire threat coming from the East, numerous other Middle Eastern chroniclers followed his example by writing about the so-called Tartars, whom 'god may curse', as most of them repeat constantly. In their eyes, the Mongols were the embodiment of violence. Detailed descriptions of their strategies and inhuman behavior found their way into the historical accounts, revealing the authors' perception of the Mongols' actions as being extraordinary and extremely vicious. The Mongols became 'the Other', manifestly different in their physical appearance, behavior, and mode of warfare, less civilized and more barbarous. Horror, disgust, and shock in the face of cruelty are conveyed by these accounts, which are aimed at bringing transgressions of morals, ethics and the laws of society to light. Though there also exist several accounts of crusaders' actions in the Holy Land describing a high level of violence, the Mongol violence seemed to have a different quality for the chroniclers. An explanation for this phenomenon may be that the crusaders could be classified by their religion, their behavior and their origins while the Mongols remained, at least in the first decades, foreign and mysterious. In view of the divergent accounts and works of historiography, it is rather difficult to gauge the Mongol violence and the ways in which it was experienced.

In recent years, new research has been done to classify texts that deal with antique and medieval violence with the aim of understanding their messages and gauging the violence conveyed therein. The biggest problem one is confronted with seems to be presented by the various master narratives underlying the texts. And this is an issue in handling Middle Eastern texts that deal with the Mongol conquests as well. Before one can begin to analyze the description of violence in these accounts, therefore, one has to classify the texts and detect their aims. Decoding the implicit messages is a difficult task for the modern reader, but it can help assess whether and to what extent a society experienced the violence of the Mongols differently from violence in general. On the one hand, it is undeniable that the Mongols appeared extremely violent and brutal to the contemporaries of the thirteenth century, which is not surprising since their realm and their power were predominantly based on military violence. On the other hand, however, the Mongols have always been described in the Arabic-Persian texts as human beings, and they became more and more human in their description as time went by. Whereas the chronicler Ibn al-Athir had to

[15] Ibn al-Athir 2008, 204.

rely on second hand information and rumors to write his accounts, later chroniclers were in direct contact with the Mongols, and some of them were even employed by the latter in order to write their history. It is no wonder, then, that the perception of Mongol violence and the image of the Mongols changed in a positive way. To be sure, difficult questions remain: To what extent was the Mongols' violence truly unparalleled, and to what extent did the perceived 'Other-ness' of the Mongols give rise to the impression of their extraordinary cruelty in the first place? Was it intensifying contacts with the Mongols and the concomitant, increasing familiarity with them that humanized their image in the eyes of the conquered? Or was it sheer dependence on the goodwill of the rulers that put chroniclers under pressure to convey a positive image of the Mongols, psychologically aided, perhaps, by an 'identification with the aggressor'?

In the first of the contributions comprising this volume, the historian Juliane Schiel from Zürich investigates two catastrophic events that have been engraved in the Western medieval consciousness, the Mongolian invasion of 1241 and the Ottoman expansion with the fall of Constantinople in 1453. On the basis of Schumpeter`s concept of creative destruction, further developed by the art historian Horst Bredekamp, she analyses Dominican sources such as the reports by the Hungarian friar Julian from 1237 or by the Italian bishop Leonardo Giustiniani of Chios from the 15th century. The abovementioned events represented pivotal moments in the history of the respective orders. The historian Katharina Schmidt characterizes the Mongols in her contribution as "specialists of violence" owing to their particular way of looking at and using violence. The emic and etic perspectives on the Mongol society, as reflected the Secret History, the oldest piece of Mongol literature, and European travelogues such as Ystoria Mongalorum by John of Plano Carpini, respectively, show that the Mongols developed, at Chinggis Khan`s instigation and on the basis of a high level of aggression within their society, a special form of psychological knowledge and highly rational forms of psychological warfare that were largely unknown in Europe at the time. Johannes Gießauf from Graz/Austria provides an overview of the various European sources on the Mongols and of the ways in which the unexpected invasion was explained and integrated into the existing frameworks of interpretation. Stereotypes such as the biblical nations Gog and Magog, harbingers of the apocalypse, helped the Western world understand the extraordinary experience of violence. The American historian Charles Bowlus explains the predatory nomadism in the Carpathian Basin with a focus on the Magyar example from the 9th and 10th centuries and contrasts it with the Mongol nomadism of the 13th century. He emphasizes the logistic advances in nomadic warfare that can be observed in the case of the Mongols and argues that an empire such as the Mongol one would have been out of the reach of earlier nomadic attempts at expansion. Reuven Amitai from Jerusalem turns the spotlight on the recent research on Hülegü's military offensive into Iraq and Northern Syria. He reconsiders the role of the Ilkhanids in the Middle East and sheds light on aspects of the Mongol presence there other than violence. He examines the thesis that all the events which took place under Chingis Khan, Hülegü and Tamerlane were probably conflated into one, with the result that only the negative aspects of their rule remained in the cultural memory. Frank Krämer, a historian of the Middle East from Heidelberg, analyzes the Mongol conquest of Bagdad in 1258. He attempts to reconstruct the events of the years 1253 to 1258 during Hülegü's westward campaign. Arabic accounts of the Middle Ages show that the city was already in decline and partly destroyed before the Mongols arrived. Dr. Judith Fröhlich, a specialist on Japanese history, deals with the ways in which memories of the 13th century Mongol invasions were kept alive in Japan, especially in the southern part of the country where the invasion attempts had taken place. She argues that the contemporaries did not perceive the Mongolian invasions as an event that differed markedly, in terms of its extraordinariness or the threat it represented, from the numerous civil wars which shook the country from time to time. Only through their reinterpretation in the 19th century did the Mongolian invasions gain national significance as a metaphor for the foreign "Other". Jule Nowoitnick, a specialist in Mongol and German literature, investigates in her contribution the historicizing of Chinggis Khan in selected works of popular culture in the 20th century, namely historical novels. She emphasizes that the contemporary perspective on the Mongols has been dominated by two main master narratives: the so-called "Pax Mongolica", on the one hand, and the first Great Khan as a cold and merciless conqueror, on the other. The motif of "Mongol violence" is generally central to Chinggis Khaan`s image in the Western world, according to Nowoitnick, as it serves at once as cause and effect with regard to the way he is perceived. Julika Singer, an art historian with a focus on modern Japanese art and visual culture, analyzes the depictions of the Mongolian invasions in Japanese history textbooks from the late 19th century. She also throws light upon their relationship to other visual media that appeared in government-related contexts such as banknotes and officially endorsed paintings. She points out that the sublimation of violence and the emphasis on the victorious outcome of the Japanese defense against the Mongolian invasions were meant to promote a notion of invincibility and a powerful collective consciousness among the citizens of the young Japanese nation-state.

I. Theories and Strategies of Extraordinary Violence

JULIANE SCHIEL (Zürich)

The Mongol and the Ottoman Threat: A Comparison Between Two Experiences of Violence

Introduction

The Mongol invasions of the 13th century can be counted among the most terrifying and fascinating events in the history of mankind. Within less than fifty years, Genghis Khan, the leader of a small tribal society on the northern border of China under the Jin Dynasty, and his successors set up the largest contiguous empire ever, extending from Manchuria to Eastern Europe and from Siberia to the Hindu Kush and Mesopotamia. In the process, they had defeated powerful empires, devastated major cities and areas, and subjugated entire peoples in East and West to their rule.

The degree of violence and destruction was certainly extraordinary, and the general feeling of uncertainty and chaos that the sudden invasions had provoked was undoubtedly strong. But how can we tell whether the Mongol invasions introduced a new dimension of violence and whether the ravages they had caused were unprecedented? What methods and concepts can historians use to measure the extent of the catastrophe and to describe the event in an adequate way?

Historians have the choice between a materialist and a perceptionalist approach. One can either focus on the hard data concerning physical facts and "neutral" evidence regarding the sequence of conquests, the number of casualties, and the nature of the weapons that were employed etc. Or one can try to reconstruct the subjective experience of violence and destruction by studying the reports of eyewitnesses handed down to us. The materialist approach usually allows more general statements on the overall extent and nature of the event whereas the perceptionalist approach provides insights into personal experiences of contemporaries and into the actual quality of violence and destruction. Of course, the two approaches are not mutually exclusive but complementary. In fact, both may and must be used side by side. Narrative accounts are needed to deepen the materialist results and to fill the hard data with life, while on the other hand statements from eyewitnesses must be counterchecked by archeological findings and other records to test the reliability of the source.

Whether we focus more on the materialist or on the perceptionalist aspect of an event depends mainly on the questions we are asking.

However, neither of the two approaches would lead to clear results without comparison. To ask whether the Mongol invasions introduced a new dimension of violence – as the title of this conference suggests – necessarily means to ask in what ways their conquests were different or extraordinary compared to other events of their kind. This is where I would like to start my reflections on the topic. I will address the question by comparing the Mongol invasions to the Ottoman expansion, and more precisely, to the fall of Constantinople about two hundred years later in 1453. In doing so, I choose a rather perceptionalist approach, assuming that the quality (and not the mere extent) of violence and destruction is best examined by what the anthropologist Clifford Geertz has European called a "thick description" of narrative texts.[1] As a traditional historian of the Middle Ages, I will concentrate on the interpretation of the Mongol and Ottoman conquests as they were seen by the Latin West, and more precisely, by Dominican monks. I will be less concerned here with the concrete acts of violence committed by Mongols or Ottomans during their conquests. Instead, I will focus on the images of violent destruction they imprinted on the minds of the people in the West. But before I turn to the analysis and comparison of Dominican accounts of the foreign invasions, I would like to first make some general methodological remarks.

The Concept of "Creative Destruction"

Both the Mongol invasions of the 13th century and the Ottoman conquest of Constantinople in 1453 were historical events which fundamentally changed the political landscape and power structure of the world system on a macro level.[2] Both provoked dramatic shifts in the world's perception and its interpretation. Their destructive power was extraordinary, as they made things happen which were not thought possible, things which were "un-thinkable", so to speak. Although, in both cases, the Latin West was indirectly rather than directly touched by the actual acts of violence, the invasions shook Western assumptions about the future tide of events to the core and unleashed an unforeseen intellectual potential, as the West attempted to adjust to the new situation.

[1] Clifford Geertz, "Thick Description: Toward an Interpretive Theory of Culture," in *The Interpretation of Cultures: Selected Essays*, ed. Clifford Geertz (New York: Basic Books, 1973), 3-30.

[2] Reuven Amitai and Michal Biran, ed., *Mongols, Turks, and Others. Eurasian Nomads and the Sedentary World* (Brill's Inner Asian Library 11, Leiden/Boston: Brill, 2005), 1-11.

In the case of the Mongol invasions, it was mainly the sudden appearance of the unknown troops from Far East which provoked the exceptional degree of chaos and confusion. Until the first rumors of the new power reached the West, peoples of Latin Europe had no idea about the actual extent of the Asian continent. For them, the terrestrial paradise was located somewhere in remote India, which was thought to represent the end of the world. In their imagination, the "Orient" was mainly inhabited by Christians of different confessions and by Muslims. The crusades had reopened the dialogue between the churches from East and West and raised the hope for a final victory of Christianity over Islam as a sign of the imminent return of Jesus Christ.[3] Neither the Bible nor the old scriptures handed down from Antiquity contained information regarding the existence of a nomadic people living east of India and corresponding to Genghis Khan and his troops, whose appearance took the West by surprise. The Mongol invasions therefore necessitated a re-reading of the written records for the purpose of reconciling tradition and experience and making sense of what had happened.

The defeat of Byzantine Constantinople, in comparison, shocked the minds of the Western peoples because of the symbolic force of the event. Unlike the Mongol invasions, the event was not unexpected, but was rather counted among the unavoidable catastrophes of mankind. In a way, the conquest of Constantinople represented the biggest prophecy fulfilled in history, as Stéphane Yerasimos put it, and this is exactly why the event was so disturbing.[4] Since the days of the first Christians, the Roman Empire had been associated with the last of the four world empires enumerated by the biblical prophet Daniel (Dan. 2; 7). After the fall of Rome, the idea of an *urbs orbis* was transferred to Constantinople, also known as "Rome of the East".[5] Thus, for Chris-

[3] Cf. for example "Burcardi de Monte Sion Descriptio Terrae Sanctae," in *Peregrinatores Medii Aevi Quatuor. Burchardus de Monte Sion. Ricoldus de Monte Crucis. Odoricus de Foro Julii. Wilibandus de Oldenborg. Quorum duos nunc primum edidit duos ad fidem librorum manuscirptorum recensuit*, ed. J. C. M. Laurent (Lipsiae: Hinrichs, 1864), XII,8; Oliver of Paderborn, "Historia Damiatina," in *Die Schriften des Kölner Domscholasters, späteren Bischofs von Paderborn und Kardinalbischofs von S. Sabina Oliverus*, ed. Hermann Hoogeweg (Bibliothek des Literarischen Vereins in Stuttgart 202, Tübingen: Literarischer Verein, 1894), ch. 62-9, p. 264-7; Robert B. C. Huygens, ed., *Lettres de Jacques de Vitry (1160/1170-1240), évêque de Saint-Jean-d'Acre* (Leiden: Brill, 1960), 83-7; 93-7.

[4] Stéphane Yerasimos, "De l'arbre à la pomme: la généalogie d'un thème apocalyptique," in *Les traditions apocalyptiques au tournant de la chute de Constantinople: actes de la table ronde d'Istanbul (13-14 avril 1996)*, ed. Benjamin Lellouch and Stéphane Yerasimos (Varia turcica 33, Paris: L'Harmattan, 2000), 153-92, here: 165.

[5] Mischa Meier, *Das andere Zeitalter Justinians. Kontingenzerfahrung und Kontingenzbewältigung im 6. Jahrhundert n. Chr.* (Hypomnemata. Untersuchungen zur Antike und zu ihrem Nachleben 147, Göttingen: Vandenhoeck & Ruprecht, 2003), 11-22.

tians of the Greco-Roman tradition, the Last Judgment was close when Constantinople fell. So far, however, the Ottomans had not been understood as the apocalyptical people who would announce the end of time. In fact, up to 1453, the Western perception of the Ottomans had been very ambiguous and was dominated by the Latin animosities against Arabs and Greeks.[6] The conquest of Constantinople, therefore, forced Latin Christendom to reconsider its attitude towards the Ottomans.

How can we analyze and describe events that unleash such fundamental shifts in the perception of world and history? How can we describe them better than solely in terms of crisis and change, taking into account as well the intellectual potential delivered by the unexpected turn of events?

The methodological approach I would like to suggest here is based on the principle of "creative destruction" going back to the Austrian economist Joseph Alois Schumpeter. In the 1940s, Schumpeter stated in his analysis of the dynamics of capitalism that the destruction of a functioning system was an integral part of capitalism as it was a necessary condition for creativity and innovation. In his book titled "Capitalism, Socialism and Democracy", he described the economic structure of a capitalist system as a process of mutation permanently revolutionizing its own structure from within by constantly destroying and reinventing itself.[7]

A few years ago, this concept was revived by the art historian Horst Bredekamp in order to serve as a theoretical framework for the humanities, and for cultural studies in particular. In his work on the architectural history of the Basilica of Saint Peter in Rome, Bredekamp was able to show how construction and destruction were closely connected and entangled with each other. New forms could not be thought without the destruction of old ones. Bredekamp therefore claimed that the building history of Saint Peter should no longer be seen as an addition of construction works from different constructors but as repeated negations in the form of destructions.[8]

This theoretical pattern of "creative destruction" proves quite useful for the analysis and description of drastic historical events like the Mongol invasions or the fall of Constantinople, as I would like to demonstrate in this paper. In

[6] Cf. for example eyewitness statements of La Broquière in 1438, or the speech Enea Silvio held in front of Pope Nicolas V, King Ladislav from Hungary and a couple of cardinals in 1452, quoted by Edwin Pears, *The Destruction of the Greek Empire and the Story of the Capture of Constantinople by the Turks* (New York: Greenwood, 1968), 175-6.

[7] Joseph Alois Schumpeter, *Kapitalismus, Sozialismus, Demokratie.* Einführung von K. Seifert, 7. erweiterte Ausgabe (Tübingen/Basel: Francke, 1993), ch. 7, here esp. 137-8.

[8] Horst Bredekamp, *Sankt Peter in Rom und das Prinzip der produktiven Zerstörung. Bau und Abbau von Bramante bis Bernini* (Kleine kulturwissenschaftliche Bibliothek 63, Berlin: K. Wagenbach, 2000), 9.

analogy to Schumpeter's study on capitalism and Bredekamp's work on the Basilica of Saint Peter, the dialectics of destruction and recreation, devastation and reinvention will be shown as inherent characteristics of those events. The Mongol and Ottoman conquests not only destroyed houses and killed people, but they also demolished established systems of thinking and traditional interpretations of the world's history. Both events gave rise to an interpretative vacuum which had to be filled, releasing new creative energy for reinvention and renovation of the world's order. The event and its interpretation are related and intertwined by the dialectics of "creative destruction" and "destructive creativity".

Eyewitnesses of destruction and violence

In order to demonstrate the practical use of this concept for a better understanding of violence and destruction caused by events such as the Mongol invasions and the Ottoman conquest, I compare two eyewitness accounts. Both texts were military reports written by Dominican monks, and both were letters addressed to the pope, head of the Roman Church. One of the authors had seen the direct consequences of violence and destruction; the other had even experienced them himself. One of them, named Julian, was born in 13th century Hungary and brought the first reliable information on the fighting tactics and political goals of the Mongol Golden Horde to the West. The other – his name was Leonardo Giustiniani of Chios – grew up in the Aegean in the 15th century and experienced the siege and conquest of Constantinople as a defender on the side of the Orthodox Greeks. The Order of Preachers to which they adhered counted among the most reliable supporters of the papacy, and its members belonged to the intellectual elite of the Latin West – in mid-13th century as well as two hundred years later.[9]

In a way, the dates of composition of these two letters, 1237 and 1453, may mark the beginning and the end of the great era of the mendicant orders. In 1237, the Order of Saint Dominic was only a bit more than twenty years old, but its convents already numbered three hundred, spreading from Southern France all over Europe as far as Poland, Dacia, Greece, and the Holy Land.

9 Julianus, "Epistola de vita Tartarorum," in Heinrich Dörrie, ed., Drei Texte zur Geschichte der Ungarn und Mongolen. Die Missionsreisen des fr. Julianus O.P. ins Uralgebiet (1234/5) und nach Russland (1237) und der Bericht des Erzbischofs Peter über die Tartaren, in *Nachrichten der Akademie der Wissenschaften in Göttingen. Philologisch-historische Klasse* 6 (1956): 165-82; "Leonardi Chiensis Historia Constantinopolitanae urbis a Mahumete II captae per modum epistolae die 15 Augusti anno 1453 ad Nicolaum V Rom. Pont.," in *Patrologiae cursus completus. Series Graeca* 159, ed. J.-P. Migne (Paris: Migne, 1866), 923-44.

The *Constitutiones*, the legal basis of the Order, had just been completed, remaining effective for the next few hundred years, and the pope was to extend the number of privileges assured to the new monastic orders of the mendicants and to make it a powerful instrument of the Roman Curia. In 1453, the Preachers' brethren still occupied important functions within the Roman Church and dominated the theology and philosophy taught at universities. They had played a crucial role in the negotiations for a Church Union with the representatives of Byzantine Greece and at the Union Council of Ferrara-Florence in 1439. And yet, from that time onwards, the mendicant friars were no longer the catalytic and driving force in Western Europe. The new intellectual elite now became dominated by the humanists from Italy and Greece.[10]

In the following, I will take a closer look at these two authors and their texts in order to compare their ways of describing and dealing with violence and destruction.

Julian of Hungary and the Mongol invasions

When Julian wrote his letter to the pope in 1237, the Dominican Order had become a major player in Hungary. Since their first settlements in 1220/21, the expansionist ambitions of the Hungarian king to make Hungary a stronghold of Western Christendom against the pagan East had converged with Dominican aspirations to combat the dualist heresies in the Balkans and Carpathians. When the Teutonic Order was expelled from Hungary in 1225 and when Béla IV became the new king of Hungary in 1235, Dominican Preachers came to occupy central political and ecclesiastical positions in Hungary and to act as the right hand of the king.[11] At that time, a note in the *Gesta Hungarorum* was

[10] Berthold Altaner, *Die Dominikanermissionen des 13. Jahrhunderts. Forschungen zur Geschichte der kirchlichen Unionen und der Mohammedaner- und Heidenmission des Mittelalters* (Breslauer Studien zur historischen Theologie 3, Habelschwerdt: Frankes Buchhandlung, 1924); Raymond Loenertz, *La Société des Frères Pérégrinants. Etude sur l'Orient dominicain* (Dissertationes Historicae 7, Rom: ad S. Sabinae, 1937); Claudine Delacroix-Besnier, *Les Dominicains et la Chrétienté grecque aux XIVe et XVe siècles* (Rom: Collection de l'Ecole Française de Rome, 1997).

[11] Lászlzó Makkai, "Transformation into a Western-type State. 1196-1301," in *A History of Hungary*, ed. Peter F. Sugar, Péter Hanák and Tibor Frank (Bloomington/Indianapolis: Indiana University Press, 1991), 23-33; Z. J. Kosztolnyik, *Hungary in the Thirteenth Century* (East European Monographs 439, New York: Columbia University Press, 1996); *Erik Fügedi*, "La formation des villes et les ordres mendiants en Hongrie," *Annales: Economies, Sociétés, Civilisations* 25 (1970): 966-87; Nikolaus Pfeiffer, *Die ungarische Dominikanerprovinz von ihrer Gründung 1221 bis zur Tatarenverwüstung 1241-1242* (Zürich: Verlag von Gebr. Leemann & Co, 1913).

discovered stating that the Christian Hungarians stemmed from pagan nomads living near the Volga, speaking the same language and still awaiting religious conversion and political reunification.[12]

No better pretext could have been found to strengthen the existing convergences between the Hungarian royalty and the Dominican Order, and Julian of Hungary was sent twice to the region named in the chronicle in order that the pagan ancestors might be found and the Holy Gospel and Hungarian rule brought to them. With regard to Julian's first visit, probably in 1234/35, it is reported that he actually found pagan people who spoke Hungarian and that he went back to explain to his compatriots how to find them.[13] When he tried to visit the same region the next time in 1237, however, he was prevented from doing so, the Mongol invasions having devastated most of the places he had visited and described the first time.

The letter he wrote to the pope after his precipitous return was no longer concerned with the expansionist ambitions of the Hungarian king and the Dominican Order but with the extraordinary quality of violence and destruction he had witnessed. The whole text reflects the ambiguity and dialectics between chaos and rearrangement as well as between demolition and reinvention unleashed by the events.

Thus, Julian began his report with a tale on the provenance of the Mongols.[14] Before relating the unheard news of the desolation of Central Asia and Eastern Europe, he first of all sought to give them a place in the history of mankind. By asserting that the Mongols descended from the biblical Ismail and that Genghis Khan, here called Gurgutam; had started his conquests as a local campaign of revenge for the sake of the wooed Amazon, he assigned them an origin and an initial motive for their invasions, and thereby attempted to "normalize" the Mongol invasions from the Christian historical perspective of his time.[15]

[12] The *Gesta Hungarorum* is known to be the first written record of the history of Hungary handed down to us, probably written by a former notary of Béla IV., cf. [Anonymus (Belae Regis Notarius)], *Die "Gesta Hungarorum" des anonymen Notars: die älteste Darstellung der ungarischen Geschichte*, ed. Gabriel Silagi (Ungarns Geschichtsschreiber 4, Sigmaringen: Thorbecke, 1991).

[13] The information which Julian brought back from his first mission was written down by one of his confrere, Riccardo. Cf. Riccardus, "De facto Ungarie magne," in Heinrich Dörrie, ed., Drei Texte zur Geschichte der Ungarn und Mongolen. Die Missionsreisen des fr. Julianus O.P. ins Uralgebiet (1234/5) und nach Russland (1237) und der Bericht des Erzbischofs Peter über die Tartaren, in *Nachrichten der Akademie der Wissenschaften in Göttingen. Philologisch-historische Klasse* 6 (1956): 151-61.

[14] Julianus, "Epistola de vita Tartarorum," cf. footnote 9, here: I,1-29.

[15] How important it was to attribute to each people a provenance and a place within the Christian *ordo* has recently been outlined by: Marina Münkler, "Die Wörter und die Fremden: Die

He then went on to list the Mongol conquests since 1218. Although his narration of the military facts proves to be quite a reliable one, Julian added to his report information that fundamentally contradicted his initial attempt at "normalization". Namely, he reported that Genghis Khan soon started to believe that he had been chosen by God to submit the entire world to his rule.[16] This information must have been most disturbing to Christian readers in the West, as they expected apocalyptical peoples called Gog and Magog, mentioned in the Old Testament, to come from the Far Northeast to announce the end of time by conquering and devastating the whole world. Yet, Julian did not explicitly link the Mongolians' professed godly mandate to the historical tradition. His report thus evoked disquieting associations without bringing clarification.

When, at the end of his list of Mongol conquests, Julian came to describe the most recent devastations he had witnessed himself, he quoted a letter from the leader of the Golden Horde addressed to the Hungarian king. In this letter, the Mongol prince repeated his self-conception of his rule and required the unconditioned surrender of the Hungarian king if he wanted to escape death and destruction.[17] Again, Julian was unable to interpret the document and to give it a clear meaning. He quoted the letter in direct speech, and instead of commenting it, he concluded his report with a long and most disparate list of information of greater and lesser import on diverging tales of provenance, the composition of the Mongol army and the nature and character of Mongol women.[18]

monströsen Völker und ihre Lesarten im Mittelalter," in *Hybride Kulturen im mittelalterlichen Europa. Vorträge und Workshops einer internationalen Frühlingsschule*, ed. Michael Borgolte and Bernd Schneidmüller (Europa im Mittelalter; Berlin: Akademieverlag, 2009), in print; on the topic of origins and provenance cf. also: Kordula Wolf, *Troja – Metamorphosen eines Mythos. Französische, englische und italienische Überlieferungen des 12. Jahrhunderts im Vergleich* (Europa im Mittelalter 13, Berlin: Akademie Verlag, 2009).

16 Julianus, "Epistola de vita Tartarorum," cf. footnote 9, here: I,32: *Ex his audacior effectus et fortiorem se reputans omnibus super terram, progressum cepit facere contra regna totum mundum sibi subiugare proponens.*

17 Julianus, "Epistola de vita Tartarorum," cf. footnote 9, here: IV,9-16: *Ego, Chayn, nuntius regis celestis, cui dedit potentiam super terram subicientes mihi se exaltare et deprimere adversantes, miror de te, rex Ungarie, quod cum miserim ad te iam tricesima vice legatos, quare ad me nullum remittis ex eidsdem; sed nec nuntios tuos vel litteras mihi remittis. Scio quod rex dives es et potens, et multos sub te habes milites, solusque gubernas magnum regnum. Ideoque difficile sponte tua te mihi subicis; melius tamen tibi esset et salubrius, si te subiceres sponte mihi! Intellexi insuper quod Cumanos servos meos sub tua protectione detineas. Unde mando tibi quod eos de cetero apud te non teneas, et me adversarium non habeas propter ipsos! Facilius est enim eis evadere quam tibi, quia illi sine domibus cum tentoriis ambulantes possunt forsitan evadere. Tu autem in domibus habitans, habens castra et civitates, qualiter effugiens manus meas?*

18 Julianus, "Epistola de vita Tartarorum," cf. footnote 9, here: V,1-VI,7.

Only once did he interrupt this enumeration of minor details to state that this news might prove how close the scourge of God (*flagellum Dei*) was and that people needed to prepare for the end of time.[19]

The unexpected confrontation with the Mongol invasions had provoked a sentiment of confusion and uncertainty. Obviously, Julian did not dare to put the information he had collected together into a coherent and unified interpretation of the event. He refused to give a definite meaning to what had happened. At the same time, his collection of diverse information and explanations opened new fields and unleashed new potential for a reorganization and reinvention of the world order. If the Mongols descended from Ismail, perhaps the Mongols, and not the Muslims, were the great antagonists of Christianity? If the protagonists of the first Mongol upheaval had disquieting names such as Gurgutam and Gureg and believed that they acted on godly instruction in devastating the whole world, perhaps their names were linguistic variations of the well-known Gog and Magog who were expected to escape one day from the remote Caucasus region and to bring about the end of mankind? Might it be that the unknown invaders from the East were not only sent to mete out punishment but also to announce the arrival of the Last Judgment? Many "maybes", many hypotheses appeared with the potential to reopen the Western view of world history. Julian gave no definitive answers, but his carefully placed question marks were able to initiate a process of reinvention and recreation.

Leonardo Giustiniani of Chios and the Ottoman conquest of Constantinople

About two hundred years later, another Dominican monk, Leonardo Giustiniani of Chios, cried out in horror at the acts of violence and destruction he had witnessed during the Ottoman siege and conquest of Constantinople. The date of 1453 not only signified the loss of the capital of the Byzantine Empire. It also destroyed the fragile equilibrium of the politically fragmented region of the Eastern Mediterranean. Since the Latin conquest of Constantinople in 1204, changing alliances and unstable regimes had characterized the Aegean, the region where Leonardo was born and raised. Numerous actors from Greece, Italy, Spain and France were engaged in the area searching for influence and power.[20] The political relations and cultural entanglements between Latins and Greeks varied from place to place, and the identities of the inhabi-

[19] Julianus, "Epistola de vita Tartarorum," cf. footnote 9, here: V,9: *Ceterum cum tale Dei flagellum adveniat et adproximet ad filios Ecclesie sponse Christi, quid super his agendum quidque faciendum sit, Vestre Sanctitatis discretio dignetur sollicite providere.*

[20] Peter Lock, *The Franks in the Aegean, 1204-1500* (London/New York: Longman, 1995).

tants of the Aegean were as manifold as the political situation itself. The Order of Preachers had to adjust to this peculiar situation, and it did so by forming alliances with local authorities, especially with Genoa and its colonies in the Eastern Mediterranean. Indeed, Dominican activities converged more and more with those of the Italian sea power. Thus, Dominican settlements in Greece and the Aegean were particularly important in the Genoese strongholds in former Byzantine territories, and alliances and hostilities of the Genoese governments influenced Dominican attitudes towards and relations with other players in the region.[21]

Hardly any personality better demonstrates the complex system of fragmentation and entanglement in the late medieval Aegean than Leonardo Giustiniani of Chios. Genoese by parentage, Aegean by provenance and Dominican by vocation, Leonardo was a border crosser between different spheres and a prototype of the hybrid culture of Eastern Mediterranean. He behaved as a churchman defending the interests of the Roman Curia in the Eastern Mediterranean, and at the same time, he acted as a diplomat serving the Gattilusj, the local dynasty of Lesbos, and representing their interests in the West. He was a theologian as much as he was a humanist. In his function as Archbishop of Mitylene and the inquisitor of the Eastern provinces of his Order, he cracked down on the Orthodox Greeks who were unwilling to submit to the Roman faith. In addition, he spoke Greek fluently and brought Byzantine philosophy to Italy.[22]

When Mehmed II decided to attack Constantinople, Leonardo, together with Cardinal Isidor from Kiev, resided in the Byzantine capital, seeking to put the decision of the Union Council from Ferrara-Florence into practice. His report of the conquest was not the first to bring the disturbing news to the West, but it was the most detailed and was copied and recopied by churchmen and humanists alike, in Latin, Greek and the vernacular.[23]

As in the reports of the Hungarian monk Julian, the descriptions and explanations given by the eyewitness were most contradictory, reflecting the degree of chaos and confusion caused by the turn of events. Thus, characteristics attributed to the respective camps and protagonists were not clear and uniform but multiple and often inconsistent. Even the author himself appeared in different roles, giving the "us" a different meaning according to the specific context:

[21] Claudine Delacroix-Besnier, *Les Dominicains et la Chrétienté grecque aux XIVe et XVe siècles* (Rom: Collection de l'Ecole Française de Rome, 1997), ch. 3.

[22] Marios Philippides, "The Fall of Constantinople 1453: Bishop Leonardo Giustiniani and his Italian Followers," *Viator. Medieval Renaissance Studies* 29 (1998), 189-225.

[23] Marios Philippides, "The Fall of Constantinople 1453," cf. footnote 22, here esp. 210; G. Moravcsik, "Bericht des Leonardus Chiensis über den Fall von Konstantinopel in einer vulgärgriechischen Quelle," *Byzantinische Zeitschrift* 44 (1951), 428-36.

sometimes he saw himself as belonging to the Latins from the Aegean, and sometimes to the Latins from the West; most of the time, however, he regarded himself as a citizen of Constantinople – whether Greek or Latin. Furthermore, his characterizations of the Ottomans, the Greeks and the Latins changed constantly within the text. Most of the time, the Ottomans appeared as the military opponents whereas the Greeks were described as the major moral adversary. Mehmed and his troops were said to be very professional in warfare[24], though cruel and barbarous in their behavior towards their enemies[25], but at the same time they were characterized as being anxious and fearful.[26] On the one hand, their tactics and techniques equaled or even exceeded the deeds of the great warriors of the past, as the various classical comparisons integrated into his report suggest.[27] On the other hand, their victory was exclusively due to their numerical advantage and the knowledge they had received from Christian converts.[28] The orthodox Greeks, on the contrary, were criticized for their obstinacy in the affair of the Church Union,[29] and they were said to turn a deaf ear

[24] Cf. for example "Leonardi Chiensis Historia Constantinopolitanae urbis," cf. footnote 9, here: 928D: *Lignis instrumentisque advectis solerti cura, uti imperatum, actum est, ut mox per cuniculos tentarent fundamenta suffodere penetrareque omnifarium urbis murum.*

[25] "Leonardi Chiensis Historia Constantinopolitanae urbis," cf. footnote 9, here: 933B; and esp. 941D–942B, where Leonardo describes the pillage of the city, the desecration of Hagia Sophia and the destruction of its holy relics: *Concite igitur omnes pedites decurrunt, quosque resistentes gladio feriunt, imbeciles, decrepitos, leprosos atque infirmos trucidant. Obsequentibus viam parcunt. Sanctissimae Sophiae admirandum templum, quod nec Salomonis aequat, profane atque infidi ingredientes, nullam sacris aris reverentiam neque sanctis imaginibus habent, quin potius exterminant, oculos sanctorum suffodiant, sanctorum quoque reliquias vel dilacerant, vel dispergunt sacrilegae manus; mox sancta Dei vasa usurpant, argentums aurumque tam sanctarum imaginum, quam vasorum sacrorum, sacculis inferciunt. Fit clamor et ululatus ad coelum; omnis sexus, homo omnis, omne aurum, omne aes, omnis supellex, omnisque urbis substantia in praedam vertitur. Securibus scrinia scindunt; fundos perfodiunt pro thesauris; qui tanti reperiuntur, et novi, et veteres, ut nulla sit urbs a saeculo quae tantis affluat, et hi omnes absconditi in manus eorum pervenerunt.*

[26] "Leonardi Chiensis Historia Constantinopolitanae urbis," cf. footnote 9, here: 937A: *Etenim quanquam maximus numerus esset, quanquam infinitis sagittis machinassent urbem, utpote ad muros invadendos timidi, vecordes, victoriam diffidebant.*

[27] "Leonardi Chiensis Historia Constantinopolitanae urbis," cf. footnote 9, here: 927C: *Tantum eorum ordinem instruendis machinis, tantam promptitudinem, tantam acierum providentiam quidam aut Scipio, aut Annibal, aut moderni belli duces admirati fuissent*; ibid., 929A: *Crates deinde innumeras ex virgultis viminibusque contextas, cattos oblongos scalasque rotatas, curarus castellatos taliaque machinamenta, quae vix Romani adversus Poenos construxissent*; cf. also: ibid., 931A; 937D.

[28] "Leonardi Chiensis Historia Constantinopolitanae urbis," cf. footnote 9, here: 928B; 933D–934A; 927B; 930D.

[29] "Leonardi Chiensis Historia Constantinopolitanae urbis," cf. footnote 9, here: 927B: *Non ergo unio facta, sed unio ficta, ad fatale urbem trahebat excidium; quo divinam iram maturatam in hosce dies venisse cognovimus*; cf. also: ibid., 926A–B; 929D–930B.

to prophecies and warnings calling for retreat.[30] They were described as selfish and avaricious traitors of the homeland, refusing to pay their duties and taxes for the fortification of the city walls[31], and they were said to be weak, anxious and stupid in their defense of the Byzantine capital.[32] The Latins from the East and the West, finally, were presented as the real heroes of the battle[33]; but at the same time, they were chastised for their refusal to lend support to the Greeks, their incapacities and their failures, while the author conjured up the good old times of the First Crusades.[34]

Like the changing attributions, the answers to the question of who was to be held responsible for the disaster varied throughout the text as well. Here, a twofold structure of the account becomes apparent. Leonardo's text comprised not only a military report of the Ottoman conquest in 1453 but also moral reflections on the failure of the Church Union of 1439; that is, the text contained a military and a moral dimension. The first, oriented on the actual course of events, was concerned with the strategic mistakes committed by Latins and Greeks alike which led to the final defeat of Constantinople in 1453.[35] The second, lying underneath the first, listed the reasons for Leonardo's own failure in implementing the Church Union with the Greeks of Constantinople and accused the members of the Orthodox Church of being faithless and untrust-

30 "Leonardi Chiensis Historia Constantinopolitanae urbis," cf. footnote 9, here: 926C: *Annon summi Dei nuntii (o Graeci!) vestram perditionem jugiter praedixerunt? Qui aures, ut aspis, impie obturastis, et sanctam Ecclesiam catholicam matrem fidelium obaudistis.*

31 "Leonardi Chiensis Historia Constantinopolitanae urbis," cf. footnote 9, here: 934A; 942A–B.

32 "Leonardi Chiensis Historia Constantinopolitanae urbis," cf. footnote 9, here: 935B–C; 936D; 943B.

33 Cf. for example "Leonardi Chiensis Historia Constantinopolitanae urbis," cf. footnote 9, here: 929B: *Itaque Teucrus demolitum, quam primum restauratum ut conspexit murum: Non Graecorum, inquit, sed Francorum hoc ingenium est, ut tanta resistentia fiat, tanta pugna: quos nec innumerae sagittae, nec machinarum ligneorumque castrorum horror, nec intermissa obsessio deterret.*

34 "Leonardi Chiensis Historia Constantinopolitanae urbis," cf. footnote 9, here: 929C–D: *O Genuenses jam quodammodo cicurati (…). Ubi sunt prisci inclyti Genuenses, qui Galatam, accincti gladio, uti qui reparabant Hierosolymam, condiderunt? Illi cum effuso cruore et aere; vos ne aes vestrum cupidi et sanguinem effunderetis, cum vecordia illam mundo decoram Teucro tradidistis, si tamen tradere potuistis.*

35 Leonardus detected five military causes for the downfall of Constantinople: First, the West, especially Genoa and Venice, did not send sufficient and timely support whereas Pera pretended neutrality. Second, the Byzantine Emperor failed to call for more discipline within the Christian army. Third, the Greek population of Constantinople refused to pay extra taxes for the fortification of the city walls. Fourth, Manuel Jagarus and Neophytus had misappropriated public money allocated for the defence of the city. And finally, Giovanni Giustiniani, who was in command during the final defensive battle, provoked the collapse by his precipitated retreat after a minor injury. Cf. "Leonardi Chiensis Historia Constantinopolitanae urbis," cf. footnote 9, here: 935D; 936C; 940C–941B.

worthy. In Leonardo's view, their false behavior towards Rome had incurred the wrath of God, and the loss of Constantinople appeared to him to be the just punishment for their sins.[36]

Obviously, Leonardo was unable to resolve the conceptual chaos that the event had brought about in his head. The coexistence of the two plots, the military and the moral one, reveals disorder and destruction. The disaster of 1453 had fundamentally shaken his personal and professional environment. The boundaries between the good and the bad, between the Self and the Other had become blurred and had to be redefined. But at the same time, his report contains starting points for a reorganization of the overall setting in the Eastern Mediterranean and of the self-perception of the Latin West. His causal linkage of the two events, the failed Church Union in 1439 and the fall of Constantinople in 1453, opened the field for a new vision of the world. The fragile and flexible world order of the multicultural Aegean had been demolished, and the conception of a universal and united Christianity under the aegis of Rome had collapsed. The answer suggested in Leonardo's report, though he did not give it full treatment, was segregation and self-restriction. The Latins had to concentrate on themselves; they were the survivors chosen to become the new and only bastion of Christendom against a powerful and ever-growing world of infidels.

"Creative Destruction" and "Destructive Creativity" – Dominican accounts in comparison

What can we learn from the comparative study of eyewitness accounts on two different far-reaching events?

First, both letters reflect the dialectics of "creative destruction" and "destructive creativity". They both contain destruction and disorientation as well as a new potential for creativity and reinvention.

[36] Cf. for example "Leonardi Chiensis Historia Constantinopolitanae urbis," cf. footnote 9, here 926B: *Non haec causa est, quod unionem, sed quod unionem non veram, sed fictam fecistis. Hac de re merito indignatum Deum: hac de re justa animadversione in hostium manus vos esse deductos*; ibid., 926C: *Idcirco non mirum si in poenam tanti criminis insperata mox tempestas invaluit; quam Spiritu sancto docti quoque a multis annis futuram esse praedixerant*; ibid., 927B: *Non ergo unio facta, sed unio ficta, ad fatale urbem trahebat excidium; quo divinam iram maturatam in hosece dies venisse cognovimus*; ibid., 929D: *Vide, beatissime Pater, quam dignum, quam rectum judicium! Celebrarunt unionem Graeci voce, sed opere negabant*; ibid., 943B: *Et qui unionem fidei comtempserunt, jam quoque dispersi in unum peccati poena convenire non possunt.* Also cf. ibid., 926A; 930A–B; 934A; 935B–C; 936D; 942A–B.

Second, for both authors a meticulous account of anything that could be of interest formed a first step in coping with the events. Thus, open contradictions were not dissolved but left to stand side by side within the text. Although both looked for explanations and tried to interpret what had happened, neither attempt led to a clear statement or a coherent interpretation. Information, not explanation, was given priority.

Third, if we compare the letters studied in this paper with other Dominican descriptions of the Mongol invasions or of the Ottoman conquest, another observation can be made. Eyewitness accounts tend to differ from second-hand reports in that, in most cases, persons who were present at an event seek to collect information whereas copyists and second-hand chroniclers tend to look for coherent explanations. Eyewitnesses often concentrate on facts and the actual course of events, recorders on their meanings. Accounts like the ones written by Julian and Leonardo often contain contradictory and incoherent elements, whereas second-hand reports tend to make things clear and well-defined. Where eyewitnesses express a series of "maybes" and question marks, second-hand chroniclers look for answers.

Two examples may illustrate the argument. The French Dominican Vincent of Beauvais updated the first version of his famous world chronicle, the *Speculum historiale*, by the end of the 1240s by adding three more *libros* mainly dealing with the current Mongol threat.[37] His history of the Mongols was based on two mendicant eyewitness accounts, the *Historia Tartarorum* of the Dominican monk Simon of Saint-Quentin and the *Historia Mongalorum* of the Franciscan friar John of Plan Carpini. Vincent of Beauvais was a very diligent copyist, but where the two accounts deviated from each other, the French chronicler chose to streamline the story.[38]

By the middle of the fifteenth century, the Spanish Dominican John of Torquemada, cardinal in Rome and a personal adviser to Pope Pius II, composed a treatise on the Turks in reaction to the fall of Constantinople and in

[37] Vincentius Bellovacensis, "Speculum historiale," in *Vincentius Bellovacensis, Speculum quadruplex sive Speculum maius. T. 4.* (Douai 1624. Reprint Graz: Akademische Druck- und Verlagsanstalt, 1965), XXIX-XXXI.

[38] Thus, Simon of Saint-Quentin describes the Hungarian defeat against the Mongols in 1241 as an important apocalyptic event announcing the Last Judgement, whereas John of Plan Carpini characterises it simply as God's punishment. Vincent, in his chronicle, eliminates the Franciscan interpretation and elaborates the apocalyptic view on the event. Vincentius Bellovacensis, "Speculum historiale," cf. footnote 37, here: XXX,149, in comparison to: Johannes von Piano Carpine, "Historia Mongalorum," in *Die Mongolengeschichte des Johannes von Piano Carpine. Einführung, Text, Übersetzung, Kommentar*, ed. Johannes Gießauf (Schriftenreihe des Instituts für Geschichte 6, Graz: Selbstverlag des Instituts für Geschichte der Karl-Franzens-Universität, 1995), 86-123, here: prologue 2.

preparation for the congress of Mantua.[39] Instead of dealing with the current military threat and the chaos and destruction the events had caused, John of Torquemada furnished an intellectual examination of the political and theological background of the conquerors. The Spanish cardinal tried to cope with the Ottoman threat by falling into line with the traditional historical and religious narrative, leaving the disturbing eyewitness accounts aside.

In terms of Schumpeter's concept outlined at the beginning of this paper, we may say that the actual degree of "creative destruction" is most likely to be discerned in eyewitness accounts such as the ones by Julian and Leonardo whereas the potential of "destructive creativity" can better be studied in second-hand reports such as chronicles and treatises. Eyewitnesses furnish the materials for a creative reinvention of the world's order, and their readers and receivers take those bricks and try to give them shape.

Fourth, in spite of the similarities between Julian's and Leonardo's ways of meeting the challenge, the two texts also reflect the different conditions of the Dominican Order in 1237 and 1453, respectively. In the first half of the 13th century, Dominicans reinvented the world around them. Unforeseen catastrophes gave them an initial impetus for change and multiplied their creative potential. In the middle of the 15th century, Dominicans witnessed the gradual collapse of their former positions in- and outside Europe. The fall of Constantinople was truly a catastrophe for the Dominican Order. Rather than seeking new forms to cope with the challenges of their time, however, they propagated resolution and persistency in defending their prestigious position within Western society. Thus, Julian helped to broaden the horizon of the Latins and push their frontiers further east while Leonardo called the people in the West to return to clear demarcations, to defend their heritage and to concentrate on their own universe, the European perspective.

My fifth and last point concerns the question raised in this workshop: the dimension of violence and destruction of the Mongol invasions. Obviously, no general conclusions can be made from the two accounts studied in this paper. For Julian, the specific quality of violence and destruction lay in the mere existence of the Mongols from the Far East forcing an extension of the Latin world map and in the Mongol's self-appointment as the world's emperor. For Leonardo, it was the simple fact that Constantinople actually fell into the hands of the infidels which was the most disturbing. Both, however, were less interested in the concrete acts of violence committed by the foreign invaders than in the meaning underneath the overall events. The description of violence did not contribute to a better understanding of what had happened, and neither Julian

39 Ioannes de Turrecremata, "Tractatus contra principales errores perfidi Machometi et Turcorum," Brussels 1475-80 (Copinger 5259).

nor Leonardo used their account of violent acts to enhance the degree of catastrophe experienced.

Here again, a comparison with second-hand reports proves useful. In most of the texts I know, eyewitness accounts are characterized by a relatively dry and unemotional style of portraying violence and destruction. Facts are listed instead of emotions being described. In contrast, second-hand accounts tend to strengthen the violent character of the events and often embellish the descriptions with brutal details.

Once more, two examples may demonstrate the argument. Vincent of Beauvais, the French chronicler already mentioned, not only disambiguated contradicting and confusing elements of the eyewitness accounts, he also systematically opted for the most brutal description he found. When Simon of Saint-Quentin and John of Plan Carpini reported the same battle or the same event with different intensity, Vincent of Beauvais adopted the version which portrayed the Mongols as violent and unscrupulous savages.[40]

In the middle of the 15th century, the Italian Dominican Jacob of Campora came to speak in front of Emperor Frederick III and King Ladislav from Hungary and gave them a vivid account of the Ottoman conquest of Constantinople in an attempt to persuade them to lead a crusade against the Turks.[41] Jacob of Campora had been bishop of Caffa on the northern side of the Black Sea when Constantinople fell. Having returned to the West, he presented himself as a specialist on Eastern affairs and gave an account of the Ottoman conquest as if he had been an eyewitness of the event although he was not. Unlike Leo-

[40] Cf. for example the information given about the burial ceremonies for Mongol noblemen. Simon's description is much crueler than John's. Vincent prefers the violent version and thereby emphasises the image of the Mongols as a brutal and atrocious people. Vincentius Bellovacensis, "Speculum historiale," cf. footnote 37, here: XXIX,86, in comparison to: Johannes von Piano Carpine, "Historia Mongalorum," cf. footnote 38, here: III,13.

[41] Iacobus Campora, *Oratio facta coram invictissime Cesare Romanorum imperatore Friderico tercio moderno in Gratz die prima februariis 1456 per dominum Ia. Campora in sacra theologia professorem ac dei et apostolice sedis gratia episcopum Cassensem.* The speech held at the Imperial Court in Graaz is handed down to us in four different manuscripts (Melk, Stiftsbibl. 736 (N13) (xv), f. 234r-237r; Munich, Staatsbibl., Clm 78 (xv), f. 250-4; Rein 87 (xv), f. 168-172v; Vienna, Nat. Bibl. 4322 (xv), f. 10v-16). So far, no edition of the text has been published, but a transcription and translation will appear in the appendix of my PhD thesis in 2011: Juliane Schiel, Schreiben gegen die Krise. Dominikanische Perspektiven auf den "Mongolensturm" und den "Fall Konstantinopels" im Vergleich (Berlin: Akademieverlag, in-print). Until then, we can rely on two partial editions of the speech Jacob held before the Hungarian king Ladislav. The content of the two speeches is almost identical. Cf. N. Iorga, *Notes et extraits pour servir à l'histoire des croisades au XVe siècle, IVe série: 1453-1476* (Paris/Bucarest: Académie Roumaine, 1915), 57-63; Agostino Pertusi, ed., *La caduta di Constantinopoli.* 2 Vol. 3rd Edition (Milano: Mondadori, 1997), here: vol. 1 ("Le testimonianze dei contemporanei"), 192-7.

nardo's report, Jacob's description contained little information on military details of the battle but was primarily concerned with the extraordinary degree of violence exhibited by the conquerors.[42]

In view of the above, it therefore seems more promising to look for the *peculiar* rather than the *new* dimensions of violence which characterized the Mongol invasions. The Mongol invasions did not introduce a new dimension of violence, or at least no more than any other major military conquest in the history of mankind. Instead of asking what was *new* in the sense of "extraordinary" and "exceptional", we may instead ask what was *particular* about the violence experienced by the Mongol invasions. Rather than measure the degree of violence and set up hierarchies between different experiences of violence, it might be more fruitful to attempt a "close reading" of the acts of violence we detect in our source material. "Thick descriptions" (in the sense of Clifford Geertz) may help distinguish the Mongol invasions from other events in their *peculiarity* rather than *exceptionality*.

[42] What made up a small paragraph in Leonardo's report occupies several pages in the manuscripts containing Jacob's speech. "Leonardi Chiensis Historia Constantinopolitanae urbis," cf. footnote 9, here: 941D–942B (cf. also footnote 25) in comparison to Iacobus Campora, *Oratio facta coram invictissime Cesare*, cf. footnote 41, where the description of the pillage occupies two folio pages, see for example the manuscript from Vienna, Nat. Bibl. 4322 (xv), f. 11v-12v, from: *Nam, cum Ysmaelite illam olim sanctam urbem ingressi sunt* (…), to: (…) *O, mira rerum perversitas*.

KATHARINA SCHMIDT (Heidelberg)

„With hearts of iron and swords for whips"[1] – The Mongols as "Specialists of Violence"

> *Interdiction, morality and culture – they all arise from the experience of collective killing. It isn`t rationality that brings someone to peace, but the awareness of irredeemable guilt. No contract restrains him from violence, but the tyranny of his conscience. (…) The violence seems to be tamed, the urge for aggression choked. However, in the underground the desires continue to exist. They want to erupt, want to violate the interdiction, want to sweep out guilt and conscience.*[2]

It was a fateful moment in Hungarian history, when the Hungarian knights around their King Bela IV. were huddled in panic near the small river Sajó behind a mighty wagon fort that was to become their deathtrap.[3] The Mongolian horsemen approached at first in ghostlike silence and then, with a horrible clamor, surrounded and slaughtered almost the whole Hungarian army, so that all rumors about the apocalyptic people Gog and Magog[4] seemed to come true. Having left the country nearly depopulated, the Mongols pursued King Bela down to the Dalmatian coast, as he had offered the Cumans, whom they had enslaved, a hiding place.[5] They had looted the country meticulously beforehand so that the few survivors were forced to fill their stomachs with earth and dust while some sources even report about cases of cannibalism caused by

1 SHM, § 195 (cf. footnote 25).

2 Translatet from: Wolfgang Sofsky, *Traktat über die Gewalt*, (Frankfurt 2005), 210f.

3 Cf. the contemporary report of Rogerius of Torre Maggiore, Carme Miserabile, ed. Ladislaus Juhász, in SRH II, (Budapest 1938), 543-588, here § 28.

4 The interpretation of the Mongolian Invasion as the arrival of the apocalyptic tribes Gog and Magog, following Pseudo-Methodius, who had used this concept in order to explain the Muslim conquest during the 7th and 8th century, has been analyzed in detail by various studies namely Axel Klopprogge, *Ursprung und Ausprägung des abendländischen Mongolenbildes im 13. Jahrhundert. Ein Versuch zur Ideengeschichte des Mittelalters* (Wiesbaden 1993), 53f.; Felicitas Schmieder, *Europa und die Fremden. Die Mongolen im Urteil des Abendlandes vom 13. bis in das 15. Jahrhundert*, (Sigmaringen 1994), 259-275.

5 Cf. Peter Jackson, *The Mongols and the West, 1221-1410*, (Harlow 2005), 60f who also argues that the Mongols sudden withdrawal was primarily caused by the completion of the revenge campaign against King Bela IV. and the fugitive Cumans.

catastrophic food shortage.[6] To contemporary witnesses, the Mongolian invaders just seemed to have unleashed the cruel, violent and merciless demon that, according to the Sociologist Wolfgang Sofsky, is concealed in every human being, suppressed only by the shackles of culture. In recent sociological research, Sofsky`s theses have been subject to intense debate, as they clearly contradicted the older approaches, centered around Norbert Elias` theories of civilization.[7] In a certain way, his approach is an inversion of the likewise linear and teleological ideas of his predecessors: While violence, according to the older theories, has become more and more civilized and culturally tamed in the course of the history of mankind, Sofsky emphasized that violence has become ever more drastic and unlimited due to its growing suppression.[8] From a historical point of view, both attempts lead in their radicalness to a dead end. Violence and its excessive use cannot be regarded in terms of a linear development, as can be observed in the case of the Mongolian society of the 12th and 13th centuries.

Speaking about excessive violence in a cross-cultural framework requires, regardless of the specific historical context, a careful examination of the term "violence". Generally, two larger trends dominate the sociological-historical debate on the definition of violence: Most researchers choose to exclusively focus on the phenomenon of physical violence, sometimes complemented by the factor of intentionality, while a minority of scholars supports the inclusion of mental violence.[9] The political scientist Johann Galtung expands his definition even to "structural violence" by including all actions that prevent a single person or a whole social group from attaining self-realization.[10] A central problem with the investigation of violence, especially in a cross-cultural context, is

6 For example: *Carmina de regno Ungariae destructo per Tartaros*, ed. Oswald Holder-Egger, in MGH SS 29, (Hannover 1892, RP Stuttgart 1975), 607; *Chronicon, quod conservatur in monte S. Georgii*, ed. Béla Pukánszky, in SRH II, (Budapest 1938), 282: *Auch so ist so grosser hunger gewest, daz dy mutter ire kinder haben gessin, vnd dy lewte haben das ertrich von einem berge vor mel mussen essen, als dy cronica sagit Martiniana.*

7 These theories were outlined by Elias, summarized in the compendium *Über den Prozess der Zivilisation. Soziogenetische und psychogenetische Untersuchungen, Band 2: Wandlungen der Gesellschaft* (Amsterdam 1997).

8 Cf. Wolfgang Sofsky, *Traktat über die Gewalt*, (Frankfurt 2005), 223f.

9 A helpful review of the main research on violence was given by Trutz von Trotha, "Zur Soziologie der Gewalt", in *Soziologie der Gewalt*, ed. Trutz von Trotha (Opladen 1997), 9-56. Pieter Spierenburg, too, argues in his preface following David Riches that the term violence should be restricted to the „realm of the intentional infliction of physical hurt", Pieter Spierenburg, "Violence: Reflections About a Word", in: *Violence in Europe. Historical and Contemporary Perspectives*, ed. Sophie Body-Gendrot, Pieter Spierenburg, (New York 2008), 16.

10 Cf. Johann Galtung, "Violence, peace and peace research", *Journal of Peace Research* 6 (1969), 167-191.

the issue of objectivity and the general validity of every definition. There are societies in which certain kinds of beating are by no means regarded as violence although they satisfy the requirement of physical injury as well as that of intentionality. What appears from outside a given culture as a violent action may be considered within that culture as being totally free of violence. On the other hand, even in the same society and culture, acts of violence are often perceived differently from various perspectives. Many sociologists argue that an investigation of the consequences of violence always results in taking up the perspective of the victim while analyzing the reasons for violence leads to a stronger identification with the perpetrator.[11]

The Mongols considered violence, especially against a non-Mongolian victim, not as something negative or in need of justification but rather as a natural part of their culture. Moreover, violence does not necessarily require any form of aggression or other emotional motives.[12] One central approach in the research of violence demands a third perspective through the eyes of a noninvolved observer. In the case of the Mongols, a combination of an emic and etic perspective makes it possible to avoid one-sidedness. Cultural relativity with respect to the Mongolian perspective can be expanded by the exterior viewpoint of European travelers such as the two Franciscans John of Plano Carpini and William of Rubruk. With regard to the terminological problem, European languages themselves show many differences among the various terms denoting violence. The German word „Gewalt" includes many, partly positive aspects, namely in the field of governance and executive power, expressed for example by the term „Staatsgewalt".[13] However, the English word "violence" has an exclusively negative connotation and implies an unjustified action against someone`s will.[14] In the Latin language as well, *potestas*, the ability to achieve something, is clearly distinguished from *violentia,* an injurious treatment of a person without his or her permission. In the perspective of the medieval Christian Western civilization, the Aristotelian definition of violence, in particular, was the key issue of the theological-philosphical debate. Following

11 Cf. Trutz von Trotha 1997, 18f.

12 This phenomenon was analyzed, for example, by Heinrich Popitz, *Phänomene der Macht*, (Tübingen [2]1992), 74-78, who also warned against the „Ausklammerung jeder Zweckrationalität" that he has often noticed in the recent research on the topic of violence and its social meaning.

13 Even if it is possible to distinguish between state violence and private violence in Europe since the 16th century (according to Spierenburg 2008, 42f), for the Middle Ages it is extremely hard to say whether somebody used force as a representative of an institution or as a private person.

14 Cf. David Riches, "The Phenomenon of Violence", in *The anthropology of violence*, ed. David Riches, (Oxford/New York 1986), 1-3.

Aristoteles, Thomas Aquinas defined violence as something *extra naturam* that happens *nihil conferente vim passo*,[15] without the help of the suffering person.[16] The Western concept of violence had its main focus on the perversity of any violent action that is devoid of legitimacy and without a special justification. However, the Mongolian terminology is diametrically opposed to this way of thinking. Violence as an abstract, general term is widely unknown to the 13th century sources. Instead, there is an enormous variety of terms which can be associated with the semantic field of violence: Various manners of death and injuries as well as methods of torture and execution. Considering this cultural background and its dissimilarity to European perspectives, it seems to be all the more important to find a definition with transcultural validity. It should minimize the semantic ambiguity of the German word „Gewalt" on the one hand, and allow a terminological opening that is necessary to fully understand the Mongolian concept of violence on the other. In my study, violence firstly means a behavior that, secondly, displays or should display a certain kind of domination over a person or a group of persons while, thirdly, their mental or physical present state is deeply changed.[17]

When Chinggis Khan, probably the best-known Mongol, died in 1227 during a retaliation campaign against the Chinese kingdom of the Tanguts, the boundaries of his empire surpassed all dimensions that a Nomadic realm has ever achieved. In less than 50 years, Temüjin, later named Chinggis Khan, created out of a small Nomadic tribe along the river Onon the uncontested rulers of the whole Central Asian steppe.[18] Already the first European travelers were puzzled by the enormous size and the amazing organization of the huge Mongolian empire, a mystery that challenges even today`s scholars: How was it possible for such a poor and badly equipped tribe to subjugate so quickly the oldest and most booming civilizations? Recent scholarship often points to the highly mobile horse-archer in combination with certain tactics such as arrow

15 Thomas von Aquin, *In octo libros physicorum Aristotelis expositio*, ed. Mariano Maggiòlo, (Turin/Rom 1965), V.10, 365b.

16 Cf. Henrik Wels, "Die aristotelische Gewaltdefinition, ihre Verbreitung und ihre Verknüpfung mit dem freien Willen", in *Mittelalter im Labor. Die Mediävistik testet Wege zu einer transkulturellen Europawissenschaft*, ed. Michael Borgolte et al., (Berlin 2008), 350-357.

17 From my point of view, the aspect of intentionality is too general as there are always certain examples of intentionally caused injuries like medical treatment that are by no means violence. On the other hand, violence practiced with the intention of taking control over someone or someone`s property is correctly denoted as such as it causes harm.

18 Unlike their nomadic predecessors, the Mongols managed not only to achieve reign over the Inner Asian steppe, but also to subdue hitherto unconquered sedentary neighbours, cf. David Morgan, *The Mongols*, (Oxford et al. 1987), 5f.

storms and feigned retreats.[19] But the Hungarians had used the same methods 300 years earlier and yet failed against Otto the Great`s armies. Compared to their enemies, the Mongols were often extremely outnumbered as well, as can be seen in the Hungarian case at Muhi. Surely, the attackers` inner unity was of central importance, owing to a strict but fair new system of justice called yassa that was established by Chinggis Khan on the basis of traditional Nomadic customs and rules. In addition, Peter Jackson emphasizes the importance of the breaking-up of old family units in the Mongolian army by the Khan which resulted in a new common identity reaching beyond particularistic family relations.[20]

An important but hitherto only superficially investigated reason, however, is the specific way in which the Mongols used violence and dealt with violent actions in their own society, which in turn can be attributed to their cultural experiences during the 12th century. The sociologist Norbert Elias argues that, beyond a certain point, violence has to be compensated for and directed out of a society in order for its collective survival to be secured. As an example, he refers to the European Crusades that, according to him, were caused, among others things, by the need to channel outward the increased potential for violence that had accumulated among the professional but very often underemployed knights in the European societies of the High Middle Ages.[21] Similar circumstances can be observed in the socio-cultural development of the central Asian Mongols at the end of the 12th century.

Since the middle of the century the nomadic tribe increasingly came under intensifying pressure from neighboring tribes such as the Chinese Tanguts or other nomadic people like the Merkit, who constantly tried to conquer the Mongolian territory.[22] The Secret History of the Mongols, the oldest piece of Mongolian literature, was written around 1228, in the main probably by a person from the inner circle around Chinggis Khan. To a large extent, the book can be compared to Western medieval chronicles: It starts with the beginning of the world and a genealogy of Chinggis Khan`s family, which descended

[19] The tactic of feigned retreat has been described in detail by Timothy May, *The Mongol Art of War. Chinggis Khan ant the Mongol Military System*, (Pennsylvania 2007), 74f.

[20] Cf. Jackson 2005, 41f.

[21] Cf. Elias 1997, 57-66.

[22] In addition, Paul Ratchnevsky points out that the Mongolian society experienced a deep crisis during the 12th century, as the powerful confederation between several Mongolian tribes had collapsed and a power vacuum emerged. The formation of a new social stratum, the *nokör*, a group of voluntary followers that provided Chinggis Khan`s main personal support, also resulted from this crisis and its wide social, economic and political impact. (cf. Paul Ratchnevsky, “Die Rechtsverhältnisse bei den Mongolen im 12.-13. Jahrhundert”, *Central Asiatic journal* 31, 1987, 64-110).

from a grey wolf and a fallow doe. The episodes are chronologically arranged and become greatly more detailed beginning with the birth of the later Great Khan. The Secret History belongs without any doubt to the genre of historical writings, but it also contains lyric poetry illuminating the most important events in the Khan`s life.[23] As he was, above all, a great warrior from the Mongolian perspective, the poetry revolves around battles and victories. Thus, violence is often present in the lyric passages, an aspect that must be taken into account in an interpretation of violent actions in the Mongolian society. Chinggis Khan, or Temüjin, as he was called before his election, is in fact the main character of the Secret History, but unintended by the author, the Secret History also provides a deep insight into the Mongolian ethnogenesis. The author documents the transformation of his society under the growing external pressure that resulted in a constant decline of nomadic traditions and moral values.[24] The Great Khan`s father was maliciously poisoned by a group of the Tatar tribe in transgression of the traditionally highly valued law of hospitality while his family sank into poverty.[25] The struggle for supremacy was deadly and involved the 13-year old Temüjin killing his own brother Bekter with an arrow through his face.[26] Violence had become omnipresent in Mongolian daily life, and regular raids between the various clans caused mistrust even within the same family. Normally, women and horses were the main booty that regularly changed hands and were taken away, tied by a rope, to the neighbouring camp of the new owner.[27] Revenge was the only motivation by which the Mongols and the young Temüjin were governed, especially after the rape of his wife Börte by the Merkit.[28] Temüjin took cruel revenge after his rise to power

[23] The latest and best translation with an excellent commentary was published by the Mongol-specialist Igor de Rachewiltz, *The secret history of the Mongols/1&2, (Brill's Inner Asian library; 7,1-7,2)*, (Leiden et al. [2]2006), cf. here especially the Introduction, XXV-CXIII (henceforward abbreviated as SHM).

[24] The awareness of a deep crisis during the 12th century and an increased potential for violence was still alive in the collective memory, as the author of the Secret History demonstrates: *The starry sky was turning upon itself, The many people were in turmoil: They did not enter their beds to rest, But fought against each other. The crusty earth was turning and turning, The entire nation was in turmoil: They did not lie on their coverlets to rest, But attacked each other. (…) When men met, weapons in hand. (…) It happened at a time Of mutual fighting. (…) It happened at a time When one man slew another.* (SHM, § 254).

[25] Cf. SHM, § 67-68.

[26] Cf. SHM, § 77.

[27] Cf. SHM, § 56.

[28] There was a comprehensive concept of vengeance, called *ösö* in Mongolian, in the Mongolian society of the early 13th century that shows the dimension of violence between several tribes. Cf. Roberte Hamayon, "Mérite de l`offensé vengeur, plaisir du rival vainqueur. Le mouvement ascendant des échanges hostiles dans deuy sociétés mongoles", in *La Vengeance*, ed Raymond Verdier, (Paris 1986), 107-140.

and wiped out the Merkit almost completely. The Merkit, according to the author, *Were exterminated, down to The offspring of their offspring: They were blown to the winds like hearth-ashes. (…) We emptied the breasts of the Merkit people Who take their revenge as a man does, And we tore their livers to pieces. We emptied their beds And we exterminated their relatives; The women of theirs who remained We surely took captive!*[29]

The ethno-sociologist Georg Elwert developed in the nineties the concept of "markets of violence" based on his studies about pre- and post-colonial African societies.[30] Elwert found, particularly in cases such as the Rwandan genocide that were often considered to be extremely emotional and uncontrolled, a highly rational behavior on the part of a small group of regional elites. The key element of his concept is the triangle comprising "violence", "time" and "trade", of which the last term also means "expense". Within this framework, it can be said that some warlords aim to establish a market of violence, mostly in so called „Violence open areas" that lack a system of rules or that have lost the hitherto accepted controlling authority. In order to stabilize these markets of violence, a second level of legitimization becomes necessary. Thus, besides the real, mainly economic reasons, the warlords emphasize cultural, religious and nationalistic motivations that are of great importance in securing a permanent, large-scale military support. The violence used by these warlords is, according to Elwert, a typical example of „strategic violence" characterized by the inclusion of third persons who are used as instruments. It involves an enhancement of the planned and mostly unemotional „instrumental violence", found, for example, in the pre-modern warfare of the archer, which was only possible with an inner calmness and distance. As the Mongols were traditionally users of this kind of violence, there was perhaps a certain predisposition for developing forms of strategic violence A good example to illustrate a typical Mongolian behavior in the context of Elwert`s concept is the topic of friendship and solidarity. In the warrior`s rhetoric of the Secret History, blood brotherhood with a close friend, called *anda,* was at first sight a highly valued good that was celebrated with extensive rituals.[31] However, this sanctified tie was devalued and destroyed quite quickly in cases of conflicting military or economic interests. The early stage of the Mongolian expansion corresponds with Elwert`s concept of an emerging market of violence in a largely uncontrolled area. As already pointed out by Norbert Elias, the actual

[29] SHM, § 112-113.

[30] Cf. Georg Elwert, "Gewaltmärkte. Beobachtungen zur Zweckrationalität von Gewalt", in *Soziologie der Gewalt*, ed Trutz von Trotha, (Opladen et al. 1997), 86-103; Georg Elwert, „Dynamics of violence. Processes of Escalation and de-escalation in violent group conflicts", *Sociologus. Zeitschrift für empirische Ethnosoziologie und Ethnopsychologie* 1, 1999, 85-102.

[31] Cf. Morgan 1987, 34.

intentions of the rulers were far-reaching, as in the Mongolian case, aiming for a permanent monopoly of violence in the areas they dominated.[32] Elwert emphasizes various steps such as the acquisition of a special knowledge of psychic manipulation during this process. On the basis of this development and under certain circumstances, specific warrior societies can emerge that I would like to call „specialists of violence“ due to their particular way of looking at and using violent methods. However, what characterizes the Mongols as “specialists of violence”, and how can their social development during the formation of their empire be observed in the contemporary sources?

While the treatment of the subjugated enemy was initially characterized by revenge, arbitrary cruelty and greed for booty, the behaviour of the new Khan became increasingly calculating and rational as time went by. For future attacks, he gave the following order: *If we overcome the enemy, we shall not stop for booty. When the victory is complete, that booty will surely be ours, and we will share it among ourselves. If we are forced by the enemy to retreat, let us turn back to the point where we began the attack. Those men who do not turn back to the point where we began the attack shall be cut down!*[33] The intensity of violent descriptions increases henceforth even more, but it is limited exclusively to the mistreatment of enemies and social outsiders as well as to Chinggis Khan`s punishment of those who disregarded orders. Regardless of rank or merit, even former friends and close confidants were publicly whipped when they did not observe the new laws. However, the Khan did not just change the former system of rules but pursued rigorously a general „democratization“ of violent actions in his society. The author of the Secret History describes the new laws in detail, repeatedly emphasizing their highly innovative character as well as their merciless rigidity.[34] In spite of this strictness, obedience to the Khan`s new system of justice was far-reaching, at least according to the impres-

32 Cf.Elias 1997, 331f.

33 SHM, § 153.

34 Cf. SHM, § 227: *Elders of the companies, do not reprimand my guards, who have enrolled as guards equal to you, without my permission and merely on the ground of seniority. If any of them breaks the law report it to me. Those liable to execution We shall certainly cut down. Those liable to be beaten We shall certainly compel to lie down and have them beaten. If you yourselves merely on the ground of seniority lay hands on my guards who are equal to you and strike them with a rod, as requital for strokes of the rod you shall be repaid with strokes of the rod, and as requital for fists you shall be repaid with fists.* This impression was confirmed by William of Rubruk, who described not without surprise the strict system of justice within the Mongolian society: *Murder they punish by the death sentence, and also cohabiting with a woman not one`s own. (...) Robbery on a grand scale they likewise punish by death. For a petty theft, such as one sheep, so long as a man has not been caught doing it often, they beat him cruelly, and if they deal him a hundred strokes, then they have to have a hundred rods.* (Translation, Christopher Dawson, *Mission to Asia*, (Toronto 1966, RP 1980), 105)

sion given by the author of the Secret History. Several members of a defeated tribe were caught after having broken a promise, but they accepted their destiny at once without any resistance: *We did not keep to the words we spoke. Now make us comply with them! And, admitting their oath, they held out their necks to the sword. Making them to admit their oath and causing them to comply with their words, he executed them and cast off their bodies there and then.*[35] According to the author`s intentions, of course, this story was meant to demonstrate the Khan`s authority and assertiveness, but it also provides an insight into the consequences of the new laws. Mercy and generosity, fundamental nomadic virtues, had lost their value in favor for steadfastness and reliability. A similar system of justice had never been seen before in the Mongols` world.

The Khan`s fundamental reorganization of the Mongolian society bore fruit as John of Plano Carpini was able to observe during his visit to various Mongolian camps: *These men, that is to say the Tatars, are more obedient to their masters than any other man in the world, be they religious or seculars; they show great respect to them nor do they lightly lie to them. They rarely or never contend with each other on word, and in action never. Fights, brawls, wounding, murder are never met with among them. Nor are robbers and thieves who steal on a large scale found there; consequently their dwellings and the carts in which they keep their valuables are not secured by bolts and bars.*[36] Chinggis Khan realized during his rise the tremendous dynamics of the potential for violence in the Mongolian society and was able to channel and direct it against the enemy. However, the use of violence within the community of the Mongols was subjected from now on to strict rules and thus practically eliminated. In this respect, the ritualization of violence played a major role, visible not only in the Mongolian sources themselves but also in the etic perspective of Western travelers. The Franciscan William of Rubruk who arrived at the Mongolian court in Karakorum in 1253 investigated the Mongolian culture and society in detail. Astonished at the Mongolian rituals of marriage, he wrote in his report: *And so when anyone has made an agreement with another to take his daughter, the father of the girl arranges a feast and she takes flight*

[35] SHM, § 136.

[36] Johannes de Plano Carpini, Historia Mongolorum quos nos Tartaros appellamus, in *The Texts and versions of John de Plano Carpini and William de Rubruquis*, ed. C. Raymond Beazly, (Millwood 1967), 43-74, here § 4,2: *Predicti homines, videlicet Tartari, sunt magis obedientes dominis suis quam aliqui homines qui sunt in mundo, sive religiosi sive seculars, et magis reverentur eosdem, neque de facili mentiuntur eis. Verbis ad invicem raro aut nunquam contendunt, factis vero nunquam; bella, rixe, vulnera, homicidia inter eos nunquam contingunt. Predones etiam et fures rerum magnarum non inveniuntur ibidem: unde stationes et currus eorum ubi habent thesaurum suum, series aut vectibus non firmantur.* (Translation Dawson 1980, 14f).

to relations where she lies hid. The father declares: "Now my daughter is yours; take her wherever you find her." Then he searches for her with his friends until he finds her; then he has to take her by force and bring her, as though by violence, to his house.[37] In many respects, this procedure is redolent of the nomadic treatment of cattle; but furthermore, it demonstrates the importance of violence that is observable in almost every ritualized act in the Mongolian society. The existing potential for violence was shifted onto a virtual level and compensated for in this way. Such rituals deflected the tensions between the male members of the society, often caused by the typical nomadic struggle for booty, into the less dangerous field of virtual "gender violence". The resistance of the bride raises her value, a custom that can also be observed in other Central Asian societies.[38] The difference compared to the Mongolian example, however, consists in the man`s reaction. He does not try to convince her verbally but uses violence to subjugate her. This violent ritual had a central function of ensuring harmony within the society. Besides other benefits, the ceremony offered the possibility to dissipate violent energy without any negative consequences for the social community.

The way in which the Mongols compensated for violent experiences with outside forces can be accurately observed in the case of the Chinese Tangut empire that revolted several times against the Mongol rule and forced the Mongols to carry out a number of costly retaliation campaigns: *After he had plundered the Tang`ut people (...) and after having exterminated the Tang`ut people`s mothers and fathers down to the offspring of their offspring, maiming and taiming, Činggis Qa`an gave the following order: "While I take my meals you must talk about the killing and destruction of the Tang`ut and say, "Maimed and tamed, they are no more."*[39] The Khan`s main objective was obviously a ritualization of the soldiers` bloody experiences aimed at keeping the memory of the great victory permanently alive and offering a possibility of reducing the aggression that arose during the battles. In this way, remembrance of the victory became a constant source of warriors` motivation. Acting tactically and with a precise aim, Chinggis Khan demonstrated his deep psychological knowledge of the effectiveness of applied violence and its potential.

[37] Itinerarium Willelmi de Rubruc, in *Itinera et relationes Fratrum Minorum saeculi XIII et XIV (Sinica Franciscana 1)*, ed. Anastasius Van Den Wyngaert, (Florenz 1929), VII,5: *Cum ergo aliquis fecerit pactum cum aliquo de filia accipienda, facit pater puelle convivium, et illa fugit ad consanguineous ut ibi lateat. Tunc pater dicit: "Ecce filia mea tua est, accipe eam ubicumque inveneris." Tunc ille querit eam cum amicis suis donec inveniat eam, et oportet quod vi capiat eam et ducat eam quasi violenter ad domum suam.* (Translation, Dawson 1980, 104).

[38] Guilelmus de Rubruquis, *Reise zu den Mongolen 1253-1255*, trans. and com. Friedrich Risch (Leipzig 1934), 70.

[39] SHM, § 268.

The Secret History contains many lyric passages obviously derived from this process of motivation that preceded, in particular, important battles against initially superior enemies. Collective singing was aimed at supporting the social cohesion of the soldiers; in addition, but the texts of these songs were meant to incite them and to make them focus on an unhesitating application of violence during the battle.[40]

Compared to other nomadic societies, the diversity of violent actions on the battlefield went far beyond the normal, physically dominated mode of nomadic warfare.[41] Mental as well as physical violence shaped the interaction with the enemy from the first contact up to his death or enslavement. Much importance was attached to the impression to be made on enemy soldiers and, in particular, to the terror that was to be stirred up among them. Often, entire nations submitted to the Mongols merely on the basis of rumors, terrified by their reputation for cruelty, thereby sparing Mongolian resources and forces as a result.[42] The Secret History reports how the Khan ordered during the campaign against the Naiman that every soldier should light up five camp fires in order to frighten the enemy and to mask the numerical inferiority of the Mongols. Totally in panic and demoralized by the fear of the expected cruelty, the Naiman were defeated easily.[43] The Franciscan John of Plano Carpini described similar methods such as the use of puppets which were placed on horses to multiply the horrible image of the attacking Mongol hordes, most effective especially against besieged cities.[44] The Mongols did not only adapt Chinese besieging techniques but also invented their own methods, such as the use of prisoners as human shields in order to quickly fill the moats of a city with earth and other materials and not least with their own bodies.[45] A city was

[40] Cf. for example SHM, § 105 where Chinggis Khans anda Jamuqa initiated such a collectively sung song: *Taking our revenge, Wiping out the Uduyit and U`as Merki, We shall rescue our Lady Börte! Taking our vengeance, Crushing all the Qa`at Merkit, We shall rescue your wife Börte, Causing her to return! (…) We shall kill his wives and children To the last one. Of his door the sacred frame, We shall smite so it shatters; We shall utterly destroy his people Till nothing will be left.*

[41] Much research has been to integrate the Mongols into the typical nomadic warfare-tradition, often in combination with a chronological survey of several nomadic societies in the history of mankind, such as Ali Al-Wardi, *Sozilogie des Nomadentums* (Neuwied et al. 1972); Fred Scholz, *Nomadismus. Theorie und Wandel einer sozio-ökologischen Kulturweise*, (Stuttgart 1995); recent historical research has been dominated by a concept following the ideas of Ibn Chaldun of an antagonism between sedentary and nomadic society. In spite of the inspirations it provides toward an understanding of nomadism, it harbors the risk of ignoring the specific characteristics of individual nomadic societies and their warfare.

[42] Cf. May 2007, 79f.

[43] Cf. SHM, § 193.

[44] Cf. Johannes de Plano Carpini, § 6,14.

[45] Cf. May 2007, 113f.

normally enclosed by a huge wall, but due to the tenacity of the Mongolian attackers and the ferocious violence which they demonstrated against prisoners day after day, the citizens soon lost all hope. This process was accelerated by specific forms of psychological warfare. John reports that *sometimes they even take the fat of the people they kill and, melting it, throw it on to the house, and wherever the fire falls on this fat it is almost inextinguishable.*[46] Although Carpini`s record is the only Western document on the Mongols` use of human fat, it seems to be authentic, as he probably had not had any previous experience with the material`s combustibility, but of course it could just have been a horror story told by his Mongolian hosts.[47] However, regardless of whether they really used such a horrifying method of warfare, the Mongols certainly knew the impact of such rumors on their enemies. Carpini himself became an agent of the Mongols` tactics so that, long before an actual attack, the self-confidence of the would-be enemies was weakened and their fear increased.

Once a city was conquered, another form of Mongolian violence became evident: The Mongols knew exactly how to break the defeated enemy`s will in order to minimize their resistance after the victory and to turn them into totally obedient slaves. Normally, total massacres were avoided, as they were costly in terms of time and energy, and the Mongols need the subjugated population for their next campaigns. Total extermination was only used after rebellions and in cases of extreme resistance, especially to discourage neighbouring countries and cities from carrying out similar acts. Nevertheless, if a city had not capitulated before its conquest, all adult men, except useful craftsmen, were executed while women and children up to a certain age were enslaved and later sold.[48] However, even the process of killing was quite systematic and efficient without any trace of chaos and murderous frenzy, unlike the contemporary Western examples of mass murder. Carpini reports being not only disgusted but also astonished by the Mongols` strict calculations after the conquest of a hostile city: *While they are pitched before the fortification they speak enticing words to the inhabitants making them many promises to induce them to sur-*

[46] Johannes de Plano Carpini, § 6,15: *immo solent aliquando accipere arvinam hominum quos occidunt, et liquefactam proiciunt super domos. Et ubicumque venit ignis super pinguedinem illam, quasi inextinguibiliter ardet.* (Translation Dawson 1980, 37).

[47] Cf. Johannes Gießauf, *Die Mongolengeschichte des Johannes von Piano Carpine*, (Graz 1995), 189, who reports on the Mongolian general Bayan and his use of human fat in order to grease his siege machines.

[48] This was also confirmed by the report of the Secret History on the treatment of beaten enemies. Submission without resistance normally resulted in mercy (for example SHM, § 176) while massacre and enslavement was the regular punishment when there was no capitulation (for example SHM, § 186). Cf. Pavel Poucha, *Die geheime Geschichte der Mongolen als Geschichtsquelle und Literaturdenkmal. Ein Beitrag zu ihrer Erklärung*, (Prag 1956), here especially *Mongolische Armeeorganisation und Kriegsführung*, 110-165.

render into their hands. If they do surrender to them, they say: „Come out, so that we may count you according to our custom," and when they come out to them they seek out the artificers among them and keep these, but the others, with the exception of those they wish to have as slaves, they kill with the axe. If they do spare any others they never spare the noble and illustrious men, so we are told, and if by chance the unexpected happens and some nobles are kept, they can never afterwards escape from captivity either by entreaty or by bribe. All those they take prisoner in battle they put to death unless they happen to want to keep some as slaves. They divide those who are to be killed among the captains of a hundred to be executed by them with a battle-axe; they in their turn divide them among the captives, giving each slave to kill ten or more or less as the officers think fit.[49]

After having been conquered, a population was systematically counted and divided into various categories. The plundering of the city had to await the end of the executions. Carpini could not understand why nobles and prominent citizens were killed while only low-ranking craftsmen were spared. However, the Mongols did not care for receiving ransom after laborious negotiations, as it would have meant in Elwert`s triangle an extremely great loss of time from the perspective of a warfare that hinged upon mobility and speed. Killings performed by the victims` own fellow citizens also made up a part of the cost-benefit-calculation and had various advantages: The Mongolian forces were spared additional strains, the time needed for the executions was reduced and, above all, the would-be slaves were mentally broken, and their way back seemed to be forever blocked by the forced murder of their own relatives.

Carpini described in detail not only the treatment of conquered cities but also the general military procedures that correspond almost entirely with the records of the Secret History. The Franciscan was extremely interested in the Mongols` military potential as he wanted his report to serve as a warning and information for his Western supporters. So it is highly credible when he writes: *When they are going to make war, they send ahead an advance guard and*

[49] Johannes de Plano Carpini, § 6,16-17 : *Sed cum iacent ante munitionem, blande eis loquuntur et multa eis promittunt, ad hoc ut se eorum manibus tradant. Et si illi se eis reddiderint dicunt : „Exite ut secundum morem nostrum vos numeremus". Et cum illi ad eos exeunt, querunt qui sunt artifices inter eos et illos reservant; alios autem, exceptis illis quos volunt habere pro servis, cum securi occidunt. Et si aliquibus aliis parcunt, ut dictum est, nobilibus et honestis hominibus nunquam parcunt. Et si forte aliquo casu contingente reservant aliquos nobiles, nec prece nec pretio ultra de captivitate possunt exire. In bellis autem quoscumque capiunt occidunt, nisi forte velint aliquos reservare, ut habeant eos pro servis. Occidendos autem dividunt per centenarios, ut cum bipenni interficiantur ab eis; ipsi vero post hec dividunt per captivos, et unicuique servo ad interficiendum dant decem aut plures aut pauciores secundum quod maioribus placet.* (Translation Dawson 1980, 37f).

these carry nothing with them but their tents, horses and arms. They seize no plunder, burn no houses and slaughter no animals; they only wound and kill men or, if they can do nothing else, put them to flight. They much prefer, however, to kill than to put to flight. The army follows after them, taking everything they come across, and they take prisoner or kill any inhabitants who are to be found. Not content with this, the chiefs of the army next send plunderers in all directions to find men and animals, and they are most ingenious at searching them out.[50] The campaign was divided into three separate stages that were to assure a maximum of gains. The first vanguards acted above all as an instrument of terror; plundering and taking of booty were strictly forbidden. By this division of labour, the collecting of the booty in a second stage was made less costly in terms of time and energy. The highly mobile looters, the *predones*, scoured at last the whole territory in small groups for forgotten goods and people. Rogerius of Torre Maggiore, an eyewitness of the Mongols` raid in Hungary in 1241, described the citizens` panic after they had emerged from their walled city following the Mongols` apparent withdrawal. Suddenly, another Mongolian division came back, killed the survivors and collected the belongings that they had just fetched out of their hiding places outside the city walls.[51] In the eyes of the victims, the Mongolian campaign simply seemed to be a never-ending nightmare, but in the light of the information provided by the Secret History, the Mongols` behavior was by no way senseless or uncoordinated. The question of whether the use of this extreme violence was justified or even needed a transcendental legitimization was mostly irrelevant to the Mongols, and the same can be said of the specific personality or religion of the victims. In the Secret History itself the Mongols` victims were almost never given individual faces. Normally, they appeared as a mass of subjects under the name of a tribe or a nation, and the author proudly emphasized how the Khan treated and enslaved every conquered object without making any distinction as to whether it was human or not.[52] That "dehumanization" of the enemy, as Carpini shows, was already intensified in the run-up of a campaign by verbal humiliation: *Moreover, in regard to this point it should be known that the*

[50] Johannes de Plano Carpini, § 6,11: *Cum ad bellum procedere volunt, precursores premittunt, qui nichil secum portant preter filtra sua et equos et arma. Isti nichil rapiunt, domos non comburunt, bestias non occidunt, sed tantum homines vulnerant et mortificant et, si non possunt aliud, mittunt in fugam. Multo libentius tamen occidunt quam fugant. Post istos sequitur exercitus, qui cuncta que invenit accipit; et homines etiam, si inveniri possunt, capiunt vel occidunt. Nichilominus tamen principes exercitus ex omni parte mittunt predones post hoc ad inveniendum homines et iumenta, qui valde sagaces sunt ad querendum..* (Translation Dawson 1980, 35).

[51] Cf. Rogerius of Torre Maggiore, § 34.

[52] Cf. for example the extinction of the Merkit, SHM, § 112.

Tatars much prefer men to shut themselves into their cities and fortresses rather than fight with them in the open, for then they say they have got their little pigs shut in their sty, and so they place men to look after them as I have told above.[53] The enemies were reduced to faceless animal-like masses, so that a rational, emotionless execution of the conquest became much easier.[54]

The examples mentioned show from an emic and etic point of view the significant role that violence and its channeling played in Mongolian society. If one compares certain manifestations of this phenomenon with the pre-modern African societies investigated by Elwert, many parallels become obvious. Many of Elwert`s societies aimed for a domination of a market of violence in the same way as the Mongols did at the beginning of their rise to power. However, they soon developed an ideological concept of rule that was meant to secure their position as permanent monopolists of violence and their ruthless expansionism. The society of slave-hunters in the kingdom of Dahomé, for example, aimed during its domination of pre-colonial West Africa for a limited domination of a market of violence in the same way as the Mongols did at the beginning of their rise to power.[55] However, they soon developed an ideological concept of god-given rulership that was meant to secure their position as permanent monopolists of violence and their ruthless expansionism. In Dahomè, extreme experiences of violence were compensated for by an aggressive warriors` cult which resembles in many ways the Mongolian handling of violence described in the Secret History. On a second level of motivation, there existed in Dahomé a certain concept of the beyond in which the blood of slain enemies served as food for the ancestors. As for the Mongols, they believed that powerful slain foes would strengthen their position in the afterlife and thus slaughtered hundreds of captured enemies on the occasion of their Khan`s death. Violence also shaped in both societies the treatment of the subjugated persons who were used as human shields in order to minimize the risk of their own soldiers. The paralyzing effect of terror was a well known and central method of warfare. In Dahomé, human sacrifices were celebrated in the presence of guests invited from other countries while the Mongols spread rumors about massacres and cruel executions. Both societies discovered during their

[53] Johannes de Plano Carpini, § 8,13: *Sed ad hoc sciendum est quod Tartari plus diligunt quod homines se in civitatibus et castris claudant, quam quod pugnent cum eis in campo. Dicunt enim illos suos esse porcellos in ara conclusos, unde ponunt custodes, ut superius dictum est.* (Translation Dawson 1980, 49).

[54] Cf. Michel Wieviorka, *Die Gewalt*, (Hamburg 2006), 159f, who regards humiliation of the victim by putting him on the same level with an animal as the central issue in understanding extraordinary violence against defenseless enemies, as it allows the perpetrator to act without an awareness of guilt or mercy.

[55] Cf. Elwert 1997, 96f.

expansion the efficiency of controlled violence and learned how to use it most effectively and without any danger to the stability of their own society.

The well-known researcher and Mongolist Igor de Rachewiltz emphasized in his research the importance of the Mongols` concept of divine rule for their special use of violence.[56] In fact, this idea of a universal sovereignty received by Heaven, the Mongolian Tengri, mainly developed by Chinggis Khans successors, was only the facade, a secondary motivation for an extremely rational form of violence. On the basis of a high level of aggression within their society, the Mongols developed at Chinggis Khan`s instigation a special form of psychological knowledge that was largely unknown in Europe at the time. Between 1206 and 1260, the Mongols became “specialists of violence”, a phenomenon that was not singular in human history but rather tied to various specific premises. In conclusion, I would like to put up the following 10 points for discussion, not only as the central characteristics of the Mongolian use of violence but also as the main features of specialists of violence in general. Based on Elwert`s model of violence, these characteristic items are meant to facilitate intercultural comparisons of the concepts of violence in various societies; they are also useful for detecting transcultural flows between the Mongolian and the European ways of thinking. Discussion of extraordinary violence requires above all a rating scale of universal validity regardless of culture or religion.

10 points to identify a “specialist of violence”

1. Social background a: increasing potential for violence
2. Social background b: area of uncontrolled violence
3. Establishment of a market of violence
4. Searching for a second level of motivation
5. Strict regimentation of violence within the society
6. Ritualization of violent wartime experiences
7. Rationalization of violent actions
8. Maximization of the external effects of violence
9. Creation of a specific mental and physical profile of the enemy
10. Dehumanization and de-individualization o f the enemy

[56] “Since the crime of turning a deaf ear to the Mongol court`s order of submission was not, in the conception just described, merely an offence against the emperor, but an overt rebellion against Heaven`s Decree, punishment for the offender had, of course to be proportionate. Hence the frightful massacres and destructions, and the complete lack of pity towards the civilian population, which was often annihilated. Here again we find an exact parallel in the practice of the crusading armies.” (Igor de Rachewitz, “Some remarks on the ideological foundations of Chingis Khan’s Empire”, *Papers on eastern history* 7, 1973, 25).

JOHANNES GIESSAUF (Graz)

A Programme of Terror and Cruelty. Aspects of Mongol Strategy in the Light of Western Sources.

At the beginning of the thirteenth century, the Mongol emperor Chingiz-Khan mobilized a war machine that succeeded, within the space of a few decades, in overwhelming the greater part of the known world. In 1235, his third son and successor Ögödei launched a new attempt to put into practice his father's idea of Mongol world-conquest. He unleashed Mongol forces under the command of his nephew Batu, the son of Chingiz-Khan's eldest son Jochi, towards the west.[1] The strategic commander of the Mongol armies, however, was undoubtedly the experienced general Sübötei.[2] Between 1236 and 1240, the Russian Principalities collapsed under the weight of successive Mongol attacks[3], and in the winter of 1240-1241, Batu and Sübötei were ready to enter Latin Christian

1 The plan to conquer the West was one of the main decisions of the „*quriltai*" of 1235. Cf. *Geheime Geschichte der Mongolen*. Herausgegeben von Manfred Taube. München 1989, § 270, p. 200-202; *The History of the World-Conqueror by `Ala ad-Din `Ata-Malik Juvaini*. Translated from the text of Mirza Muhammad Qazvini by John Andrew Boyle with an Introduction by D. O. Morgan. Manchester 1997, 196-200 (henceforth: Juvaini, *History*); *The Successors of Genghis Khan*. Translated from the Persian from Rashid al-Din by John Andrew Boyle. New York-London 1971, 54-56 (henceforth: Rashid, *Successors*); W. Abramowski, Die chinesischen Annalen von Ögödei bis Güyük. Übersetzung des 2. Kapitels des Yüan-shih, *Zentralasiatische Studien* 10 (1976), 130. For the Mongol idea of world-conquest cf. J. Masson Smith, The Mongols and World-Conquest, *Mongolica* 5 (1994), 206-214.

2 Probably no Mongol general played a greater role than Sübötei in establishing and maintaining the early Mongol empire. He was destined to be the mastermind of this campaign because he had been – together with general Jebe – commander of those Mongol troops, which had undertaken a raid through Armenia, Georgia and Russia in the years 1220/24. Due to his successes, he held the honorary title „*ba'atur*" („valiant"). Cf. P. D. Buell, „Sübötei Ba'atur (1176-1248)," in *In the Service of the Khan*. Wiesbaden 1993, 13-26, R. A. Gabriel, *Genghis Khan's Greatest General. Subotai the Valiant.* Westport 2004.

3 On the conquest of the Russian Principalities cf. B. Spuler, *Die Goldene Horde. Die Mongolen in Rußland 1223-1502.* Leipzig 1943, 16-20; G. Vernadsky/M. Karpovich, *The Mongols and Russia*. New Haven [2]1953, 48-52; J. Fennell, *The Crisis of Medieval Russia 1200-1304.* London-New York 1983, 76-96; J. Martin, *Medieval Russia (980-1584).* Cambridge 1995, 135-140; L. de Hartog, *Russia and the Mongol Yoke. The History of the Russian Principalities and the Golden Horde 1221-1502*. London-New York 1996, 29-34.

territory for the first time.[4] The right wing of their army passed through Galicia into Poland, where they defeated the combined forces of Poles and Germans near Liegnitz (Legnica) in Silesia on 9 April 1241.[5] At the same time, Batu and Sübötei had been advancing into Moravia and Hungary, where they achieved a victory on the banks of the river Sajó near Mohi on 11 April. A large part of Hungary was occupied for more than a year and utterly devasted. The defeated Hungarian king Bela IV fled before the Mongol advance and Qadan, a son of the Great-Khan Ögödei,[6] was given the task of capturing him. First, Bela tried to take refuge with Duke Frederick II of Austria, who was contemptuous of the Hungarians' plight and extracted a large ransom from the king before sending him on his way to Croatia.[7] There, Bela hoped to find refuge in Zagreb, but the Mongols followed him in pursuit since the extirpation of the enemy's rulers and nobles was one of the main goals of the Mongol strategy.[8] Therefore, Bela

4 On the Mongol invasion of Europe cf. G. Strakosch-Grassmann, *Der Einfall der Mongolen in Mitteleuropa in den Jahren 1241 und 1242.* Innsbruck 1893; J. J. Saunders, *The History of the Mongol Conquest.* London 1971; H. Göckenjan/J. R. Sweeney, *Der Mongolensturm. Berichte von Augenzeugen und Zeitgenossen 1235-1250.* Graz-Wien-Köln 1985, 36-63; H. Göckenjan, „Der Westfeldzug (1236-42) aus mongolischer Sicht," in *Wahlstatt 1241. Beiträge zur Mongolenschlacht bei Liegnitz und zu ihren Nachwirkungen.* Würzburg 1991, 35-75; J. Gießauf, „Der Traum von der Weltherrschaft. Eine Skizze der politischen Geschichte des mongolischen Großreichs vom Tode Chinggis Khans bis zum Zerfall in Einzelkhanate," in *Die Mongolei. Aspekte ihrer Geschichte und Kultur.* Graz 2001, 53-60; P. Jackson, *The Mongols and the West 1221-1410.* Harlow 2005, 58-86.

5 Cf. U. Schmilewski, *Wahlstatt 1241. Beiträge zur Mongolenschlacht bei Liegnitz und zu ihren Nachwirkungen.* Würzburg 1991.

6 According to Rashid ad-Din (Rashid, *Successors,* 27s.) and Yüan shih (L. Hambis, *Le chapitre CVII du Yuan Che. Avec des notes supplémentaires par Paul Pelliot.* Leiden 1945, 71s.) Qadan was the sixth son of Ögödei and a concubine named Erkene. Cf. Göckenjan/Sweeney, *Der Mongolensturm,* 263s., n. 14; J. Gießauf, *Die Mongolengeschichte des Johannes von Piano Carpine. Einführung, Text, Übersetzung und Kommentar.* Graz 1995, 169, n. 473.

7 On the "Austrian hospitality" see J. Gießauf, „Herzog Friedrich II. von Österreich und die Mongolengefahr 1241/42," in *Forschungen zur Geschichte des Alpen-Adria-Raumes. Festgabe für em. O. Univ.-Prof. Dr. Othmar Pickl zum 70. Geburtstag.* Graz 1997, 173-199.

8 Cf. the report of Juvaini on Chingiz-Khan's order to pursue the Chorezm-Shah: „*He claimed: It is necessary to make an end of him before men gather around him and nobles join him from every side*" (Juvaini, *History,* 143). Cf. also *Die Mongolengeschichte des Johannes von Piano Carpine.* Einführung, Text, Übersetzung und Kommentar von J. Gießauf. Graz 1995 (henceforth: Carpine, *Historia*), cap. VI, 16, p. 104: „ *Et si aliquibus aliis parcunt, ut dictum est, nobilibus et honestis hominibus nunquam parcunt ...* " and cap. VIII, 3, p. 108: „*Intendunt etiam delere omnes principes, omnes nobiles, omnes milites et honestos viros de terra, ut superius dictum est, et hoc faciunt sub dolo et artificiose in subditos suos*". Already in 1237/38, the Hungarian Dominican Friar Julian related similar details following his mission to „Greater Hungary" on behalf of Bela IV : „*Omnium regnorum que obtinent, reges et duces et magnates, de quibus est spes quod aliquando possint facere resistentiam, interficiunt sine mora*"

moved to Trogir (Trau) and then to a nearby island on the Dalmatian coast which the Mongols could not reach for lack of ships. After ravaging Croatia and attacking Trogir unsuccessfully, Qadan withdrew his troops to reunite with the main body of the army since Batu had ordered the sudden and unexpected withdrawal of Mongol forces from East Central Europe.[9] They returned east via Zeta, Serbia and Bulgaria, all of which they looted as they passed through.[10]

Stupefied and shattered, the Europeans could hardly comprehend what had happened to them. When we read contemporary chronicles, we are confronted with bloody images of the Mongols and their ruthless atrocity. In Western sources, the name *Tartars* was applied to the Mongols and their subject peoples. This term, a corruption of the tribal name *Tatar* and apparently deriving from *Tartarus*, the Latin term for the hell of classical mythology, was used quite specifically because it carried all the terrible connotations of the danger to the West: the *Tartars* were agents sent from hell, breaking forth from the mysterious East, the land of Gog and Magog, to unleash their fury upon the Christian world as instruments of divine chastisement.[11] The trail of death and horror which they had left behind across Eastern Europe was seen in apocalyptic terms. Having consulted ancient writings – especially the utterances of the sibyline prophecies of Pseudo Methodius, according to Thomas of Spalato –, many thought the Mongols were the people whose appearance was prophesied to precede the coming of Antichrist.[12] We are confronted with such images, for

(= H. Dörrie, Drei Texte zur Geschichte der Ungarn und Mongolen. Die Missionsreisen des fr. Julian OP. ins Uralgebiet (1234/5) und nach Rußland (1237) und der Bericht des Erzbischofs Peter über die Tartaren", *Nachrichten der Akademie der Wissenschaften in Göttingen. Phil. hist. Kl.* 6 (1956), 125-202, cap. 3,5, p. 176).

9 On the various theories historians have offered concerning this withdrawal, cf. G. S. Rogers, An Examination of Historians' Explanations for the Mongol Withdrawal from East Central Europe, *East European Quarterly* 30 (1996), 3-26.

10 Cf. J. V. A. Fine, *The Late Medieval Balkans: A Critical Survey from the Late Twelfth Century to the Ottoman Conquest.* Ann Arbor [4]1996, 145.

11 On Latin sources alluding to the assumed provenance of the Mongols from the „*Tartarus*" cf. C. W. Connell, Western Views of the Origin of the "Tartars": An Example of the Influence of Myth in the Second Half of the Thirteenth Century, *Journal of Medieval and Renaissance Studies* 3 (1973), 117-119; A. Klopprogge, *Ursprung und Ausprägung des abendländischen Mongolenbildes im 13. Jahrhundert.* Wiesbaden 1993, 155-159; Gießauf, *Die Mongolengeschichte*, 28, n. 104.

12 Thomas Archidiaconus, *Historia Salonitana* ed. Fr. Rashīd al-Dīn, in *Monumenta Spectantia Historiam Slavorum Meridionalium XXVI, Scriptores vol. 3.* Zagreb 1894, 171 (henceforth: Thomas, *Historia*): „*Tunc plerique litterati viri veteres scrutantes scripturas, coniiciebant maxime ex dictis Methodii martiris, has fore illas gentes, que precedere debent antichristi adventum.*" On the interpretation of Mongols as Gog and Magog see M. Steinicke, *Apokalyp-*

example, in the „Chronica Maiora" of Matthew Paris. Despite his geographical distance from the events described, the monk of St. Albans is one of the best-known European chroniclers of the Mongol invasion.[13] However, like the majority of chroniclers of these events, he had never seen a *Tartar* with his own eyes. He shared the dominant view of the Mongols that we can find in the majority of the European reports of the 1240's: The Tartars are the devil's horsemen from a mysterious quarter of the earth, pagans who lack a generally recognized law and indulge in unusual, even bizarre, customs.

Nevertheless, not everybody accepted millenarian speculations. We also possess first-hand narratives that provide descriptions of Mongol customs and practices and which are free of apocalyptic interpretations. However, the number of surviving eyewitnesses who had had direct contact with the Mongols was rather small, and only a few of these eyewitnesses and principal reporters, in turn, were able to look beyond the impression of apparently unjustified and senseless slaughter.

In the last decades, studies by Bigalli, Connell, Bezzola, Fried, Reichert, Klopprogge, Schmieder, Münkler and Ruotsala have analysed the entire course of European-Mongol relations and expanded our knowledge of the Western image of the Mongols in the Middle Ages.[14] Building on their findings, this paper focuses on early narratives which are free of apocalyptic speculations

tische Heerscharen und Gottesknechte. Wundervölker des Ostens in abendländischer Tradition vom Untergang der Antike bis zur Entdeckung Amerikas. Phil. Diss. Berlin 2002, 84-124.

13 Matthew collected news, especially letters, about the Mongols from every part of Europe and mentioned them in his work. Cf. Matthaeus Parisienis, *Chronica Majora.* Edited by Henry Richards Luard (Rolls Series. Rerum Britannicarum Medii Aevi Scriptores 57), 7 Vol. London 1872-83, III, p. 488s.; IV, pp. 76-78, 109-119, 270-277; VI, pp. 75-84, 113-116. On Matthew Paris and his Mongol narratives cf. J. J. Saunders, „Matthew Paris and the Mongols," in *Essays in Medieval History Presented to Bertie Wilkinson.* Toronto 1969, 116-132; G. A. Bezzola, *Die Mongolen in abendländischer Sicht (1220-1270). Ein Beitrag zur Frage der Völkerbegegnungen.* Bern 1974, 63s.; K. Rudolf, Die Tartaren 1241/42. Nachrichten und Wiedergabe: Korrespondenz und Historiographie, *Römisch historische Mitteilungen* 19 (1977), 91-99; H. E. Hilpert, *Kaiser- und Papstbriefe in den Chronica Majora des Matthaeus Paris.* Stuttgart 1981, 27-43, 153-164.

14 D. Bigalli, *I Tartari e l'Apocalisse. Ricerche sull'eschatologia in Adamo Marsh e Ruggiero Bacone.* Firenze 1971; Connell, Western Views, 115-137; Bezzola, *Die Mongolen*; J. Fried, Auf der Suche nach der Wirklichkeit. Die Mongolen und die europäische Erfahrungswissenschaft im 13. Jahrhundert, *Historische Zeitschrift* 243 (1986), 287-332; F. E. Reichert, *Begegnungen mit China. Die Entdeckung Ostasiens im Mittelalter.* Sigmaringen 1992; A. Klopprogge, *Ursprung und Ausprägung*; F. Schmieder, *Europa und die Fremden. Die Mongolen im Urteil des Abendlandes vom 13. bis in das 15. Jahrhundert.* Sigmaringen 1994; M. Münkler, *Erfahrung des Fremden. Die Beschreibung Ostasiens in den Augenzeugenberichten des 13. und 14. Jahrhunderts.* Berlin 2000; A. Ruotsala, *Europeans and Mongols in the Middle of the Thirteenth Century. Encountering the Other.* Helsinki 2001.

and which consider the causes of the success of the Mongol armies. In this context, I want to take a closer look at first-hand accounts that show an awareness of two of the key factors of Mongol strategy, i.e. accounts that contain hints of the considerable attention the Mongols paid to propaganda and psychological warfare, which they carried out by means of cruelty and intimidation.[15]

The first chronicler to emphasize the important role which terror played in Mongol strategy was Roger of Torre Maggiore who writes: *„Soon rumours spread that the Tartars had occupied the German village of Thomasbrücke where they slaughtered everyone not fit for slavery. Hearing such news, my hair stood on end with fright, my whole body started trembling and my tongue refused its duty because of the unavoidable and terrible death which awaited me. In my mind's eye, I saw the slaughterers, and the cold sweat of death made the blood freeze in my veins. I saw people in fear of death, unable to control their hands and weapons, unable to raise their arms or legs and only staring into space. And what more? I laid my eyes on people half-dead from panic.“*[16]

This vivid description of the dreadful fear of the Mongols is found in Roger's report commonly known as „Carmen Miserabile“. The canon of the

[15] More than thirty years ago, Denis Sinor wrote an article on Mongol strategy taking a particular interest in the importance of the long-range planning and the rigid timetable of Mongol military operations (D. Sinor, „On Mongol Strategy,“ in *Proceedings of the 4th East Asian Altaistic Conference*. Taiwan 1975, 238-245). However, the role of cruelty and intimidation in Mongol warfare was not part of his considerations. The same applies to his article on Inner Asian warriors (D. Sinor, The Inner Asian Warriors, *JAOS* 101 (1981), 133-144). Jean Richard deals in his paper about the causes of the Mongol victories at least with the deployment of captives as arrow shields (J. Richard, Les causes des victoires Mongoles d´aprés les historiens occidentaux du XIIIe siècle, *Central Asiatic Journal* 22 (1979), 112s.). The best overview of this topic so far has been given by Hansgerd Göckenjan, who took a particular interest in spies and scouts (H. Göckenjan, Kundschafter und Späher. Ein Beitrag zur Strategie und Taktik reiternomadischer Kriegsführung, *Acta Orientalia Accademiae Scientiarum Hungaricae* 53 (2000), 187-202). Cf. also the analysis of the role of massacres and cruelty in Mongol warfare by C. Commeaux, *La vie quotidienne chez les Mongols de la conquètte*. Paris 1972, 141-147.

[16] *Epistola magistri Rogerii in Miserabile Carmen super destructione regni Hungarie per Tartaros facta* ed. L. Juhász, in *Scriptores rerum Hungaricarum tempore ducum regumque stirpis Arpadianae gestarum* vol. 2. Budapest 1938, cap. 34, p. 579 (henceforth: Rogerius, *Carmen*): *„Post hec statim invaluere rumores, quod dictum Pontem Thome Theutonicorum villam in aurora Tartari occupaverunt et, quos tenere noluerant, horrenda crudelitas acerbitatis gladio dire iugulavit. Quo audito incorruerunt pili carnis mee, cepit corpus tremere ac pavere, lingua miserabiliter balbutire perspiciens, quod dire mortis articulus, qui iam vitari non poterat, imminebat. Trucidatores cordis oculis intuebar, caro sudore mortis frigidissimum emittebat. Videbam et mortales mortem expectantes assidue non posse manus et arma extendere, erigere brachia, pedes ad deffensionis loca movere, oculis terram prospicere. Et quod plura? Homines conspiciebam ex timore nimio semivivos."*

Hungarian city of Várad (now Oradea in Rumania) had been taken prisoner by the invaders in 1241 and had lived several months under their dominion before he was able to escape. His account, probably written immediately after the unexpected withdrawal of the Mongols in 1242, represents one of the major Western narratives of the Mongol invasion of Europe, and there is nothing to discredit his descriptions of that which he had witnessed.[17] In analogy to to Persian, Chinese or Russian sources, he relates the unheard-of Mongol severity in punishing citizens of towns which had tried to resist the Mongol assaults. The Mongols used to call a town which showed no intentions of surrendering to the besiegers „mo balyq", which means „bad city". All citizens of the so-called bad cities were driven together outside the city's walls and slain.[18] These actions were intended to be a warning of terrible retaliation for other cities and were aimed at intimidation. The message of the Mongols was clear: peaceful surrender or an anticipatory declaration of allegiance could enable a ruler to keep his throne and allow a population to escape a massacre; resistance almost invariably meant decimation or extermination.[19]

Very similar information about the Mongol tactic of demoralizing the foe by means of cruelty can be obtained from the Mongol chapters in the „Historia Pontificum Salonitanorum atque Spalatensium" of Thomas of Spalato, which belongs to the most outstanding sources of the 1240's about the Mongols.[20] Thomas pursued a career as canon of the cathedral chapter of Spalato (Split), and in 1230, he was elected archdeacon, a post he held until his death in 1268. It is likely that he began to write his „Historia" between 1245 and 1251. Thomas's Mongol narrative comprises four chapters of the „Historia" which treat the sequence of events in Hungary and Dalmatia from the first rumours of the approach of the Mongols in the late 1230's to their departure in the spring of 1242.[21] The flamboyant manner in which he portrays the *Tartars* shows that, to him, they are a plague, people who lack compassion and humanity. Although

[17] On his life and work cf. F. Babinger, „Maestro Ruggiero delle Puglie, relatore prepoliano su i Tartari," in *Nel VII. centenario della nascita di Marco Polo.* Venezia 1955, 51-62; Bezzola, *Die Mongolen*, 86-89; Göckenjan/Sweeney, *Der Mongolensturm*, 129-138; on some considerations about the transmission of the text cf. T. Almási, The *Carmen Miserabile*: Some Issues Concerning the Transmission of the Text, *Chronica* 3 (2003), 84-93.

[18] On such massacres in the realm of the Chorezm-Shah cf. Juvaini, *History*, 121, 131, 145. Cf. Göckenjan/Sweeney, *Der Mongolensturm*, 52s.

[19] On possible demographic considerations behind these massacres, see J. Masson Smith, Demographic Considerations in Mongol Siege Warfare, *Archivum Ottomanicum* 13 (1993/94), 329-334.

[20] On his life and work, cf. J. R. Sweeney, Thomas of Spalato and the Mongols: A Thirteenth-Century Dalmatian View of Mongol Customs, *Florilegium* 4 (1982), 156-183; Göckenjan/Sweeney, *Der Mongolensturm*, 227-235.

[21] Thomas, *Historia* cap. XXXVI-XXXIX, 132-178.

Thomas condemns them in severest terms, he is curious about their origins and customs and includes relevant information in his „Historia“. Despite his conception of the *Tartars* as a *„pestilential nation“*[22], his Mongol chapters exhibit a high degree of factual accuracy. Apart from his own observation, Thomas's sources must have been refugees who streamed into Split in 1242, fleeing in terror from the troops of the Mongol prince Qadan. He says that his description of the Mongols is given *„according to what I have been able to hear from more inquiring persons who have looked into the matter.“*[23] Thomas writes: *„At this time this monstrous slaughterer* [= Qadan] *ordered his men to drive all the captives together on a plain – men and women as well as boys and girls. Gathering them together like a flock of sheep, he made his executioners behead them all. Everyone broke into loud lamentations, and at the wail of people being slain, the whole world seemed to quake. All captives were cut down, and like sheaves in a cornfield, their corpses were strewn on the plain. But the Tartars did not plunder the dead so that it would become clear that they had not slaughtered them out of lust for booty. The whole host of murderous people, taking their ease in camp camaraderie in the midst of those dead, began to dance and feast with great delight and to shake with great mocking laughter, as though these fine men had performed some great deed."*[24]

According to Thomas, the Mongols did not show any interest in booty after the battle of Mohi. They concentrated their efforts on pursuing and killing their exhausted and terrified enemies because this was the best way to prevent further Hungarian resistance.[25] Very similar observations were made by Roger

[22] Thomas, *Historia* cap. XXXVI, 132: *„gens pestifera Tartarorum“.*

[23] Thomas, *Historia* cap. XXXVII, 168: *„Nunc vero de natura et habitu gentis illius* [= Tartarorum], *prout ab his audire potui, qui rem curiosius indagarunt, pauca narrabo“.*

[24] Thomas, *Historia* cap. XXXIX, 174: *"Tunc truculentus carnifex iussit omnem captivitatem, quam ex Hungaria duxerat, congregari in unum, multitudinem magnam virorum et mulierum, puerorum et puellarum, fecitque omnes in quandam planiciem duci. Et cum omnes quasi quidam grex ovium coadunati fuissent, missis spiculatoribus, omnium fecit capita amputari. Tum ingens audiebatur ululatus et planctus, totaque terra moveri a voce pereuncium videbatur. Iacuerunt autem omnes in illa prostrati planicie, quemadmodum spicarum manipuli sparsim solent in agro iacere. Et ne cui videretur, quod cedis huius immanitas spoliorum sit avidatate patrata, nullas ab eis vestes detrahere voluerunt; sed tota multitudo funeste gentis in circuitu occisorum illorum per contubernia discumbentes, ceperunt in magna leticia comedere, choreas ducere magnosque cachinnos ludendo movere, quasi multum aliquid perpetrassent boni."*

[25] Thomas, *Historia* cap. XXXVI, 163: *"Iacebant autem per vias infelicium opes, vasa aurea et argentea, purpurea indumenta, et arma copiosa. Sed Tartarorum inaudita crudelitas nil curans de spoliis, omnem pretiosarum rerum parvi pendens predam, in sola hominum cede crassarunt. Cum enim viderent iam itineris labore defessos, nec posse ad arma manus extendere, nec pedes ulterius ad fugam laxare, tunc ceperunt hinc et inde iaculis infringere, gladiis obtruncare, nuli parcere, sed omnes feraliter trucidare."*

of Torre Maggiore, who writes about Mongolian slaughterers who were not interested in looting.[26] On another occasion, Thomas of Spalato reports that, during the winter of 1241/42, the Mongols rode up and down the left bank of the Danube, where they had piled up their slain enemies, with the corpses of children impaled on lances – in Thomas's words, „*like fish on a spear*“ – to instil fear into the Hungarians.[27]

John of Piano Carpine gives a matter-of-fact description of Mongol tactics devoid of such dramatic sketches. He simply states: „*When the Tartars make war, they send ahead an advance guard, and they carry nothing with them but their tents, horses and arms. They seize no booty, burn no houses and slaughter no animals; they only wound and kill men or, if they can do nothing else, put them to flight. They much prefer, however, to kill them than to put them to flight.*“[28]

John of Piano Carpine, a Franciscan friar who had played a leading role in the establishment of the Franciscan Order in Europe, had been dispatched in 1245 by Innocent IV as papal envoy to the Mongol court. He and his Polish companion, Brother Benedict, were the first European travellers of the 13th century who penetrated to the core of the Mongol Empire. John, however, was not only charged with the delivery of two papal bulls addressed to the „*King of the Tartars*“[29]; he also had the task of furnishing the Pope with first-hand intel-

[26] Rogerius, *Carmen*, cap. 30, p. 573: „*Argentea quoque vasa et aurea, serice vestes et alia hominibus oportuna per campos et silvas a fugientibus proiecta, ut ipsi velociori cursu manus insequentium evaderent, non habebant aliquos collectores. Tartaris tantum interfectionibus hominum insistentibus de spoliis minime curare videbantur*". Cf. Göckenjan/Sweeney, *Der Mongolensturm*, 213, n. 163.

[27] Thomas, *Historia* cap. XXXVI, 167s.: „*Et ut metum incuterent his, qui erant ex altera parte Danubii, collectam multitudinem occisorum in acervos plurimos super ripam fluminis locaverunt. Alii vero puerulos lanceis affigentes, quasi pisces in veru, per horas alvei baiulabant.*"

[28] Carpine, *Historia,* cap. VI, 11, p. 103; English translation: *The Mongol Mission. Narratives and Letters of the Franciscan Missionaries in Mongolia and China in the Thirteenth and Fourteenth Centuries*. Translated by a Nun of Stanbrook Abbey, Edited and with an Introduction by Christopher Dawson. London-New York 1955, 35. On the advance guard (*precursores*) cf. G. Dörfer, *Türkische und mongolische Elemente im Neupersischen* vol. 4, Wiesbaden 1975, 148s.; Göckenjan, Kundschafter und Späher, 194s.

In similar words, the Franciscan friar C. de Bridia gives an overview of the duties of the Mongol advance guards: *"Cumque Tartari propinquare ceperint, premittunt uelocissimos cursors, qui terreant ex inspirato homines et occident, ne possit contra eos exercitus subito congregari"* (*Hystoria Tartarorum C. de Bridia Monachi*. Edidit et annotationibus instruxit A. Önnerfors, Berlin 1967, cap. 56, p. 34). C. de Bridia, however, cannot be regarded as an authentic and independent source because his *Hystoria Tartarorum* is only a summary of the reports of Carpine and his companion Benedict the Pole. On his work, cf. Gießauf, *Die Mongolengeschichte,* 55s.

[29] The two letters of pope Innocent IV (1245 March 5 „*Dei patris immensa*“ and 1245 March 13 „*Cum non solum*“) are addressed „„... *regi et populo Tartarorum*“. Cf. MGH Epistulae saeculi

ligence about the *„devil's envoys and servants of hell*“[30]. Following his two-year mission to Central Asia, he compiled, in two redactions, a detailed dossier on the hitherto relatively unknown enemy. His „Historia Mongalorum“, which was by far the most widely known of all the early accounts of Mongols, provides information that can be shown to be largely trustworthy.[31] He was the first European who properly understood the significance of the Mongol army organization and presented an outline of it. Two chapters of his book are dedicated to Mongol warfare and to suggestions for practicable European countermeasures.[32] Alongside strategy, his interest is focussed on other military questions such as discipline, horsemanship, the equipment of the mounted warrior and his personal weapons.

The common denominator of the quoted sources is the insight that one important factor of Mongol success was the weakening and demoralization of the foe by means of cruelty. Beyond that, we see from these quotations that some Western reporters were able to comprehend the fact that the Christian world was not confronted with the bloodthirstiness of barbarians but with a complex plan of total warfare and deliberate terror.[33]

XIII selectae: II, 72s., n. 102, and 74s., n. 105; K.-E. Lupprian, *Die Beziehungen der Päpste zu islamischen und mongolischen Herrschern im 13. Jahrhundert anhand ihres Briefwechsels.* Città del Vaticano 1981, 141-145, n. 20 and 146-149, n. 21; for further details see Gießauf, *Die Mongolengeschichte,* 35, 77.

30 *„... Sathane nuntios tartarique ministros“* as Innocent IV used to call them in a letter of 21 July 1243 (= MGH Epistulae saeculi XIII selectae: II, 3s., n. 2).

31 On his life, his mission and his work cf. Giovanni di Pian di Carpine, *Storia dei Mongoli* a cura di Paolo Daffinà, Claudio Leonardi, Maria Christiana Lungarotti, Enrico Menestò, Luciano Petech. Spoleto 1989, 49-92; Gießauf, *Die Mongolengeschichte,* 73-84; F. Schmieder, *Johannes von Plano Carpini. Kunde von den Mongolen 1245-1247*, Sigmaringen 1997, 14-31; J. Gießauf, „Johannes von Piano del Carpine. Provinzialminister 1232-1239,“ in *Management und Minoritas. Lebensbilder Sächsischer Franziskanerprovinziale vom 13. bis zum 20. Jahrhundert.* Kevelaer 2003, 2-18.

32 Carpine, *Historia,* cap. VI (p. 101-104) and VIII (p. 107-111): *„De bello, et ordinatione acierum, et armis, et astutiis in congressione, et crudelitate captivorum, et oppugnatione munitionum, et perfidia eorum in iis qui se reddunt eisdem“;* and: *„Quomodo bello Tartaris occuratur, et quid attendunt, et de armis et ordinatione acierum, et quomodo occuratur eorum astutiis in pugna, et munitione castrorum et civitatum, et quid faciendum est de captivis“*).

33 Similar conclusions were drawn by Vernadsky/Karpovich, *The Mongols,* 116s., Bezzola, *Die Mongolen,* 88, Göckenjan/Sweeney, *Der Mongolensturm*, 52-54 and D. O. Morgan, *The Mongols.* Oxford 1987, 92, who states: *„Chingiz's principle seems to have been much the same as President Truman's over Hiroshima and Nagasaki. The apparent rationale was that if the population of one city was subjected to a frightful massacre, the next city would be more likely to surrender without resistance, thus avoiding unnecessary Mongol casualties. The morality of this approach to warfare is no doubt open to discussion, but there can be no disputing that it worked.“* On the „topos“ of the wild and animal-like barbarian cf. K. Lechner, *Hellenen und Barbaren im Weltbild der Byzantiner. Die alten Bezeichnungen als Ausdruck eines*

A second significant aspect of Mongol strategy combined this programme of psychological warfare with the practical advantage of providing a buffer in the initial stages of an attack: the ruthless employment of captives as arrow shields.

We find very detailed descriptions of this traditional Mongolian tactic in, for example, the „Secret History of the Mongols" of the thirteenth century[34], the reports of Persian historians like Juvaini[35] and in contemporary Chinese sources like Meng-Ta pei-lu, which offers the most precise outline[36]. The Mongols began with the capture of small settlements in a region in order to provide themselves with sufficient manpower that could help them capture larger towns and cities nearby. In heavy assaults, captives were given the task of advancing ahead of the Mongol army to weaken the enemy troops which, having become exhausted, were finally overrun by the Mongols.

Several other Eastern sources confirm this account[37], and similar information can be found in nearly all the major trustworthy Western reports in which we hear about the custom of driving prisoners in front of the main army as arrow shields.[38] They were used to fill up the moats of besieged towns, to erect siege engines under fire from the defenders and finally to head the storming parties. Only a few supervising Mongols took part in these suicide missions to

neuen Kulturbewusstseins, Phil. Diss. München 1954, especially 107-114; B. D. Shaw, Eaters of Flesh, Drinkers of Milk: The Ancient Mediterranean Ideology of the Pastoral Nomad, *Ancient Society* 13/14 (1982/83), 5-31; J. Gießauf, *Barbaren – Monster – Gottesgeißeln. Steppennomaden im europäischen Spiegel der Spätantike und des Mittelalters*. Graz 2006.

34 Geheime Geschichte der Mongolen § 265, p. 198.

35 Cf. Juvaini, *History*, 107: „*When the town* [= Buchara] *and citadel had been purged of rebels and the walls and outworks levelled with the dust, all the inhabitants of the town, men and women, ugly and beautiful, were driven out on the field of the musalla. Chingiz-Khan spared their lives; but the youths and full-grown men that were fit for such service were pressed into a levy for the attack on Sarmaqand and Dabusiya.*" Very similar ibidem pp. 53, 92s. and 100.

36 The following passage summarizes the German translations of the Meng-ta pei-lu and the Hei-Ta shih-lüeh. Cf. *Meng-Ta pei-lu und Hei-Ta shih-lüeh. Chinesische Gesandtenberichte über die frühen Mongolen 1221 und 1237.* Nach Vorarbeiten von Erich Haenisch und Yao Ts´ung-wu übersetzt und kommentiert von Peter Olbricht und Elisabeth Pinks. Wiesbaden 1980, 53 and 191.

37 Cf. B. Spuler, *Die Mongolen in Iran. Politik, Verwaltung und Kultur der Ilchanzeit 1220-1350.* Leipzig 1939, 415, 418; D. H. Martin, The Mongol Army, *Journal of the Royal Asiatic Society* 1943, 67s.; Liu K'i, „Aufzeichnungen von den Vorgängen in Ta-Liang," in *Zum Untergang zweier Reiche. Berichte von Augenzeugen aus den Jahren 1232-33 und 1368-70.* Wiesbaden 1969, 14.

38 Cf. the Hungarian Dominican friar Julian cap. 3, 6-10 (= Dörrie, Drei Texte, 176s.); Matthaeus Parisiensis, *Chronica Majora* IV, p. 76; Rogerius, *Carmen,* cap. 37, 582; Thomas, *Historia,* cap. XXXVII, 170; Carpine, *Historia,* cap. VIII, 6, p. 108s.

prevent the captives from fleeing.[39] However, these captives did not only serve as human targets to minimise casualties among the Mongols; they also fulfilled a psychological role. The justified Mongol expectation was that the defenders under siege would be reluctant to kill their own relatives and compatriots as they were driven forward in front of the attackers. The intention behind these atrocities – to strike terror into the hearts of opponents – was indeed successful, as is shown by the evidence of several cities that surrendered promptly to the Mongols.[40]

Concerning the treatment of captives and subdued peoples, we owe the best Latin summary report to John of Piano Carpine, who writes: „*They send a detachment of captives and men of other nationalities who are fighting with them to meet the enemy head-on, and some Tartars may perhaps accompany them. .... Moreover, when it pleases the masters, they take all the young men with their wives and children and compel them to follow them with all their household; henceforth, they are counted as Tartars, or rather as captives, for although they are numbered among the Tartars, they are never shown the respect that the latter enjoy but are treated as slaves and are sent into every kind of danger like other prisoners; they are the first to be in battle, and if a swamp or a dangerous river has to be crossed, they have to try the passage first.*“[41]

In another passage, the Franciscan writes that the Mongolian captains of a hundred divide those captives who are to be killed among other captives whom they want to keep as slaves and force the latter to kill the former – ten or more of their compatriots.[42]

The facts of Mongol cruelty and massacres speak for themselves. They could produce terror so stupefying that, as Ibn al-Atir records, a single Mongol

[39] From Juvaini, *History*, 53, we learn that some of these Mongols were criminals sentenced to death whose lives had been spared on condition that they took part in such dangerous operations. Cf. also *Meng-Ta pei-lu und Hei-Ta shih-lüeh,* 163, n. 7; Göckenjan, Kundschafter und Späher, 194.

[40] In my opinion, Stephen Turnbull's conclusion about the efficiency of Mongol terror in the Middle East is probably accurate: ... *it is interesting to note the ease with which Genghis Khan captured cities in the central Asian Muslim world compared to similar operations in China. The Chinese had learned to live with nomad hordes over the centuries and were used to their ways, but to the subjects of the Khwarazm Shah the Mongols were strange, alien savages, and it was this barbarian factor that Genghis Khan exploited so well*" (S. Turnbull, Man or Monster? The Real Genghis Khan, *Military Illustrated* 184 (2003), 31).

[41] Carpine, *Historia,* cap. VI, 14, p. 103s. and cap. VII, 11, p. 107.

[42] Carpine, *Historia,* cap. VI, 17, p. 104: *"In bellis autem quoscumque capiunt occident, nisi forte velint aliquos reservare, ut habeant eos pro servis. Occidendos autem dividunt per centenarios, ut cum bipenni interfeciantur ab eis; ipsi vero post hec dividunt per captivos, et unicuique servo ad interficiendum dant decem aut plures aut pauciores secundum quod maioribus placet"*. For a convincing interpretation of this text cf. Schmieder, *Johannes von Plano Carpini*, 144s., n. 143.

horseman could enter a Persian village and begin killing people while no one dared to raise a hand to stop him. Furthermore, the chronicler had heard that one Mongol took a man captive but had no weapon with which to kill him. He told his prisoner to lie with his head on the ground without moving. The terror-stricken man did so and remained there until the Mongol returned with his sword and cut his head off.[43] It is quite obvious that Ibn al-Atir exaggerated with respect to details. What seems important to me, however, is the clearly visible effect of Mongol strategy behind this story. Because of the brutal success of the Mongols, their enemies were often in a state of terror and, in effect, were already defeated psychologically before they were even engaged in battle. The Mongols fostered their terrible image in order to fool their victims into thinking that they were superhuman mounted demons appearing out of nowhere to destroy utterly the known world.[44] One can find confirmation for this psychological advantage of the *Tartars* in the simple statement of the Franciscan Friar Jordan of Giano in his letter to Duke Henry of Brabant: "... *sola nominis sui* [= Tartari] *formidine multos in fugam convertunt*"[45]. At the beginning of the fourteenth century, the Byzantine historian Georgios Pachymeres confirms in similar words that the Mongols used their horrible reputation as a psychological weapon that made the emperor shiver with dreadful fear.[46]

To summarize this examination of the Western sources of the 1240's with additional reference to the eastern chronicles of the thirteenth century, it may be concluded that some of the early writers left the well trodden tracks of interpretation to a remarkable extent. Reporters like Rogerius, Thomas of Spalato and particularly John of Piano Carpine did not use the standard apocalyptic or barbarian models to explain Mongol atrocity but were able to recognize the concept of violence and fear as an intrinsic part of Mongol strategy. In this respect, they were undoubtedly pioneers in transforming the *Tartars* into human beings – cruel, greedy and irritating, of course, but still human beings – and cutting them down to size. In their reports dealing with the crushing defeats by the hitherto unknown enemies, the authority of topos was undermined

[43] I follow the French translation of the Persian text from M. C. d' Ohsson, *Histoire des Mongols depuis Tchinguiz-Khan jusqu'à Timour Bey ou Tamerlan* vol. 3, Le Haye-Amsterdam 1834-35, 69s.

[44] Cf. the thoughts of the Arabian doctor Ibn al-Labbad: "*Sie* [= Tartaren] *töten ausnahmslos und unbarmherzig. Es ist, als ob ihr Zweck die Austilgung der Menschengattung wäre ... Es erhellt hieraus, dass sie nicht so sehr nach Besitz und Vermögen streben, sondern nach Zerstörung der Welt, damit sie zur Wüste werde*" (= J. v. Somogyi, Ein arabischer Bericht über die Tataren im „Ta'rīḫ al-Islām" von aḏ-Ḏahabī, *Der Islam* 24 (1937), 115).

[45] Jordan's letter of May 1241 in Mattheaeus Parisiensis, *Chronica Majora* VI, p. 84.

[46] Georges Pachymérès, *Relations historiques*. Édition, introduction et notes par A. Failler, traduction Française par V. Laurent. Paris 1984, II, 24, p. 187: εννοειν ώστε και έως εκείνου και τουνομα μόνον εισ φόβον ηγεισθαι και δεδιέκαι.

by the power of individual experience. As a result, several years later, the anonymous author of the annals of the chapter of Krakow had no problems in revealing the secrets of success of this strange people: neither outstanding strength nor courage but the deliberate employment of immeasurable atrocity and cunning[47]. The Europeans had become acquainted with Mongol strategy; this did not help much in battle against the well-trained steppe nomads, but knowledge of the enemy and its consequent demystification increased the inclination to seek countermeasures instead of being preoccupied with lamentations about the scourge of God.

47 *Annales Capituli Cracoviensis* in MGH SS XIX, 598 ad annum 1241: „[Thartari]... *illesi ad propria per Hungariam, totum mundum ex sua crudelitate gravi horroris percellentes formidine, redierunt. Quos tamen non robur virium efficit formidandos, nec robusti brachii fortitudo, verum sola cruenta crudelitas ac infidelitas versucia fraudulenta."*

II. Nomadic Violence under the Microscope

CHARLES R. BOWLUS (University of Arkansas)

Predatory Nomadism in the Carpathian Basin. The Magyar Example (860-955)

In 1988, Archibald R. Lewis and J. R. S. Phillips published books that interpreted medieval European history within a broader Afro-Eurasian context. These tomes, written independently of one another, come to a similar conclusion: to understand the rise of the West to its dominant position in the early modern epoch, it is necessary to look deeply into the era that we know as the middle ages. Lewis's book is a short interpretative essay titled *Nomads and Crusaders — A.D. 1000-1368* in which he points out that Latin Christendom was virtually free from the incursions of predatory nomads from Inner Asia during the High Middle Ages (ca. 1000-1350) while other 'advanced' Afro-Eurasian societies struggled to keep raiders from the steppes and deserts at bay.[1] Phillips's book, *The Medieval Expansion of Europe*, is somewhat longer, but not excessively so considering the magnitude of the subject.[2] He too emphasizes the role played by nomads in weakening traditional Afro-Eurasian civilizations, making some of them vulnerable to western European aggression, while opening others to travellers from the West, who benefited more from cross-cultural contacts than did their contemporaries residing in the beleaguered parts of the Afro-Eurasian landmass. Although *lux* came *ex oriente*, it also shone brightly *in occidente*.

Indeed, this period witnessed great advances in the Latin West: an era in which this civilization expanded its horizons culturally and geographically. Meanwhile, the civilizations of the Byzantine commonwealth, North Africa, the Near East, the Indian subcontinent, and the Far East tended to stagnate under mounting pressures from nomads at their gates. The Mongols, of course, were the most powerful and terrible of these intruders from the steppes, and their brief appearance in the Carpathian Basin in the mid-thirteenth century temporarily terrorized the West as well.[3] However, Mongol armies largely spared the West. Indeed, their conquest worked to benefit Latin Christendom, for

1 A. R. Lewis, *Nomads and Crusaders, 1000-1365* (Bloomington, IN: 1988).

2 J. R. S. Phillips, *The Medieval Expansion of Europe* (Oxford, New York: Oxford University Press, 1988).

3 J. Gießauf, *Barbaren—Monster—Gottesgeißeln. Steppenomaden im europäischen Spiegel der spätantike und des Mittelalters* (Grazer Universitätsverlag, Graz, 2006).

the Mongols opened up Inner Asia and the Far East for western travellers (mostly merchants and missionaries) while forcing other societies to adopt defensive postures vis-a-vis these ferocious interlopers. Mamluk regimes in Syria and Egypt, for example, successfully resisted the Mongols militarily, but they paid a price by bringing Near Eastern society under thoroughly militarized rule. China, on the other hand, was itself conquered and governed by Mongols and their surrogates. When the traditional Middle Kingdom re-emerged in the mid-fourteenth century under a native Ming dynasty, it closed down its Inner Asian frontier almost completely. Although there was a brief period in the fifteenth century in which the Ming expanded its sphere of interest into south Asia and the Indian Ocean, the regime deliberately halted this expansion circa 1430, and the great ships that had spearheaded these expeditions rotted in Chinese ports.

In contrast, after the shock of the initial confrontation with Mongols on their eastern frontiers, leaders of western Christendom found it unnecessary to establish and maintain costly defensive infrastructures against nomadic hordes who, after brief incursions into the marchlands of Europe, folded their tents and departed, never to return; and because they did not come back, the West enjoyed one more century of progress before a series of unrelated crises struck in the mid-fourteenth century. Sources tell us that Mongol leaders turned back in order to participate in the election of a new khan, and many modern historians have accepted this fact as an adequate explanation for why they did not return. Nevertheless, it is well known that Mongol armies revisited western Asia to complete the conquest of the Abbasid Caliphate and then pushed across the Syrian desert in an attempt to establish themselves on the eastern shores of the Mediterranean Sea, an enterprise that ultimately failed. Meanwhile, other Mongol armies consolidated their hold on the steppes of southern Russia and firmed up their hegemony over the forest zone to the north. It might of course be argued that Mongol armies failed to turn their attention back to Latin Christendom because it was relatively poor and offered too few returns for the cost of conquering it, in contrast with the Abbasid Caliphate, Mamluk Egypt, the Indian sub-continent, etc. This objection can be answered by pointing out that Latin Christendom's prosperity grew more rapidly in the thirteenth century than did the wealth of many other areas that occupied the attention of the Mongols.

Why did the Mongol war-machine fail to return to the West? It must be acknowledged that their arms were not ineluctably successful everywhere. They failed to conquer the Mamluk state, most of the Indian sub-continent, and Viet Nam. Their invasions of Japan ended in fiascos. They even experienced great difficulties with the Southern Sung polity, which only succumbed about one-half century after the conquest of Northern China and after there had been enormous changes in Mongol military organization. It is important here to recognize that, in most other parts of Eurasia where the Mongols failed, they kept trying. In the West, they gave up after a brief foray into the margins.

The failure of the Mongols in the West may seem puzzling because traditional paradigms of late ancient and early medieval history have emphasized the devastation and destruction wrought by Inner Asian nomads who periodically appeared on the fringes of Europe, moving from the steppes adjacent to the Black Sea across the Carpathians, then finally settling on the plains of the middle Danube (the medieval kingdom of Hungary) and, in the process, setting in motion other peoples (Germans, Slavs, Alans, etc.) who brought down such magnificent edifices as the Roman Empire. Why didn't the Mongols have a similar impact on the West as the Huns did on imperial Rome? While not all modern historians accept the notion that the 'fall' of the Roman Empire was caused by outside forces, many still do, and their paradigms are taken for granted in textbooks and popular histories.[4] Even some professional historians still insist that it was indeed the nomadic Huns (an external force) who triggered the so-called age of migrations (*Völkerwanderung*) that led to the fall.[5] Such historians, however, now must couch their arguments, for it has been conceded that the impact of the invasion was less than earlier historians believed. Throughout the forth century, Peter Heather argued, the "strength and cohesion of Germanic groups" was growing, but then he added that this fact "should not be overstated. The new Germanic powers were still no match for the Roman state. . . The Huns, however, induced too many of these more substantial (Germanic) groups to cross the frontier in too short a space of time for the Roman state to be able to deal with them effectively."[6] As I have pointed out elsewhere, despite the fact that the Huns under Attila were bent on conquest, their empire quickly fell apart following the death of this leader in 451, and, although their war bands continued to function as mercenaries in the service of other powers, they vanished completely after less than a century.[7] As for the Germans, most of them entered Roman imperial service as viceroys, federates, and mercenaries. The Roman Empire, whenever it finally ended, definitely outlasted the Huns who putatively destroyed it.

4 An important exception is D. Nicolle, *Attila and the Nomad Hordes* (Oxford UK: Osprey Publishing, 1990), who paints a more modest picture of the impact of Huns and other nomads on Europe.

5 P. Heather, "The Huns and the End of the Roman Empire in Western Europe," *English Historical Review* 90, 1995, 4-41.

6 Ibid. 42.

7 C. R. Bowlus, "Reitervölker des frühen Mittelalters im Osten des Abendlandes. Ökologische und militarische Gründe für ihr Versagen," *Ungarn Jahrbuch* 22, 1-25.

After the disappearance of the Huns, in the mid-sixth century nomadic Avars entered the Carpathian basin, causing great difficulties for the eastern portions of the Roman Empire and, as allies of the Persians, bringing the 'new' Rome, Constantinople, under siege in 626. The Avars, however, never caused much trouble in the West. The failure of the siege of Constantinople was followed by an uprising of Slavs and the formation of the so-called Samo Reich. When the khagnate was re-established ca. 650, it was generally at peace with its neighbours--though the Avar élite may have received subsidies from Constantinople to help keep Bulgars at bay. There are a few reports of some border skirmishes with the Bavarians along the Danube circa 700, but relations between Bavarians, Franks, and Lombards were generally peaceful in the eighth century, until Charlemagne launched his juggernaut against the Avars in 791.

In the ninth century, largely sedentary Franks and Moravian Slavs vied with one another to establish polities in the Carpathian Basin.

In 892, however, another nomadic people, the Magyars (also known as Hungarians) entered the basin at the invitation of the East Frankish king, and in 907 they defeated a Bavarian force to become rulers of the region. When they crossed the Carpathians to settle permanently along the middle Danube, the Magyars were primarily horse archers who made periodic incursions into western Europe. Their invasions came to an abrupt halt in 955, however, when the East Frankish king, Otto I, annihilated their swarms in an encounter, the so-called battle of Lechfeld. Histories of medieval Europe have echoed annalists and hagiographers who portrayed the Hungarians as invincible hoards of wild and undisciplined barbarians whose incursions ushered in a reign of terror that endured for more than one-half century. Meanwhile, Scandinavian and Muslim sea rovers attacked Europe from the north, west, and south. Though independent of one another, all together their depredations putatively caused the collapse of the Carolingian Empire and arrested the political, economic, and social development of Europe for at least a century. According to the paradigm, leaders in the Latin West could only respond by developing (heavy) cavalry forces to deal with the invaders in the field and by studding the landscape of Europe with fortresses to protect their movable assets.[8] From iron, stone, and mortar élites in the Latin West fashioned the 'first feudal age' to deal with these invasions.

[8] K. Leyser, *Medieval Germany and Its Neighbors 900-1250* (London: Hambledon, 1982), 43-67.

Despite its persistence, this paradigm has been out of date since Gina Fasoli demolished many of the myths concerning the Magyars in 1945.[9] The Hungarians were not a cause of the collapse of the Carolingian Empire. Rather, the Magyars understood and profited from the rivalries and internecine conflicts that persisted as the realm of Charlemagne's heirs disintegrated in the late ninth and early tenth centuries. In 1968, Szabolcs de Vajay buttressed Fasoli's conclusions, arguing convincingly that, as early as 860 (well before they finally settled in the Carpathian Basin), Magyars served Moravian leaders Rastislav and Sventipulk, both of whom were involved in conflicts with various East Frankish rulers.[10] In 892, Arnulf of Carinthia, a late Carolingian ruler, turned the tables when he employed Magyar horsemen against Sventibald. In addition, Vajay argued that some Magyars must have been involved in Arnulf's invasion of Italy in 896 which resulted in his imperial coronation. Recently, Aldo Settia has called attention to the fact that there is little evidence of massive destruction by the Magyars during their frequent later incursions into Italy,[11] and Barbara Rosenwein has observed that Berengar I, Margrave of Friuli and later king of Italy, who had a terrible reputation as a warrior, prevailed against numerous rivals partially because of his skilful use of Hungarians against his opponents.[12] Most serious scholars no longer portray the Magyars as a *gens detestanda*, who brought only death and destruction, but rather as wily military entrepreneurs who knew how to exploit their martial skills for gain while the chaotic conditions of the late Carolingian era persisted.[13] They were predators, living from the fruits of neighbouring societies rather than trying to conquer them. Western military leaders locked in struggles against one another employed Magyars because of their special martial talents based on mounted archery. Although their skills made them useful as small units of auxiliaries, the ecology of the Carpathian Basin could not support huge steppe armies, and environmental conditions in the West did not suit their tactical capabilities. The destruction of Magyar forces at the battle of Lechfeld in 955 convinced their leaders to abandon predatory nomadism and to become themselves 'guardians of the gate of Christendom', a role that their descendants played against

9 G. Fasoli, *Incursioni Ungare in Europa nel secolo X* (Bologne, Biblioteca Storica Sansoni, 1945).

10 Sz. De Vajay, *Der Eintritt des ungarischen Stämmebundes in die europäische Geschichte. 862-933* (Mainz: Studica Hungarica 4, 1968).

11 A. Settia, "Gli Ungari in Italia e I mutamenti territoriali fra VIII-X secolo," in *I barbari in Italia.* Ed. M. B. Aramone. (Libri Scheiwiller: Milan, 1984).

12 B. Rosenwein, "The Family Politics of Berengar I, King of Italy (888-924)," *Speculum* 71, 247-89.

13 M. G. Kellner, *Die Ungarneinfälle im Bild der Quellen bis 1150. Von der 'Gens detestanda zur 'Gens ad fidem Christi conversa'* (Munich: Verlag des Ungarisches Instituts, 1997).

other predatory nomads such as Petchenegs and Cumans.[14] More will be said about this below.

When the Hungarians began their settlement in 896, they were no strangers to the Carpathian Basin. They had already used their martial skills in the service, first of the Moravians and then, reversing themselves, they served the East Franks against the Moravians. This mercenary behaviour was nothing new, for, while still in Ethelköz, they had served the Byzantine Empire for profit prior to their westward trek. The Hungarians made their decision to settle permanently along the middle Danube, when Petchenegs, in the service of Bulgars, attacked defenceless Magyar camps and absconded with their women and children, a practice that was not uncommon on the Eurasian steppes. Across the great forests of the Carpathians (Transylvania), they continued their profession as classic nomadic mercenaries in their new homeland. Because they had martial skills that complemented those of élites in the West, who were warring against one another, Magyars could find willing customers for their 'service industry'. Although such terms as *mercenarius*, *solidarius*, and *stipendarius* are never used to describe the early Hungarians, they were mercenaries indeed, for they fought for material rewards that came frequently in the form of precious metals (*aurum et argentum*). Economically, it was much more rational to fight for pay or tribute than for plunder and slaves, which of course they also did. When they took plunder, however, their horses had to bear the weight and lost mobility. When they took captives, they had to guard and herd them until ransoming them for hard cash. Human chattel hampered their tactical mobility, their greatest asset.

The fact that the Hungarians frequently fought as mercenaries has to do with the very nature of their tactics and military organization.[15] Their services were in great demand for the same reasons that they were feared. Monetary rewards came to them because their tactical repertoire was based on the types of forces lacking in Carolingian and Ottonian Europe: durable light steppe cavalry who unleashed from their composite bows lethal hail storms of arrows that rained down on their opponents from great distances. Even if their pay was sometimes disguised in the form of gifts, it is clear that they fought for hire. Gift-giving in return for military service is mercenary, no matter how anthropologists might try to explain it. Magyars did their share of looting, to be sure,

[14] N. Berend, *At the Gate of Christendom. Jews, Muslims and 'Pagans' in Medieval Hungary, c. 1000-c. 1300* (Cambridge UK: Cambridge University Press, 2003) and by the same author "Hungary: 'the gate of Christendom', *Medieval Frontiers: Concepts and Practices*, ed. D. Abulafia and N. Berend (Aldershot UK: Ashgate, 2002), 195-216.

[15] For Hungarian warfare see, Charles R. Bowlus, *The Battle of Lechfeld and its Aftermath, August 955. The End of the Age of Migrations in the Latin West* (Aldershot UK, Ashgate, 2007), 19-44.

but so did mercenaries of later epochs. They were not simply rowdies 'who occasionally roughed up the natives.' The Byzantine Emperor Leo VI noted that the early Hungarians were highly disciplined and did not begin to pillage until the enemy had been thoroughly routed. There is evidence, however, that this discipline was breaking down in the middle of the tenth century, when looting contributed to the Magyar defeat at Lechfeld.[16] On the other hand, Magyars certainly were not chary when it came to taking subsidies from sedentary powers in return for military services, and they successfully demanded tribute from richer neighbours in return for leaving them in peace after having menaced them by invading their realms.

Like Huns and Avars before them, the early Hungarians came to realize that, as horse archers, they could not subjugate, occupy and govern either the Latin West or the Byzantine Empire. Their base in the Carpathian Basin was simply not large enough to allow them to become a nomadic superpower like the Mongols later became. The ecology of the basin simply could not support a force of mounted archers that was large enough to subdue neighbouring empires. Thus the Magyars had two choices. They could create a sedentary kingdom based on agriculture and small scale transhumance capable of supporting towns where specialized trades could develop, or they could create in the Carpathian Basin a society of mercenaries living as parasites from their neighbours. In the short run, the pressures to pursue careers as predatory warriors were great. However, the farmers, the herdsmen, and burgesses won out in the long run. Why?

Inner Asian specialists have attempted to answer this question by devising ecological and geographic models to estimate the number of steppe warriors who could be sustained by the pastures of the Carpathian Basin.[17] Although sources speak of great multitudes of Magyar archers, Denis Sinor concluded that the entire basin could only nourish enough horses to provide mounts for 60,000 bowmen. Rudi Paul Lindner reduced the number even more drastically. He premised his argument on the assumption that Huns, Avars, and Hungarians were first and foremost pastoralists who would not have excluded other large herbivores, cattle, sheep, and goats from their herds. Thus he reasoned that no more than half of the Great Hungarian Plain could ever have been given over to horse pasture. On the basis of that premise, he reasoned that only 150,000 horses would have been available for Attila's horde. Assuming that

[16] T. von Bogyay, *Lechfeld: Ende und Anfang: Geschichtliche Hintergründe, ideeler Inhalt und Folge der Ungarnzüge. Ein Ungarischer Beitrag zur Tausendjahrfeier des Sieges am Lechfeld* (Munich: Karpathia, 1955).

[17] D. Sinor, "Horses and Pasture in Inner Asian History," *Oriens extremus* 19 (1972), 171-84. R. P. Lindner, "Nomads, Horses and Huns," *Past and Present* 92 (1981), 3-19.

each archer required ten mounts, Lindner concluded that the Great Plain could not have provided mounts for more than 15,000 archers. "Our Huns", he wrote, "could not even have mustered two Mongol divisions or 20,000 horsemen against the Romans' much larger resources."[18] Although he primarily discussed Huns, Lindner emphasized that his analysis also applied to Avars and Hungarians whose military experiences were 'echoes of Attila'. He argued that, by the end of his reign, mounted archers constituted only a tiny portion of his army. By implication, the Magyars must have been forced to follow the same course.

Heather posited another view.[19] He suggested that 15,000 highly skilled mounted archers on any frontier of the Roman Empire would have constituted a formidable fighting force that could fend quite well for itself in a parasitic relationship with its neighbours. Settling on the fringes of the wealthy and sedentary world of the Mediterranean, steppe peoples (Huns, Avars, and Magyars) would have had powerful incentives to abandon pastoral nomadism altogether and become full-time military specialists, for whom Heather has no qualms about using the term mercenaries. Assuming that they could live more profitably from the spoils of war than from cattle, sheep and goats, Heather argued that they would surely have been motivated to curtail other forms of husbandry in order to increase the rangeland available for war horses. He posits that 'predatory nomadism' was a more economically rational use of the limited steppes of the Carpathian Basin than was pastoralism. Since Magyars could not realistically use the pastures of the Carpathian Basin to become a nomadic superpower, and since they possessed martial skills that their sedentary neighbours lacked, it was logical for them to seek a livelihood as predators.

At this point, is must be noted that Sinor, Lindner, and Heather actually underestimated the number of horses required to provide 15,000-20,000 steppe warriors with ten mounts each. Steppe warriors did not simply spring onto feral horses and dash off to rape, pillage, and burn. To produce an adequate supply of warhorses (generally geldings), steppe peoples had to manage their herds carefully. Taking into consideration the structure of herds, I have estimated that, to provide each warrior with ten mounts sufficiently mature to stand the rigors of campaigning, a herd of at least twenty-six horses would have been required — one stallion, ten mares, five of whom were pregnant, another five nursing, five foals of one to two years and two of three years. Including the ten war geldings, and the total herd necessary for each archer was thirty-six.[20]

[18] Lindner, Ibid. 14-15.

[19] P. J. Heather, "Huns, Horses, and Nomadism," *Abstracts of papers, Twenty-First Annual Byzantine Studies* (1985), 9.

[20] Bowlus, Lechfeld, 26.

Thus, a total of 720,000 horses (not 200,000) would have been needed to maintain 20,000 archers with ten war geldings each, a number exceeding the resources of the Carpathian Basin. The majority of these horses would never taste combat. In fact, at most twenty-eight percent of the total herd would consist of geldings ready for expeditions. If the steppe lands of Hungary could have supported 150,000 horses (Lindner's figure) or 300,000 (excluding all other forms of husbandry as Heather suggests), then only 36,000 or 72,000 war geldings would have been available to furnish mounts for either 3,600 or 7,200 archers assuming ten-horses per archer. No matter which of these scenarios one might choose, neither Huns, Avars, nor Magyars were capable of putting even one Mongol division in the field, at least not if each archer had a train of ten mounts.

But the assumption is also suspect that steppe warriors went off on campaigns to western Europe riding one horse while trailing a minimum of nine others on a line. Such a large number of horses would have been difficult to manage on expeditions. Extra horses were of tactical importance only insofar as they guaranteed steppe warriors fresh mounts before entering battle. Mounted archers certainly did not go into battle with strings of horses *en train*, for in such a case these bowmen could not possibly manage their horses while launching their arrows at the same time. A steppe warrior with five horses would still have been highly mobile strategically in that he could alternate his mounts frequently to maintain a pace of 100 km or more per day. Still, before entering combat, extra horses would have to be tended by men who could not engage in the fighting. It might be argued that, following an encounter, extra horses would have been necessary as pack animals for steppe warriors returning to the Alföld with booty. If, on the other hand, the archers were primarily involved in mercenary activities, seeking monetary gain rather than bulky goods, too many extra horses would not have been particularly useful. Thus, by limiting the number of horses per archer to five or less, the Hungarians could double their numbers, their firepower, and hence their value as mercenaries.

Another consideration confronting the early Hungarians was the question of the availability of pasture along the invasion routes. It made little difference how many horses could be raised on the limited steppes of the Carpathian Basin if there were not adequate pasturage to support them during expeditions in Europe. It also made sense for potential employers to engage bands that had fewer horses and a higher percentage of archers. By limiting the number of horses per archer, more grazing lands would be available for other animals back in the Carpathian Basin. Horses are expensive animals to keep. Cattle, sheep, and goats yield much more protein, hide, and fiber on the hoof than do horses, whose digestive systems are less efficient than those of ruminators. Moreover, it is important to point out that the Carpathian Basin does not consist entirely of steppe lands. There are substantial regions of fertile loess and clay soils which agriculturalists were exploiting at the time of Hungarian settlement. Thus, it made no sense for Magyars to expand their equestrian herds to the very limits of the carrying capacity of the basin if the eco-systems of the kingdoms of Italy and East and West *Francia* could not sustain large steppe armies.

To be sure, there were some very good pastures with steppe-like vegetation scattered throughout western Europe, but most of these were not large enough to nourish Hungarian horses for very long. There were islands of grasslands resembling 'stepping stones', allowing small bands of Hungarians access and egress. The Magyars learned where these routes were and the used them. Unfortunately for the invaders, their victims also knew these routes and they were aware of the fact that Hungarians needed precisely these pastures. Consequently, the defenders improvised ambushes for the interlopers when they returned to the homeland. An important reason why mercenary service was more attractive than raiding to Hungarians was that, by entering into agreements with local magnates, they could avoid ambushes and were able to secure in advance safe routes of ingress and egress.

Durable light Hungarian cavalry was in demand primarily because of formidable archery that allowed the infliction of heavy losses on the enemy without irrevocably committing themselves to close combat. Procopius, a Byzantine military historian writing in the sixth century, called the composite bows of the Huns 'miracle weapons'.[21] The emperor Maurice, however, who wrote his Strategikon less than a half century later, noted that composite bows were sensitive to inclement weather. They came unglued when damp. Consequently, he advised commanders to attack archers whenever it rained. Examples from various parts of Eurasia show that Maurice's observations were correct. Especially in the Latin West north of the Alps, where rainfall is evenly distributed throughout the year, Hungarians on many occasions were forced to stash their bows in waterproof cases and flee when torrential rains or even sudden showers caught them by surprise. The archery of steppe warriors was affected not only by rainfall, but also by micro-climatic, geographic, and above all physical factors. Composite bows were most effective when archers released arrows as rapidly as possible at an angle of approximately forty-five degrees, which ensured that arrows would fall in clusters at the maximum range of the weapon and with maximum force and killing power. In this kind of archery, precise aiming at individual targets point blank was of no importance. Archers lofted projectiles into a target zone several hundred meters away. To do this, the bowmen had to estimate the distance and the windage accurately in

[21] Bowlus, Ibid. 27.

order to make an educated guess as to the whereabouts of his enemy targets several seconds after the volley, when the missiles (powered by gravity on their downward trajectories) landed. Archers also needed open landscapes. In 955, Otto I was able to protect his forces from Magyar archery by marching his men through a forest in relief of Augsburg.

Mounted archery was obviously not effective under this and many other conditions. It was a tactic that could be devastating. Releasing hailstorms of arrows, horse arches sometimes completely destroyed opposing armies in the field; nevertheless, this tactical repertoire was too limited to allow mounted archers to become an army of conquest under the climatic conditions in the Latin West, even if the Carpathian Basin could have supported more horses. Their tactics were well suited for forces paid to accomplish specialized tasks, that is, for predatory warriors, for mercenaries, but not for conquerors.

In conclusion, this essay has argued that a close analysis of the Magyars, who in the late ninth century moved from the steppes adjacent to the Black Sea into the Carpathians and settled on the plains of the middle Danube, provide clues to explain why the Mongols failed to spread their terror from the Carpathian Basin into western Europe. Unlike Huns, Avars, and Magyars, who remained there, the Mongols quickly discovered that this western extension of the world's largest land mass is ill suited for their style of warfare. There is admittedly still much scholarly disagreement over the impact of the Mongol invasions on Europe and on European mentalities. As Nora Berend has observed, "Some scholars have even denied that the invasion left lasting effects, claiming that the chilling medieval accounts were generated not by the weight of the devastation but by the appearance of a little-known and even less understood, therefore mythified, enemy."[22] It is probable that King Bela IV, a victim of the Mongol invasion, tried to take advantage of the terror to advance the interests of the Hungarian kingdom. Berend calls attention to a royal letter written upon Bela's return, after having been driven from his realm. He maintained that the Mongols were intent on coming and conquering the whole of the Christian world. "Hungary would serve as an ideal site for the Mongols for their conquest of the West, since they could establish their camps in the country and could find ample pasture for their horses," which, as we have seen, would not have been the case because of the *lack of adequate pasture*. In this letter, however, "Hungary was thus depicted as occupying a key position. It was the gate that was to keep enemies out, but that once opened, could serve as a point of entry to a defenceless Christendom." It was necessary for other Christian powers to subsidize and assist the kingdom in order to keep this gate firmly closed. Hungary, however, unlike the regions of northern and western

[22] Berend, *At the Gate*, 205.

China, the Persian plateau, or the Ukraine, did not have a large enough steppe to allow the Mongols to belly up to the West in order to launch wars of conquest. Thus, Latin Christendom was spared and given additional time to develop its civilization, which eventually, for better or worse, became globally dominant. It was not the 'creative destruction' of the Mongols that led to the 'Rise of the West' but rather the fact that the Mongols exerted almost no pressure on western European civilization while devastating much of the rest of the Eurasian land mass.

REUVEN AMITAI (Jerusalem)

Im Westen nichts Neues? Re-examining Hülegü's Offensive into the Jazīra and Northern Syria in Ligth of Recent Research

The Hebrew University of Jerusalem

The research of recent decades, as well as some more popular presentations, have succeeded in somewhat mitigating an unequivocally harsh view of the Mongols in both scholarly and lay circles. It should be mentioned, however, that even among serious scholars of the Mongols of the older generation,[1] the positive side of Mongol rule was never forgotten. In short, the nascent approach of seeking good aspects of the Mongol rule, especially cultural effervescence, but also a certain degree of religious tolerance and general intellectual openness, has been strengthened in the last generation or so, without turning a blind eye to the cruelty and destruction of the conquests and the often heavy-handed Mongol approach to government, not the least in the realm of taxation. Among scholars writing in English, we might note the important studies by David Morgan,[2] Peter Jackson,[3] Thomas Allsen,[4] Morris Rossabi[5] and others,[6]

1 B. Lewis, "The Mongols, the Turks and the Muslim Polity," in B. Lewis, *Islam in History*, 2nd edition (Chicago and La Salle: Open Court, 1993), pp. 189-209 (notes on pp. 443-444); V.V. Bartold, *Mussulman Culture*, tr. S. Suhrawardy (Calcutta: University of Calcutta, 1934), 110-112.

2 D.O. Morgan, *The Mongols*, 2nd edn. (Oxford, Malden MA and Carlton, Victoria: Blackwells, 2007); *idem*, *Medieval Persia 1000-1797* (London: Longman, 1988), chapters 6-8.

3 P. Jackson, *The Mongols and the West, 1221-1410* (Harrow: Pearson Longman, 2005).

4 T.T. Allsen, *Commodity and Exchange in the Mongol Empire: A Cultural History of Islamic Textiles* (Cambridge: Cambridge University Press, 1997); *idem*, *Culture and Conquest in Mongol Eurasia* (Cambridge: Cambridge University Press, 2001).

5 M. Rossabi, "The Legacy of the Mongols," in B.F. Manz (ed.), *Central Asia in Historical Perspective* (Boulder: Westview, 1994), 27-44; *idem*, *Khubilai Khan: His Life and Times* (Berkeley: University of California Press, 1988).

6 A good place to start is the articles collected in L. Komaroff and S. Carboni (eds.), *The Legacy of Genghis Khan: Courtly Art and Culture in Western Asia, 1256-1353* New York: The Metropolitan Museum of Art and New Haven and London: Yale University Press, 2002), as well as many of the studies discussed in P. Jackson, "The State of Research: the Mongol Empire, 1986-1999," *Journal of Medieval History*, 26 (2000), 189-210; Morgan, *The Mongols*,

who have shown this gentler face of Mongol rule, while still showing the darker side of their conquest and domination.

This approach has been taken a few steps further in the last few years by the British scholar George Lane, whose revisionist approach to the rule of Hülegü and his descendents, collectively known as Ilkhans, has been both refreshing and thought-provoking.[7] Lane has shown that the Ilkhanid period in Iran and its surrounding countries (1260-1335) was overall one of relative economic and political stability (certainly more than previously thought), and has demonstrated perhaps more strongly than any of his scholarly predecessors how truly dynamic this period was from the point of view of intellectual and cultural life. Lane also cogently argues that the Ilkhans enjoyed more local support than previously thought. One of the most important insights that Lane has presented is that we have been victims of massive confusion, perpetrated probably unwittingly by our sources, who in turn were influenced by their contemporaries, regarding the various waves of the Mongol conquest. To the popular and scholarly mind, the campaigns of Chinggis Khan in Transoxania and northwest Iran (1219-23), his grandson Hülegü's in Iran and further west from about 1255 onward, and those of Tamerlane (Temür) in the last third of the fourteenth century and the beginning of the fifteenth have all been jumbled into one. In other words, the death and destruction that characterized much of Chinggis Khan's offensive in the Muslim world, let alone the probably worse nature of Tamerlane's attacks (without the alleviating factors of the former), have unintentionally or not been attributed to Hülegü as well.

I am willing to accept this suggestion up to a point: certainly with the exception of the Assassins in their mountain fortresses, who had plenty of opportunity to experience Mongol military might and traditional methods of conquest at close quarters, basically the population of Iran did not suffer unduly from Hülegü's arrival in the region at the head of a large army.[8] Indeed, Hülegü's reorganization of the administration in this region may have been to their benefit, as officials were under tighter control, tax policy may have been better regulated and the Turco-Mongol nomads kept under a firmer hand.

chapter 9: "The Mongol Empire since 1985." For a good short summary of discussion of *Pax Mongolica* in the research literature, see: Hodong Kim, "The Unity of the Mongol Empire and Continental Exchanges over Eurasia," *Journal of Central Eurasian Studies*, 1 (2009), 15-18.

7 G. Lane, *Early Mongol Rule in Thirteenth-Century Iran: A Persian Renaissance* (Routledge-Curzon, 2003).

8 For Hülegü advance in Iran, see J.A. Boyle, "Dynastic and Political History of the Īl-Khāns." In *The Cambridge History of Iran*, vol. 5: ed. J.A. Boyle (Cambridge: Cambridge University Press, 1968); B. Spuler, *Die Mongolen in Iran: Verwaltung und Kultur der Ilchanzeit. 1220-1350*, 4th edn. (Leiden: Brill, 1985), 44-48.

I do not think, however, that this somewhat irenic description of Hülegü's campaign stands as he and his armies continued west, particularly after most of them took up position in the Azerbaijan region in the northwest of Iran (due to the conditions there that were suitable for nomadism of the Inner Asian type). In this volume, we have the paper by Frank Kraemer about the conquest of Baghdad in early 1258, which clearly demonstrates that the Mongols under Hülegü could take off their gloves when deemed necessary. In my article, I will discuss the next Mongol offensives in 1259 and 1260 into the Jazīra (Upper Mesopotamia, i.e., the region combining parts of northern Iraq, northeast Syria and southeastern Turkey) and northern Syria. I will show that when required or desirous from a Mongol point of view, the Mongols could show their true colors, or at least one aspect of their political and military culture. Perhaps in Iran, Hülegü had put on a gentler face of Mongol rule, but as he went beyond previously conquered territory, older, meaner forms of behavior could come to the fore.

I hope that the readers will forgive me if I have taken liberties with the title of the classic work by Erich Maria Remarque. I am using the phrase *Im Westen nichts Neues* for several reasons: Firstly, on the one hand, there is indeed something new on the Western front: after the period of relatively peaceful campaigning, there is a renewed use of traditional Mongol siege tactics, including the deliberate employment of terror, cruelty and destruction to bring about the weakening of the enemies' will and to punish them for the temerity to resist the Mongol vision of world conquest. Secondly, on the other hand, it also means that there is really nothing new here: it is a return to the tried and true methods of Mongol conquest from the not too distant past. Thirdly, if I might paraphrase the standard English translation of this title, all was not "quiet on the Western Front," and in fact, this campaign ushers in a period of war in this area that was to keep the Ilkhanids and their supporters busy for several decades.

In this paper, I will attempt to examine in some detail the taking by the Mongols of two cities in particular, one each in the Jazīra and northern Syria. These are Mayyāfāriqīn (Martyropolis in Greek, Silvan in modern Turkish) and Aleppo (Ḥalab in Arabic and Hebrew) respectively. Mayyāfāriqīn was ruled by an independent Ayyūbid prince, al-Kāmil Muḥammad b. al-Muẓaffar Ghāzī, while Aleppo was a possession of the most important Ayyūbid ruler at this time, al-Nāṣir Yūsuf, a direct descendent of Saladin. Al-Nāṣir, however, at this time was spending his time further south, at his main city (since about 1250) – Damascus – and in his stead left an older relative, al-Mu`aẓẓam Tūrānshāh, a son of Saladin himself. This al-Mu`aẓẓam was no spring chicken, as his father had died some 67 years before the events described here. Yet his relatively old age did not prevent him from leading a spirited fight against the Mongols, once push came to shove as it did at the beginning of 1260; although this is not a theme of the paper today, I cannot help but mention that al-Mu`aẓẓam's personal courage, presence of mind and his ability to lead contrasts sharply with the gifts of his nephew, al-Nāṣir Yūsuf, the sultan of all of Syria, and thus his direct ruler.[9]

In this paper I will attempt to base my work mainly on the contemporary Arabic sources or those compiled just after the period described, although I will have recourse to at least one later Arabic historical work that is particularly dependable, and contains clearly labeled earlier material. I am referring to *Ta'rīkh al-duwal wa'l-mulūk* by Ibn al-Furāt (d. 1405), whose relevant section is still unedited and whose unique manuscript is found in the Vatican Library. I will also have a look at how the pro-Mongol Rashīd al-Dīn (d. 1318), who wrote in Persian, presents these incidents, as well as similarly inclined other works. We will see that neither Rashīd al-Dīn nor his "colleagues" pulled their punches. In the case of Rashīd al-Dīn, the more than forty years between the events described and the writing of this text, plus the recent conversion to Islam of the Mongols, including of course Rashīd al-Dīn's patron Ghazan Ilkhan, both surely paved the way for the author to deal with the events of 1260 (as well as those of the previous years – including the conquest of Baghdad and the execution of the last Caliph) in a relatively dispassionate – if not always accurate – manner.

Before proceeding to my discussion, I would want to set the stage by presenting the main events in Hülegü's *Drang nach Westen*. In 1251, Möngke, the son of Tolui (and thus, the grandson of Chinggis Khan), became Qaghan/Qa'an or Great Khan, and this represented a significant dynastic shift within the royal family from the descendents of Ögödei to those of Tolui. Möngke soon ordered the organization of large offensives into China and the Middle East, under his brothers Qubilai and Hülegü respectively. The latter's brief was to organize and consolidate territory already conquered, to subjugate the Assassins (i.e., the Nizārī Ismā`īlīs) who controlled numerous castles in eastern and northern Iran, and to bring the `Abbāsid Caliph to bay: if he submitted, he was to be well treated, and if not he was to bear the full brunt of Mongol military might.[10] According to Rashīd al-Dīn, Hülegü was "to conquer the lands of the enemies...until you have many summer and winter camps" and he was to enact

9 For developments in this area before Hülegü's arrival, and events subsequently, see R.S. Humphreys, *From Saladin to the Mongols: The Ayyubids of Damascus, 1193-1260* (Albany: State University of New York Press, 1977), 333-363.

10 For the motivation and organization of this campaign, see T.T. Allsen, *Mongol Imperialism: The Policies of Grand Qan Möngke in China, Russia and the Islamic Lands 1251-59* (Berkeley and Los Angeles: University of California Press, 1987), 47-49; R. Amitai-Preiss, *Mongols and Mamluks: The Mamluk-Ilkhanid War 1260-1281* (Cambridge: Cambridge University Press, 1995), 8-17.

the laws of Chinggis Khan in the lands from the River Oxus up to the edge of the land of Egypt.[11] Hülegü spent a couple of years making arrangements for this large offensive, which probably involved many tens of thousands of Mongol troops, their families and herds. He set out from Mongolia in 1253, making slow progress, which befits an army encumbered by many sheep eating their way across Central Asia. By early 1256, Hülegü had reached the Middle East, and commenced his campaign against the Assassins, more-or-less conquering their strongholds by the end of the year, capturing their leader and having him put to death.[12] In early 1258, the Mongols converged on Baghdad, after some inconclusive negotiations with the Caliph, who suffered from the treachery of senior elements at his court. After a spirited but hopeless defense by the army and local inhabitants, the city was soon taken, many of its inhabitants slaughtered and the Caliph executed.[13] But I will not dawdle here, since we will hear about this episode in detail in the chapter by Frank Kraemer. A Mongol army was sent south to conquer the remainder of Iraq, and Hülegü moved north via Hamadān and then to Azerbaijan, which had already become the center of Mongol rule in the region.

It is clear that as Hülegü moved westward into the Muslim world, his view of Syria, and perhaps Egypt became clearer, and his plans for these regions more concrete. At some point, he had told Baiju, the hitherto commander of Mongol forces in the area: "You must set out, in order to deliver those countries up to the coast of the western sea (the Mediterranean), from the hands of the sons of France and England," although possibly this could be read "from the hands of the sons of the Franks and infidels." [14] There are other indications from Hülegü's reported sayings and his letters that he had set his sights on Syria and Egypt, including in the letters to al-Nāṣir Yūsuf on one hand, and later, the new ruler of Egypt, Quṭuz, on the other.[15] Before moving into Syria, however, Hülegü first had to clear the way in the Jazīra, not the least to make sure

[11] Rashīd al-Dīn (Abū al-Khayr Faḍlallāh al-Hamadānī), *Jāmi` al-tawārīkh*, vol. 3: ed. `A. `Alīzādah (Baku: Farhangistān-i `Ulūm-i Jumhūrī-yi Shūrā-yi Susiyālīstī-yi Ādharbāyjān, 1957), 3:23 = translation by W.M. Thackston, *Rashiduddin Fazlullah's Jami`u't-tawarikh: Compendium of Chronicles. A History of the Mongols* (Cambridge, MA: Harvard University, Dept. of Near Eastern Languages and Civilizations, 1998-99), 2:479.

[12] For the itinerary above, see the studies cited in note 8 above. For the size of the army, see Allsen, *Mongol Imperialism*, 203-207; for a different view, which suggests a smaller army, see the relatively new article by J.M. Smith, Jr., "Hülegü Moves West: High Living and Heartbreak on the Way to Baghdad, " in L. Komaroff (ed.), *Beyond the Legacy of Genghis Khan* (Leiden: Brill, 2006), 111-134.

[13] Boyle, "Dynastic and Political History," 346-349.

[14] Rashīd al-Dīn, ed. `Alīzādah, 3:39 (cf. the edition by M.E. Quatremère, *Histoire des Mongols de la Perse* [Paris: Imprimerie Royale, 1836], 224) = tr. Thackston, 1:487 (see note 1).

[15] Amitai-Preiss, *Mongols and Mamluks*, 21-24, 36.

that there would be no potential centers of opposition in his rear obstructing communications and making trouble while he was campaigning in Syria.

On the whole, there were not undue problems gaining control of the Jazīra, important for agriculture and trade, with its many rich cities. For example, Mosul, under the rule of the aging Atabeg Badr al-Dīn Lu'lu' had submitted to the Mongols even before the conquest of Baghdad. Irbil, some 80 kilometers to the south, was taken after Baghdad with the help of Lu'lu', and did not prove to be much of a problem from a military point of view.[16] This is how most fortified cities in this area passed into Mongol control: either they submitted peacefully, fully aware of the Mongol threat, or attempted to resist, succeeding to do so only for a short period and suffering the consequences. The example of Mayyāfāriqīn is exceptional for the longevity of its resistance, although not for its ultimate fate.

This city, in southeastern Turkey today, to the east of Āmid (today Diyarbekir), had already suffered Mongol depredations in the past: The Mongols devastated the area around Mayyāfāriqīn as early as 1231. In 1240-41 a Mongol embassy arrived there, demanded that it should surrender and its fortifications be destroyed. On this occasion, the Ayyūbid prince, al-Muẓaffar Ghāzī succeeded "in deflecting the attentions of the embassy elsewhere."[17] His son and successor, al-Kāmil Muḥammad (who came to power in 1244), thought it first prudent to offer submission to the rising power in southwest Asia, and he himself arrived at Möngke's court in February 1253, as part of a pledge that ended a Mongol siege to his city. As an aside, I will note that when al-Kāmil arrived at Qaraqorum, he found there the heirs apparent of Mosul and Mārdīn, as well as Leon, prince of Lesser Armenia. There seems also to have been present an envoy of the Ayyūbid ruler of Karak. So al-Kāmil was in good company, and was far from being atypical in attempting to pre-empt a Mongol attack on his city by submitting and becoming part of the new world order. What is unusual is that this prince, upon returning to his city in early 1257, threw off his allegiance to his new masters, and began preparing for the inevitable showdown with them.[18] My own understanding of this apparently unexpected and unwise behavior by al-Kāmil is that he had been away from the region when Hülegü arrived on the scene. Perhaps al-Kāmil did not fully grasp the fact that a tremendous army that had entered the Middle East, or perhaps the hitherto relatively peaceful advance of Hülegü (except *vis-à-vis* the Assassins) had misled

[16] Humphreys, *From Saladin to the Mongols*, 344; D. Patton, *Badr al-Dīn Lu'lu' Atabeg of Mosul, 1211-1259* (Seattle and London: Middle East Center, Henry M. Jackson School of International Studies, University of Washington, 1991), 51-64.

[17] C. Hillenbrand, "Mayyāfāriqīn," *Encyclopaedia of Islam*, 2nd edn., 6:928ff.

[18] Amitai-Preiss, *Mongols and Mamluks*, 21.

him. In any event, the die was cast for the fateful confrontation. Neither side, however, could forecast that it would be such a drawn-out affair.

A good way to look at the siege of Mayyāfāriqīn is to take one basic text (in translation), adding some other data from additional sources as well as further comments. I have chosen a passage from the large section on the Mongols by the Egyptian writer al-Nuwayrī (d. 1333), from volume 27 of his encyclopedia *Nihāyat al-arab fī funān al-adab* ("The highest aspiration in the categories of culture"):

> Also in the [*hijrī*] year 656 (which began 8 January 1258), Hülegü sent a part of his armies to Mayyāfāriqīn under [the command of] Sartaq and Qutghan Noyan.[19] In [this city] was al-Malik al-Kāmil [20] Nāṣir al-Dīn Muḥammad b. al-Muẓaffar Ghāzī b. al-`Ādil Abū Bakr b. Ayyūb. [The Mongols] put it under siege and built trebuchets (*al-majānīq*) against it from every side. [Mayyāfāriqīn's] people fought them, defended [the city] and persevered in spite of the difficult siege. Provisions became scarce among them to such a degree that they ate dogs, cats and corpses. The Mongols conquered [the city] after two years, after [its] army (*al-jund*) had ceased to exist due to the heavy fighting, taking into captivity those who survived. Al-Malik al-Kāmil, its ruler, was taken along with nine of his Mamluks. They were brought before Hülegü and killed,[21] except for one who was named Qarasunqur...The Mongol conquest of Mayyāfāriqīn was in the 658 (which began 17 Dec. 1259). When this al-Malik al-Kāmil was killed, the Mongols put his head on a spear and paraded with it around Syria, passing through Aleppo and Hama, reaching Damascus on 27 Jumādā I from this year (A.H. 658= 10 May 1260).[22] They

[19] The title *noyan* was at this time generally given to Mongol divisional commanders who were not from the royal family. Baybars al-Manṣūrī, in the parallel passage in his chronicle (and probably al-Nuwayrī's partial source), refers to both commanders as *noyan*. See below, note 26.

[20] Ibn al-Fuwaṭī (Kamāl al-Dīn Abū al-Faḍl), *al-Ḥawādith al-jāmi`a wa'l-tajārib al-al-nāfi`a fī al-mi'a al-sābi`a*, ed. M. Jawād (Baghdad: al-Maktaba al-`Arabiyya, 1351/1932-33), 240, mistakenly gives his royal *laqab* as al-Malik al-Ashraf, as does Bar Hebraeus, *The Chronography of Gregory Abû 'l-Faraj, 1225-1286,* ed. and tr. E.A.W. Budge (London: Oxford University Press, 1932; rpt. Amsterdam: APA – Philo Press, 1976), 1:434 = Ibn al-`Ibrī (Abū al-Faraj), *Ta'rīkh mukhtaṣar al-duwal*, ed. A. Ṣāliḥānī (Beirut: al-Maṭba`a al-Kāthūlīkiyya li'l-Ābā' al-Yashū`iyyīn fī Bayrūt, 1890), 483. While these pro-Mongol writers disagree with the Ayyūbid and Mamlūk sources on this minor point, they generally concur with them on the nature and outcome of the siege, and its aftermath.

[21] According to Rashīd al-Dīn, edn. `Alīzādah, 3:80 (=tr. Thackston, 1:508), al-Kāmil was brought before Hülegü at Tall Bāshir, in north Syria. This appears to indicate that this was at a relatively early part of the spring. For Hülegü's itinerary in Syria in early 1260, see Amitai-Preiss, *Mongols and Mamluks*, 26-28.

[22] This date is confirmed by the contemporary Damascus writer Abū Shāma (Shihāb al-Dīn `Abd al-Raḥmān b. Ismā`īl), *Tarājim rijāl al-qarnayn al-sādis wa'l-sābi` al-ma`rūf bi'l-dhayl alā al-rawḍatayn*, ed. M. al-Kawtharī (Cairo: Maktab Nashr al-Thiqāfa al-Islāmiyya, 1947), 205.

> marched around with it in Damascus with songs and drum-beating. His head was hung on Bāb al-Farādīs, and thus it remained until Damascus returned to the Muslims…[23]

I would like to make the following comments: firstly, the siege did not last for two years, but was "only" a year and a half long, so it started at the end of 1258, continuing until the spring of 1260. After the surprisingly spirited resistance of both the local army and the population, Hülegü sent reinforcements under his son Yoshmut (Rashīd al-Dīn also mentions the general Suntay), who took direct control of the operation, but even this additional support was initially unsuccessful.[24]

Before the campaign, al-Kāmil had made a quick trip to Syria to consult with his cousin al-Nāṣir Yūsuf, his ostensible overlord, hoping to get some support or at least coordinate their plans vis-à-vis the Mongols. Nothing directly came of this; al-Nāṣir Yūsuf was hardly capable of arranging the affairs of his own country, let alone dispatching help to a neighbor. However, once the Mongol siege of Mayyāfāriqīn started in earnest, al- Nāṣir tried to intervene indirectly: he sent the envoy `Izz al-Dīn ibn Shaddād al-Ḥalabī, later famous as a historical-geographer and biographer of Baybars, to meet with the Mongol prince Yoshmut to get him to end the attack. Ibn Shaddād has been kind enough to provide us an account of his journey, which included frightening stories, yet laced with humor, of encounters with Mongol contingents. He was also unsuccessful in convincing Yoshmut to desist in his siege. The Mongols, on the other hand, tried to use Ibn Shaddād to act as a go-between between them and al-Kāmil and to draw him out. After much wrangling and threats, also not without its comic side, Ibn Shaddād agreed, but nothing came of this activity. Ibn Shaddād was permitted to return to Syria and thereupon made his way to Egypt before the Mongol onslaught on the country the following year.[25]

The difficulties that the inhabitants were undergoing are clearly communicated by Ibn Shaddād. The Mongols were far from waging a desultory siege,

23 Al-Nuwayrī, *Nihīyat al-arab*, 27:383-384.

24 Boyle, "Political and Dynastic History," 350; Rashīd al-Dīn, edn. `Alīzādah, 3:77-80 (=tr. Thackston, 1:507-508). It should be noted that Rashīd al-Dīn places the account of the siege of Mayyāfāriqīn after the battle of `Ayn Jālūt, which might prove confusing were it not for other sources.

25 Ibn Shaddād al-Ḥalabī (`Izz al-Dīn Muḥammad b. `Alī), *al-A`laq al-khaṭīra fī dhikr umarā' al-shām wa'l-jazīra*, vol. 3: ed. Y. `Abbāra (Damascus: Wizārat al-Thaqāfah wa'l-Irshād al-Qawmī, 1978), 3:491-499; R. Amitai-Preiss, "Evidence for the Early Use of the Title Ilkhan among the Mongols," *Journal of the Royal Asiatic Society*, 3rd Ser., 1 (1991), 354-357 (reprinted in R. Amitai, *The Mongols in the Islamic Lands: Studies in the History of the Ilkhanate* [Aldershot, UK and Burlington, VT, USA: Ashgate Publishing Ltd., 2007]); Amitai-Preiss, *Mongols and Mamluks*, 23.

although it appears that they had not pulled out all the stops, for otherwise it is difficult to understand why it took them so long to overcome the resistance. The determination of the garrison, the local population and the prince should not be forgotten in this respect. Yet, whatever the reasons for the length of the siege, the results were not unexpected and were in the best Mongol tradition: those who survived were killed, with the ruler being singled out for a particularly cruel death. The ostentatious display of his head was to drive home the point of the futility and downright immorality of resisting the Mongols. Certainly, the story of the city was conveyed in "real time" to the inhabitants of neighboring countries. Thus, in the words of the contemporary Christian writer from Damascus, Ibn al-`Amīd: "The Mongols captured [Mayyāfāriqīn] by sword, and killed its ruler al-Kāmil ...looted [it] and killed whomever was in it."[26]

The story of Aleppo is similar, but there are also some basic differences. At the beginning of 1260, large Mongol forces, personally led by Hülegü Ilkhan (a title that can henceforth use with a large degree of certitude), crossed the Euphrates, taking up position at the city on 18 January. According to the north Syrian historian, Ibn Wāṣil, who was down south at this time, the following message was sent up to the governor, al-Mu`aẓẓam Tūrānshāh:

> You are too weak to fight the Mongols (*al-mughul*), and you do not have the power to fight them. We are heading for al-Malik al-Nāṣir [Yūsuf] and those with him from the army. Accept from us a governor (*shiḥna*) in the Citadel and one in the City and we will go towards al-Malik al-Nāṣir. If we are defeated, you can do what you want: either keep the governors, drive them away, and if you want kill them. And if we are victorious, we will have nothing against Aleppo and your lives will be protected.

[26] Ibn al-`Amīd (al-Makīn Jirjis), *Kitāb al-majmū` al-mubārik*, ed. C. Cahen, in "'La Chronique des Ayyoubides' d'al-Makīn b. al-`Amīd, " *Bulletin d'études orientales*, 15 (1955-57), 167 = A.-M. Eddé and F. Micheau, *Chronique des Ayyoubides (602-658 / 1205-6 – 1259-60)* (Paris: L'Académie des Inscriptions et Belles-Lettres, 1994), 104. Other contemporary or slightly later Arabic writers in Egypt and Syria with similar accounts of the siege and fall of Mayyāfāriqīn include: al-Yūnīnī (Quṭb al-Dīn Mūsā b. Muḥammad), *Dhayl mir'āt al-zamān fī ta'rīkh al-a`yān* (Hyderabad: Osmania Oriental Publications Bureau, Osmania University, 1954-61), 1:430-432; Ibn Wāṣil (Jamāl al-Dīn Muḥammad), *Mufarrij al-kurūb fī akhbār banī ayyūb*, in M. Rahim, *Die Chronik des ibn Wāṣil...Untergang der Ayyubiden und Beginn der Mamlukenherrschaft* (Wiesbaden: Harrassowitz, 2010), 177-178, 202; Baybars al-Manṣūrī al-Dawādār, *Zubdat al-fikra fī ta'rīkh al-hijra*, ed. D.S. Richards (Beirut and Berlin: Das Arabische Buch, 1998), 40-41.

Tūrānshāh replied: "We will never agree to this. There is only the sword between us." The envoy went away amazed and pained by this answer, because he knew what calamities it would bring upon the people of Aleppo.[27]

The Mongols thereupon surrounded the town, constructing a wall around it and erecting trebuchets that let loose a barrage day and night. Sappers began working to undermine the walls, but this was not ultimately necessary, since Mongol fighters were able to scale the walls after a week.

The Muslims retreated towards the Citadel in order to defend themselves in it. Those who could go up to it, did so, while there were those who threw themselves into the moat. The Mongols entered the town, putting the Muslims to the sword, killing and imprisoning them as they wished. A large number of people went up to the citadel. The next day began and it was likewise, with the Mongols continuing to kill and capture. The alleys and squares filled up with dead, as [the Mongols] had done in Baghdad.

Certain areas were protected because of [Mongol] royal orders (*farmānāt*), among these the houses of certain notables, a Sufi center (*khānqāh*), and a synagogue. Over 50,000 people were saved this way, plus there were those who hid. On Friday, 14 February, Hülegü ordered the ending of the massacre.[28]

Some additional information is conveyed by Ibn al-Furāt:

The blood of the people [of Aleppo] flowed. It is impossible to count the dead. This was even worse than in Baghdad and the Persian cities…The streets were full of corpses, and the horses stepped on them. The Mongols captured many women and children, numbering more than 100,000. Most were sold among the Franks and Armenians.[29]

Of course, we do not have to accept the exact number that is cited here for the dead, but rather that the author intends to inform us that "a lot of people" had been killed. There is little reason to doubt, however, the general evidence about the nature and extent of the massacres: it is more than just an anti-Mongol trope, as it is confirmed by pro-Mongol sources, such as Rashīd al-Dīn, [30] the

[27] Ibn Wāṣil, edn. Rahim, 196.

[28] *Ibid.*, 197.

[29] Ibn al-Furāt (Nāṣir al-Dīn `Abd al-Raḥmān b. Muḥammad), *Ta'rīkh duwal al-mulūk*, MS. Vatican Ar. 726, fol. 226b.

[30] Rashid al-Din, ed. `Alīzādah, 3:68-69 = tr. Thackston, 1:502-503.

Arabic chronicle attributed to Ibn al-Fuwaṭī,[31] and Bar Hebraeus' account.[32] Meanwhile, the siege of the citadel commenced. Led by the elderly but tireless al-Mu`aẓẓam Tūrānshāh, the defenders put up a spirited defense for a month, but eventually, they realized the hopelessness of their situation and asked to surrender on terms. This was on 11 March 1260. Al-Nuwayrī writes that:

Hülegü ordered that whoever was in the citadel would all return to their homes and property, and he would not be disturbed. The common people and foreigners went down to the places that were protected by the royal orders (*farmānāt*).[33]

Al- Mu`aẓẓam himself died a few days after this surrender, perhaps worn out and broken from the struggle and the sight of the Mongol conquest.[34]

Although it is not germane to our discussion, I think it might be interesting to follow events just a little further, to put the taking of these two cities in context. Hülegü himself remained in north Syria for a couple of months, concerning himself with the subjugation of other towns in the area and receiving assorted luminaries from elsewhere in Syria, not the least various Ayyūbid princes who came to make their submission. Early on, probably while the siege of the Aleppan citadel was in full swing, he had sent a division southward under the command of Kitbuqa, perhaps his most trusted general. Taking control of Damascus, which had been abandoned by al-Nāṣir Yūsuf, who had panicked after the unexpectedly (at least to his mind) quick fall of Aleppo, and headed towards Egypt with most of his army, Mongol raiders and scouts were sent into Palestine and Transjordan. After harrying the countryside and several cities (including Jerusalem), these raiders returned to Damascus with the lots of booty, including much livestock. Meanwhile, Hülegü and almost all of the army with him withdrew from the country, moving via the Jazīra to Azerbaijan for his summer camp. Various reasons have been suggested for this move, and I will list them without any discussion: the lack of adequate pasture and water for a large cavalry army in Syria over the summer; the lack of political certainty in the Mongol empire in wake of the news that Möngke Qaghan had died in August 1259; the need to take up a position in the southern Caucasus vis-à-vis the possible aggression from Berke Khan, ruler of the Mongols in the Steppe region north of the Black and Caspian Seas, the so-called Golden Horde; and, faulty intelligence regarding the abilities of the Mamluk army in Egypt and it

[31] Ibn al-Fuwaṭī, *al-Ḥawādith al-jāmi`a*, 342.

[32] Bar Hebraeus, *Chronography*, tr. Budge, 348 = Ibn al-`Ibrī, 487.

[33] Al-Nuwarყī, *Nihāyat al-arab*, 27:388.

[34] Ibn al-Furat, *Ta'rikh*, MS. Vatican, fol. 227a.

plans. In fact, as is well known, it was from that quarter that an army under Sultan Quṭuz set out that defeated Kitbuqa and his relatively small force at `Ayn Jālūt in northern Palestine on 3 September 1260. The Mongols were thrown out of Syria, the Mamluks gained control over most of the country (mainly with the exception of the Crusader "states" on the coast, but that is another story), the frontier between the two powers stabilized more or less along the Euphrates River, and we see the start of a 60-year war between the Ilkhanid Mongols and the Mamluk Sultanate.[35]

I would like to conclude by returning to the two campaigns that culminated in the taking of Mayyāfāriqīn and Aleppo and seeing what elements were employed by the Mongols to take them. Between the two of them, we see the full array of "tools" that the Mongols brought to bare in siege warfare: Firstly, the large concentration of forces, and the use of sophisticated engineering techniques, be it in the realm of artillery, *ad hoc* fortifications to offer protection and intensify the blockade, and sapping. Secondly, there is a demand for surrender, with the not necessarily implicit threat of terrible consequences if this "generous" offer was not accepted. One could also look at this proposal as a form of psychological warfare, to weaken the enemies' will to fight, and to sow confusion and disagreement among them.

But the use by the Mongols of psychological warfare did not end here: one way to look at their deliberate and calculated use of mass terror against earlier enemies was that it would have a cumulative effect upon would-be enemies who would think twice before attempting to resist the Mongols. In addition, the actual will and capability to resist could be seriously compromised if not completely neutralized by these ostentatious displays of might and cruelty. However, in the present context, this technique does not seem to have worked very well from the Mongols' point of view: The fate of Baghdad was fresh on people's minds in the region, and yet the leaders, soldiers and even civilians of Mayyāfāriqīn and Aleppo put up a spirited resistance until overwhelmed by superior force. In fact, in these cases, the defenders may have been propelled by recent Mongol violence to fight with additional vigor and resolution. According to Rashīd al-Dīn, this may have actually been a factor in stiffening the resistance of Mayyāfāriqīn: al-Malik al-Kāmil supposedly noted that in spite of Mongol promises, various rulers (and thus their subjects) suffered terribly.[36] On the other hand, with the news of Aleppo's fate, the main Syrian army near

[35] For the events of 1260 in Syria, see: P. Jackson, "The Crisis in the Holy Land in 1260," *English Historical Review*, 95 (1980), 481-513; R. Amitai, "Mongol Provincial Administration: Syria in 1260 as a Case-Study," in I. Shagrir, R. Ellenblum and J. Riley-Smith (eds.), *In Laudem Hierosolymitani: Studies in Crusades and Medieval Culture in Honour of Benjamin Z. Kedar* (Aldershot: Ashgate, 2007), 117-143; Amitai-Preiss, *Mongols and Mamluks*, 26-28.

[36] Rashīd al-Dīn, 3:77-78 (tr. Thackston, 2:507).

Damascus broke up, and later that year in Egypt, Quṭuz had to deal with many recalcitrant commanders who were frightened out of their wits by the possibility of fighting the Mongols. This apparent cruelty and destruction, or at least the reputation of such, could be quite effective at times.

However, it is a mistake to see this wanton death, captivity and destruction as only a coldly calculated way to wage psychological war. This cruelty and devastation were also punishment for those who refused to accept the heaven-given mandate for Mongol rule, still certainly a deeply held and unchallenged belief among the Mongol leadership (and perhaps the lower echelons too).[37] It may also reflect a still-existing distain and even revulsion towards city life by the Mongols who – leaders and common tribesmen alike – maintained their traditional nomadic lifestyle. In addition, it may indicate a lack of appreciation for the Muslims, Islam, and its culture, by the still mainly pagan Mongols.

Whatever the inspiration for this policy – and the reasons above do not contradict each other –, this was not uncontrolled violence and obliteration. When Hülegü decided that it was in his interest, he called a stop to the annihilation in Aleppo. Even more telling, the Mongols could control their urges, and thus with the taking of the Citadel there, it was decreed that all defenders would be spared, although this large fortification was largely destroyed.[38] Largesse, then, was also part of the Mongol "tool-box" for conquest and siege, and could be judiciously employed at times.

Yet, with all due respect to this magnanimity that Hülegü showed to al-Mu`aẓẓam Tūrānshāh, his troopers and the civilians who holed up with him, it was the willful destruction and death that are the leitmotifs of this episode and even more so in Mayyāfāriqīn. This brings us back to the innovative thesis of my friend and colleague Dr. Lane, who had seen with the coming of Hülegü a definite reduction of Mongol violence and the ushering in of a new form of their rule. Maybe he is right in a general sense, but on the western frontiers of

37 On this imperial ideology, see: E. Voegelin, "The Mongol Orders of Submission to European Powers," *Byzantion*, 15 (1940-41), 378-413; K. Sagaster, "Herrschaftideologie und Friedensgedenke bei den Mongolen," *Central Asiatic Journal*, 18 (1973); I. de Rachewiltz, "Some Remarks on the Ideological Foundatioins of Chingis Khan's Empire," *Papers in Far Eastern History*, 7 (1973), 21-36; J. Fletcher, "The Mongols: Ecological and Social Perspectives," *Harvard Journal of Asiatic Studies*, 46 (1986), 19, 30-32, 34-35 [reprinted in J. Fletcher, *Studies on Chinese and Islamic Middle Asia* (Aldershot, 1995), art. VIII]; P. Jackson, "World-conquest and Local Accommodation: Threat and Blandishment in Mongol Diplomacy," in J. Pfeiffer and S.A. Quinn (eds.), with the collaboration of E. Tucker. *History and Historiography of Post-Mongol Central Asia and the Middle East: Studies in Honor of Professor John E. Woods* (Wiesbaden: Harrassowitz, 2006), 3-22.

38 It was only towards the end of the thirteenth century that the citadel of Aleppo was rebuilt, and late in the fourteenth that the city's fortifications were repaired; J. Sauvaget, "Ḥalab," *Encyclopaedia of Islam*, 2nd edition, 3:88.

the nascent Ilkhanid state, it was business as usual, certainly towards much of the civilian population. In short, all was not quiet on the Western front, and would remain that way for generations.

FRANK KRÄMER (Heidelberg)

The Fall of Baghdad in 1258: The Mongol conquest and warfare as an example of violence

The 13th century was full of changes, especially in the Middle East, where some very important processes of transformation occurred. One of those changes was caused by an extraordinary event: The Mongol conquest of Baghdad and the killing of the last ᶜAbbāsid caliph. The February 10th of the year 1258, or the 27th Muharram of the year 656 of the Islamic *hijrī* calendar, is a date with a particularly symbolic character for many Muslims. Hend Gilli-Elewy even refers to it in her work as an "epochal date" in Arab and Persian history.[1] Since it stands for an event of great importance and consequence as well as threat and humiliation in Muslim history, it found its way into the "cultural memory"[2] of the Middle Eastern people.

On this particular February 10th, Mongol troops under the command of Hülegü, a grandson of Chingiz Khān, finally conquered Baghdad and sacked the city. A momentous occurrence accompanying this event was the wiping out of the ᶜAbbāsid caliphate and the assassination of the last ᶜAbbāsid Caliph: al-Mustaᶜṣim bi-ᵓllāh. At the time, this incident seems to have been widely perceived as an unbelievable and incomprehensible catastrophe which was hard to understand for the contemporary people.[3] The symbolic centre of the *umma*, the community of all Muslims, was now in the hands of the "infidel" Mongols. The Islamic religious supremacy as well as the universal concept of the caliph's rule came to an end. Or in the Words of Conermann: "Die Desintegration des islamischen Reiches erreichte damit ihren Höhepunkt."[4] The region of Iraq was separated from the other Arabic and Islamic regions further to the west. The following Mongol rule of the region, the so called Il-khanid empire,

1 Hend Gilly-Elewi, Bagdad nach dem Sturz des Kalifats. Die Geschichte einer Provinz unter il-khanidischer Herrschaft (656-735/1258-1335) (Berlin: Schwarz, 2000), 2.

2 Cf. Jan Assmann, Das kulturelle Gedächtnis Schrift, Erinnerung und politische Identität in frühen Hochkulturen (München: Beck, 1992).

3 Stephan Conermann, „*Die Einnahme Bagdads durch die Mongolen im Jahr 1258. Zerstörung - Rezeption – Wiederaufbau*“ in: Städte aus Trümmern. Katastrophenbewältigung zwischen Antike und Moderne (Göttingen: Vandenhoek und Ruprecht, 2004), 54.

4 Gilli-Elewi 2000, 3.

was not an Arabic empire at all. Bert Fragner even speaks of a reinvention of Iran after a period of 700 years.[5]

The fact that this event left deep traces and scars in the Islamic society can still be observed by examining modern Middle Eastern politics. A recent reference to this incident was made, for instance, in 2003, when American troops invaded Iraq and surrounded Baghdad.[6] Even the notorious terrorist Osama Bin Laden compared the Americans with Hülegü in one of his intermittent recorded messages to the world,. In his opinion, "Colin Powell and Dick Cheney had destroyed Baghdad worse than Hülegü of the Mongols."[7]during the last Gulf War.[8]

The mere fact that there was no need to explain Hülegü's identity to his listeners , shows that at least Osama Bin Laden was convinced that no clarification was needed.[9] Another widespread claim among the peoples of the Middle East is that the Mongols set the Arab society centuries back in time. They are said to be the reason why today, the Westerners have the leading technologies and not the Arabs.[10] But what happened back then, as the Mongols moved west with their troops and cavalry and finally conquered and destroyed Baghdad, as the old sources tell us?

5 Bert Fragner, "Ilkhanid Rule and its Contributions to Iranian Political Culture" in: Beyond the Legacy of Genghis Khan (Leiden: Brill 2006), 73.

6 Cf. Ian Frazier, "Invaders: destroying Baghdad," The New Yorker, April 25, 2005.

7 BBC News Middle East, "Full text: 'Bin Laden's message'," BBC News, http://news.bbc.co.uk/2/hi/middle_east/2455845.stm

8 This quotation is not a unique example when it comes to comparisons with Americans or "Enemies of Islam". Other Muslim fundamentalists and groups, for instance al-Zarqāwī, al-Qaraḍāwī, Ḥamās etc., use this polemic from time to time to emphasize the danger which comes from their enemies. An interesting question is how good the knowledge of the Mongols and Hülegü among not well-educated and non-academic persons is. As those speeches are addressed to common people, it seems that there are they do evoke some associations in the people's minds. For references and speeches concerning this point, cf.: Special Dispatch. The Middle East Media Research Institute, "Leader of Al-Qaeda in Iraq Al-Zarqawi Declares 'Total War' on Shi'ites, States that the Sunni Women of Tel'afar Had 'Their Wombs Filled with the Sperm of the Crusaders," Memri, http://memri.org/bin/articles.cgi?Page=archives&Area=sd&ID=SP98705#_ednref2

9 The question remains as to whether and to what extent the Mongol conquest and Hülegü are a part of the so called "cultural memory" . It might be that this part of history found its way back to the Middle East after it had been reexamined and rediscovered by western scholars in the 19th century. This needs to be further examined and discussed. An example of a renaissance caused by the West is the visit of the German emperor William II at Saladins tomb in Damascus in 1898. This event triggered a reconsidering of Saladin and his deeds in the East.

10 Bernard Lewis, *Islam in history. Ideas People, and Events* (Chicago: La Salle, 1993), 189.

1. The situation in Baghdad before 1258

When we read or hear something about Baghdad, we cannot but think about the glamorous past of this place. The medieval Baghdad in its heyday was eternalized in the compilation of the "Arabian Nights" stories during the reign of Hārūn al-Rashīd (reg. 786-809).[11] The city was glorified and presented at the peak of its brilliance, when it became the center of commerce, learning, and science. It was famous, too, for its garrison and for the power it exuded. Baghdad had probably developed into one of the largest cities of the time. According to some estimates, there were between one and one-and-a-half million inhabitants. The city reached the peak of its growth in the early 10th century during the reign of the Caliph al-Muqtadir, but the actual number of inhabitants is open to speculation and remains unclear.[12] Centuries had passed between those times and the Mongol conquest, and consequently it is no wonder that the situation in Baghdad had changed and that the city had undergone more complicated and distressing times in comparison to its peaceful past and years of glory.

But how was the situation in the early 13th century before the Mongols came into play?

Conventional wisdom has it that the Mongols arrived in 1258, devastated Bagdad and destroyed its wealth and booming culture. To this day, this cliché of the barbaric Mongols from the East who came and devastated Baghdad is a theme among scholars. Some still keep on lamenting about the loss of the caliphate and the loss of culture caused by the Mongols. In fact, everything which is connected to Baghdad's decline is still often attributed to the Mongols and their impact. The fall of Baghdad has even been described as the greatest calamity to have ever befallen the world.[13]

However, reading the sources concerning the decades or even centuries before this crucial date sheds a different light on Baghdad and the situation the Mongols came across in that city. Since the middle of the 10th century, the 'Abbāsid Caliphate was in decline, having lived on its past glory and subsequently having lost its power.[14] Thanks to a new generation of scholars, some alternative approaches have been taken over the last decade, and the sources have been re-examined, thus shedding a new light onto the later periods of the Mongol conquests in the west.

[11] F. Omar, "Hārūn al-Rashīd," in Encyclopedia of Islam, ed. Bernhard Lewis et al. (Leiden: Brill, 1960), vol. III, 232.

[12] David Morgan, *The Mongols* (Malden: Blackwell Publishing, 2007), 65.

[13] George Lane, Early Mongol Rule in Thirteenth Century Iran. A Persian Renaissance (London: Routledge Curzon, 2003), 28.

[14] Cf. Gilli-Elewi 2000, 37.

To begin with, the famous traveler Ibn Jubayr had already described in 1185 a general decline of Baghdad. He found some parts of Baghdad to be neglected, and its western parts and most of the old quarters such as Ruṣafa, Shammasiyya and Mukharrim seem to have been in ruins.[15]

In 1226, as Yaqūt tells us, the western parts of Baghdad consisted of isolated quarters, each of which was surrounded by a wall and separated from the others by wastelands of ruins.[16] Friday Mosques had increased in number, and Baghdad suffered during this period from fire, flood and severe conflicts. Already by the 11th century, enormous areas of the old Baghdad had burnt down. The famous round city of al-Manṣūr on the west bank had already crumbled into ruins long ago while, on the east side, where the newer parts of Baghdad were situated, the quarters were in better conditions. Life took place in east Baghdad around the caliphal palaces.[17] This eastern quarter was surrounded by a thick defensive wall of relatively recent origins (around 1100) with four main gates.[18] In spite of all the decay and destruction, however, Bagdad was still an immense city by medieval standards.

During the early 13th century, the political situation resembled a civil war, the city being torn by sectarian fighting between the Sunni and Shia communities.[19] These clashes reached a peak in the years 1242, 1255 and 1256. The situation got completely out of control, especially when the soldiers who were supposed to de-escalate the conflict mixed with the crowd, pillaged the quarter Karkh and burnt it down, and even took the women, making everything worse. This lack of loyalty on the part of the soldiers is partly understandable since they did not receive their payments anymore.[20] These series of events are a further indicator of the serious economic problems of the caliphate.

15 For more travel records and contemporary descriptions of Baghdad see e.g.: A. A. Duri, "Baghdad," in Encyclopedia of Islam, ed. Bernhard Lewis et al. (Leiden: Brill, 1960), vol. I, 901.

16 The city is described as being fragmented into different independent parts which operate autonomously. See e.g. Yaqūt al-Rūmī, *Kitab muʿajam al-buldān*, ed. Farīḍ ʿAbd al-ᶜAzīz al-Jundī (Beirut, 1990), 274.

17 Duri 1960, 900

18 This wall has been destroyed several times by floods or wars, for instance by the Mongol troops who besieged Baghdad in 1258. Nevertheless, this wall marked the city limits and survived until the end of the Ottoman period. Cf. Duri 1960, 901.

19 George Lane, "Chingiz Khān and Mongol Rule," in *Greenwood Guides to Historic Events of the Medieval World*, (Westport : Greenwood Press, 2004), 60.

20 (Pseudo-)Ibn al-Fuwaṭī, *al-Ḥawādith al-jamīᶜa wa-ʾl-tajārib al-nafīᶜa fi ʾl-miʾa al-sābiᶜ*, ed. Muṣṭafā Jawād (Baᶜbda: al-Maktaba al-ᶜarabiyya, 1922), 168. According to the examiniation of Muḥammad Riḍā al-Shabībī, it has been proven that ibn al-Fuwaṭī was not the writer of al-Ḥawādith al-jamīᶜa. Cf. Muḥammad Riḍā al-Shabībī, *Muʾarrikh al-ʿIrāq Ibn al-Fuwaṭī. Baḥth fī adwār al-tāʾrīkh al-ʿirāqī min mustahall al-ᶜaṣr al-ᶜabbāsī ilā awākhir al-ᶜaṣr al-muġulī* (Baghdad 1950-58). The "(Pseudo-)" preceding the author name Ibn al-Fuwaṭī reflects that

The government was too weak to keep order, and in addition, serious problems were caused by floods that occurred, for instance, in 1243, 1248 and 1253. Incidentally, in the year 1256, a flood destroyed large parts of Baghdad, even entering the markets and putting both sides of Baghdad under water. This indicates that the famous irrigation system of Mesopotamia had been neglected for years and caused some serious problems in agriculture.[21] It was probably no longer possible to maintain it for some reason, but as Adams points out, this cannot be blamed only on the Mongols. Some of these underground water channels, the so-called *qanat* had surely been destroyed by the Mongols. But for such a system, neglect is as serious as destruction, for qanat need to be regularly cleaned and maintained; otherwise, they cease to work very quickly.[22]

Above all, the inhabitants of Baghdad had had an awareness of danger, already evident since the 1220s, because the imminent threat by the Mongol troops was not a fact they could deny. It was only a question of time until something happened to them and their city.[23] In the last years before the invasion, refugees had arrived in Baghdad and were looking for shelter. As a consequence, daily life had become more and more complicated because of overpopulation, shortage of living space, and an increase in food prices, which culminated in inflation and serious economic problems.[24]

Baghdad and the region of Iraq had already experienced the conditions of an internal and external war, which demoralized the people and placed a heavy burden on the inhabitants.[25] Nevertheless, Baghdad was still, according to Bernard Lewis, "the legal center of Islam and the symbol of its unity."[26]

2. The Mongol tasks in the west

In 1251, the Great Khan Möngke held a *quriltay*, which is a gathering of Mongol leaders. This *quriltay* set the foundations of Hülegü's campaigns and changed the map of Asia thoroughly. One of the decisions made there was to send

situation and simultaneously shows that this text is still associated with his authorship. I used this marking following Stefan Conermann 2004.

21 Duri 1960, 894

22 Robert Adams, *Land behind Baghdad* (Chicago, 1965).

23 Cf. (Pseudo-)Ibn al-Fuwaṭī 1922, 27-28, 84-85.

24 Cf. Gilli-Elewy 2000, 147-152.

25 Gilli-Elewy 2000, 22.

26 Lewis 1993, 191-2.

Hülegü, who was Möngke's younger brother, to the West to accomplish some important tasks.[27]

"Mengu [Möngke] Qa'an had seen in the character of his brother Hülegü the indications of sovereignty and had detected in his enterprises the practices of conquest. [...] and charged him with the conquest of the western parts."[28]

Whether Hülegü had the aim of founding the Il-khān[29] dynasty or just wanted to complete the subjugation of Persia, which his father had not been able to accomplish[30], his intentions remain unclear and require further investigation. At any rate, it is obvious that this mission was of great importance to the Mongol ruler. As Lane writes, the composition of the vast army further indicates the significance of the expedition with which he had been commissioned.[31] His first task was the elimination of the Ismāᶜīlī Assassin sect. The second task was to secure the obedience from the Caliphate of Baghdad since it was not acceptable for a Mongol ruler to have another leader who claimed a position of universal domination.[32] The third task was the subjugation or destruction of the Ayyūbid states in Syria. The fourth and final task was the subjugation or destruction of the Mamlūk Sultanate in Egypt.

In spite of all efforts, the Mongols were not able to achieve much in the western parts of Asia. For about ten years, Mongol power had not spread much. Rashīd al-Dīn spoke of some cries for help which reached the court of the Great Khān, especially those asking the Mongols to wipe out the Assassins and the Caliph of Baghdad.[33] The vast Mongol army set out on 19th October 1253, and they were given a splendid send-off. Hülegü's most important general, Kitbuġā, a Nestorian Christian, had already been sent out on his mission half a year earlier with 12,000 soldiers so that he could harass the Assassins and prepare the way through Iran for the main army.[34]

27 The Mongols attacked the city of Baghdad twice before in 1230 and 1242 but were repulsed and had to pull their troops back.

28 ʿAlāʾ al-Dīn ᶜAṭā Malik al-Juwaynī, The History of the World-Conqueror by 'Ala ad-Din 'Ata Malik Juvaini, ed. John Andrew Boyle (Manchester: Manchester University Press, 1958), 607.

29 For a detailed explanation of the Title Il-Khan see: Reuven Amitai-Preiss, "Evidence for the early use of the title Ilkhān among the Mongols," *Journal of the Royal Asiatic Society* 3rd ser. 1 (1991).

30 Lane 2003, 15

31 Lane 2003, 18

32 „In this context Alamut and Baghdad were alternative centers of power and loyalty which could not indefinitely be permitted to survive." Morgan 1988, 59.

33 Berthold Spuler, Die Mongolen in Iran: Politik, Verwaltung und Kultur der Ilchanzeit 1220-1350 (Berlin: Akademie Verlag, 1968), 49.

34 George Lane, *Genghis Khan and Mongol rule* (Westport: Greenwood Press, 2004), 59.

It is said that Hülegü's army consisted of one fifth of all available Mongol soldiers.[35] Some sources speak of 120,000 men, but the reality is uncertain since numerical data in medieval sources are notoriously unreliable. Khān Jagatai and Batu of the Golden Horde also sent contingents of troops. Some specialists of siege warfare came from northern China for assistance. For logistical reasons, the huge troop contingent was divided into four divisions–which took slightly different routes. This variation in routes was necessary in order to provide the horses with enough pasture. The forces of Hülegü represented a truly impressive imperial army which had its counterpart in the east in the army of Qubilay Khān.[36]

The army moved on very slowly along a well-planned route.[37] It seems that there was no haste or urgency at all, which indicates that Hülegü and his troops were deeply convinced of their upcoming victory over the ᶜAbbāsids. According to Smith, the average pace must have been about 4 miles per day.[38] The roads had been cleaned and leveled, and pontoon bridges had been built over rivers to enable the passing of the troops. Pastoral bases had already been established around Azerbaijan by the Mongol Army in 1229 to support future campaigns.[39] In 1255, Hülegü reached Samarkand, and in 1256 he finally crossed the Oxus river to Khurasan, or what is presently Afghanistan. Soon afterward, Hülegü entered Ismāᶜīlī territory. The sect of the Ismāᶜīlīs had come to be feared and mistrusted by the local rulers and political and religious leaders through their aggressive missionary and clandestine military operations.[40] In fact, local Iranian vassal forces played a major part in besieging and conquering the fortresses, called eagle-nests due to the remoteness of their heavily fortified mountain retreats.

Hülegü demanded complete surrender of the Ismāᶜīlīs, for his brother Möngke, had ordered that he must not only destroy them but also turn their

[35] An important question that needs to be further discussed is which people and tribes inhabited this vast contingent. Some other very important campaigns were taking place at the same time. Qubilay was authorized by Möngke Khan to take one out of five men from the Mongol army, as Hülegü did, so they together took two men out of ten. Möngke Khan himself employed the largest number of soldiers, nine tümens, i.e. 900.000 men in his campaign against China. So it is likely that a substantial part of Hülegüs troops was not of Mongol origins and that he had to raise his army from outside Mongolia. For further information see: John Masson Smith jr., "Hülegü moves west: high living and heartbreak on the road to Bagdad," in *Beyond the Legacy of Genghis Khan*, ed. Linda Komaroff (Leiden: Brill, 2006), 112p.

[36] Cf. Lane 2003, 18.

[37] Hülegü and his Troops reached Bagdad three years and three month, or ca. 1200 days, after they had been sent off from Hamadan.

[38] Cf. Smith 2006, 113.

[39] Smith 2006, 111.

[40] Lane 2003, 59.

heads downward and their bodies upward. The Great Khan probably believed in some rumors which he heard that “four hundred Assassins in various disguises, had made their way in with the aim of killing him,”[41] as William of Rubruck reports.

It is not surprising that Hülegü was not only perceived as a conqueror but also welcomed as a king. He had even been asked by local Persian rulers to accept the throne of Persia. Hülegü’s advent seemed to symbolize a promise of the return of political stability and security. I would not go as far as Lane, who claims that “Hülegü Khan came to Persia to restore justice, stability and prosperity, to claim his inheritance and to found a new dynasty.”[42] I find it highly problematic to make definitive statements about the aims of Hülegü[43] or of the campaign in general. At any rate, however, it has been shown that, after the conquest, a new stability emerged.[44] From the start, the Mongols had allowed some local rulers, such as the Karts of Heart, the Salġurids of Shiraz, and the Qāra Khitai of Kerman, to remain as their vassals.

In 1256, after a long and hard siege, Hülegü captured the headquarter of the Assassins without fighting: Maymūn Diz was conquered.

Several other castles which were still holding out, such as Alamut and Lamassar, had to be besieged, conquered and destroyed. Since Alamut had been a centre for learning and for scholars, Juvainī, a Persian scholar in Hülegü’s service, received permission to inspect the library and to take everything he deemed valuable, such as Korans and non-heretical books as well as scientific and astronomical instruments. The rest were demolished and burnt down. Many scholars, including the famous Naṣīr ad-Din Ṭūsī, were rescued and later taken to the new capital Maġāra, which is present-day Azerbaijan in Iran.

The Assassin Grand Master Rukn al-Dīn was captured in Maymūn Diz, treated well and sent to Qaraqorum to be presented to Möngke. However, he was turned away by Möngke, and on his way back, he was murdered under

41 Guilelmus de Rubruquis, *The mission of Friar William of Rubruck his journey to the court of the Great Khān Möngke 1253-1255*, ed. Hakluyt Society (London: Hayklut Society, 1990), 220.; Ser. 2, 173), London 1990, Vol. 2, p. 220.

42 Cf. Lane 2003, 18.

43 For a contra position see Dorothea Krawulsky, *Mongolen Ilkhane und Ideologie Geschichte* (Beirut: Verlag für islamische Studien, 1989), 90. „Hülägü kam nicht nach Iran , um sich ein Reich zu erobern, sondern um als Abgesandter seines Bruders Möngke (reg. 1251-1259) und im Namen des chinggisidischen Clans den islamischen Westen zu erobern, bis eine neue Versammlung aller Prinzen und großen Heerführer, nach vollendeterAufgabe, neue Eroberungsziele festlegen würde.“

44 As Morgan writes, there are some indications in the sources which can be interpreted as saying that Möngke wanted Hülegü to come back to Mongolia after accomplishing his tasks in the Middle East. See e.g.: (Morgan 1988, 59)

circumstances that remain unclear.[45] In spite of the Mongol victory at Alamut and the surrender of their Grand Master, some other castles such as Lammassar and Girdkuh did not surrender, so they had to be besieged and conquered as well. The tactic of siege is told in an account by Rashid ad-Dīn: Girdekuh was a heavily fortified citadel in the remoteness of the Taliqan mountains. The citadel was surrounded by a system of triple thick walls. The soldiers, following the orders of Kit-Buqa, dug a deep ditch near the citadel and flanked it with a high and well-fortified wall. The soldiers were therefore able to camp behind this safe construction, and in addition, they erected another wall behind themselves to avoid the danger of an attack from behind. The Mongols had brought with them many siege machines, which were surely operated by Chinese specialists since siege warfare, at the time, was still something new and awkward for the Mongol cavalry.[46] The effect on the morale of the besieged should not be underestimated since these huge machines were truly terrifying devices. One of the machines used in this siege was called *kamani gav* (ox's bow) in Persian: a huge device consisting of a large crossbow mounted on a frame that shot bolts dipped into a burning fluid similar to pitch. The *kamani gav* must have had a range of around half a mile.[47]

After this mission had been accomplished, Hülegü turned his attention to Baghdad and the ᶜAbbāsid caliphate.

3. The Mongol conquest of Baghdad

The main problem in describing and analyzing the Mongol conquest and their campaigns is that we do not have a single master narrative. For that reason, it is extremely complicated, and nearly impossible, to reconstruct the events of 1258 in detail.[48] The various texts which have come down to us are all complicated and have to be seen in their respective contexts and times to be understood properly. Of course, we have no choice but to rely on the records of that time, but we must also be aware of the tradition in which those texts were written. The chronologies supply us with a good overview of the sequence of events, but when it comes to their description, we must always understand the position of the writer and his loyalties.[49] The following account of the Mongol

[45] Lane 2004, 60.
[46] Smith 2006, 118.
[47] Cf. Smith 2006, 127.
[48] Cf. Conermann 2004, 55.
[49] Some good overviews and surveys of the sources and their writers are given in the works of Morgan 2007, 5-25 and Lane 2003, 1-16.

conquest of Baghdad, therefore, is far from being complete, but it tries to describe the events in a chronological order.

First of all, it needs to be said that it was not necessarily the aim of Hülegü to destroy the Caliphate in Baghdad. In a speech addressed to Hülegü, as has been retold by Rashīd al-Dīn, Möngke emphasized that Hülegü und his men must head for Persia to eliminate the Lurs and Kurds[50] who were constantly practicing brigandage along the highways. If the Caliph of Baghdad came out to pay homage, however, they were not to harass him in any way whatsoever.[51]

Accordingly, Hülegü sent emissaries to the caliph telling him to raze the walls of Baghdad and to come in person to make obeisance to Hülegü. The Caliph refused and replied that he was ready to defend himself with all of Islam.[52] He advised Hülegü to go back to where he came from and treated the Mongol envoys with great disrespect.[53] In the years before, as for instance in 1238, some clashes between the Mongols and the troops of the Caliph had taken place in which the Mongols were defeated. These events may have influenced the attitude and self-confidence of the ᶜAbbasid. The Caliph al-Mustaᶜṣim bi-ᵓllāh, who had been ruling since 1242, has been pictured as an inefficient, careless, and inactive ruler. Hülegü sent a message to the Caliph while he was in Hamadan and demanded submission from him. But since 1232, the Caliph had always refused to follow such requests. Up to that point, they had not had to bear any consequences, but this was soon to change. From that time onwards, Hülägü started to make preparations for a siege of the town.

Nevertheless, Hülegü was troubled by the thought of destroying the holy city and possibly killing the Caliph. He has been described as a superstitious man who paid attention to voices foretelling divine retribution. Earthquake, drought, plague and the death of a king had been predicted by Muslim astrologers[54], so Hülegü asked Naṣīr al-Dīn Ṭūsī, a famous scientist whom he had captured at Alamut, for his advice. But, his answer was simple and short; he told him not to fear, for "Hülegü will reign in place of the Caliph" [55]

The Caliph's army had been neglected for years. In 1250/1, for example, al-Mustaᶜṣim bi-ᵓllāh had abolished the appanage for the troops and terminated

50 The Lurs and the Kurds posed a threat on several occasions and were famous for constantly carrying out raids on the highways. Cf. Lane 2003, 29.

51 Rashīd al-Dīn, *Rashiduddin Fazlullah's Jami'u 't-tawarikh: compendium of chronicles: a history of the Mongols*, ed. W.M. Thackston (Cambridge: Harward University Press, 1998-9), 231, 479.

52 Ibid.

53 On the correspondence between Hülegü and the caliph, cf. Gilli-Elewy 200, 23-26.

54 Cf. Timothy May, *The Mongol Art of War* (Yardley: Westholm Publishing, 2007), 132.

55 Quoted in: Lane 2004, 61.

their pay[56]; in addition, the caliph's army was now ill-equipped, poorly trained, and of doubtful loyalty. His army also received some support from Arab tribes from south Iraq and from a citizen militia of dubious reliability and very little training.[57] However, the Caliph still felt safe and secure in his city. He was torn between two advisors: On the one hand, Ibn al-'Alqamī, a Shiite, favored surrender because he saw the best chances for himself to survive in a possible alliance with the Mongols. According to Juzjānī, he reduced the number and strength of the Baghdad garrison.[58] Subsequently, he was reappointed to his office by Hülegü. On the other hand, there was Aybak, a Sunnite who had ambitions of usurping the Caliph's position. He advised the Caliph to trust in God and to resist.[59] Because of the sectarian riots in the City of Baghdad and the clearly pro-Sunni position of the Caliph, he could not be sure of the loyalty of the Shiites in Baghdad anymore. Most likely, the Mongol troops did receive assistance on their way to Baghdad from the Shiite population as well. In all likelihood, the caliph really refused to believe "that the Mongols would dare to attack, and no one could persuade him otherwise," as May points out.[60]

The Mongol army set out in November 1257 westwards from Hamadan to Iraq, approaching Baghdad from the North in 1258.[61] The Army consisted of three divisions. The first one, under Suġūnjāq Noyan and Bayjū Noyan, came from the northwest, passing by Irbil and crossing the Bridge of Mossul to Baghdad. They established their headquarters on the west side of the river Tigris.[62] At the same time, Kitbuġa and Ilke Noyan approached from the southeast, passing by Ġirīt and Bayāt. The main contingent under the command of Hülegü and the vice commander, the Chinese general Guo Kan, came from the east, passing by Kirmanshah and Ḥulwān.[63] The Mongol troops were also reinforced by contingents of Georgian cavalry, and some troops from the principality of Antioch probably participated as well.[64]

The plan was to cut off Baghdad from Syria and Egypt. The Syrian Desert itself did the rest for Baghdad's isolation. The conditions in the city must have been terrible. Rumors of the approaching Mongol troops spread fast, and the

56 Cf. May 2007, 131.

57 David Nicolle, The Mongol warlords: Chingiz Khān, Kublai Khān, Hülägü, Tamerlane (Poole: Firebird Books, 1990), 108.

58 Morgan 2007, 132.

59 Lane 2004, 60f.

60 Cf. May 2007, 131.

61 Morgan 2007, 132.

62 Joseph von Hammer-Purgstall, *Geschichte der Ilchane, das ist die der Mongolen in Persien: 1200-1350* (Amsterdam: Philo-Press, 1974), 146 and al-Dīn 1998-99, 262.

63 Several different versions of the movement of the troops can be found in the texts. See e.g.: (Gilli-Elewy, 26-27)

64 Nicolle 1990, 111.

rural population headed towards Baghdad to look for shelter within the city walls of Baghdad. Confusion must have reigned all over the city.

Approaching the city, Hülegü ordered his forces to assemble in formations and to march towards Baghdad from different directions so that they could threaten the city from both sides, namely the east and west banks of the Tigris. One contingent had to block the western approach to Baghdad and guard the west side of the river so that nobody could enter or escape. The Army of Bayjū crossed the Tigris using a bridge made of boats[65] constructed by engineers of Badr al-Dīn Luʾluʾ,the Atabeg of Mosul, a Mongol vassal[66]

The Mongol headquarter was established on the west side of the Tigris river. There, they were joined by other Mongol contingents under the command of Batu's nephews Bayjū, Suġūnjāq and Buka Timur. Timur led his men across the Small Tigris, aiming to attack Bagdad from the rear. Suġūnjāq, with permission from Bayjū to lead the vanguard of the western army, marched towards Baghdad.[67] Hearing these news, the little *dawātdār*[68] Mujāhid al-Dīn Aybak of the Caliph sent his army to the west bank of the river on the January 16th. The first clash took place roughly 50 kilometers[69] north of Baghdad, where at first the Mongols were driven back[70]; subsequently, however, the Caliph's army was lured into a marshy terrain. This was a major mistake on the part of the army since it was now trapped at that site. The Mongols then opened a dike, and many of the Caliph's soldiers either drowned or were cut to pieces by the Mongol troops. Few soldiers were able to escape back to Baghdad or south towards the desert.[71] Soon afterward, the Mongol troops converged upon the City. In his contemporary chronicle, (Pseudo-) Ibn al-Fuwaṭī compares them with locusts,[72] which are simply not countable.

Having arrived in Baghdad, the Mongols again resorted to building a palisade and a ditch around the besieged city, and they applied this tactics to the entire eastern city from river bank to river bank.[73] However, this time around,

65 Cf. May 2007, 132.

66 For further informations about Badr ad-Din Luʾluʾ, see: David Talbot Rice, "The Brasses of Badr al-Dīn Lu'lu," *Bullettin of the School of Oriental and African Studies, University of London* 13/3 (1950).

67 al-Din 1998-99, 280.

68 At the head of the „war party" was the little dawātdār (porte-écritoire) Mujāhid al-Dīn-Aybeg; Cf. al-Dīn 1998-99, 226.

69 The sources speak of 9 Pasarang. One Pasarang corresponds to 5.25 kilometers. Cf. al-Dīn, 280.

70 Probably, this withdrawal of the Mongol troops was more of a tactical nature. It temporarily gave the forces of the caliph an impression of victory and a feeling of superiority.

71 al-Dīn 1998-99, 280.

72 *"[...]ka-'l-jarād al-muntašhir [...]"* (Pseudo-)Ibn al-Fuwaṭī 1922, 324.

73 al-Dīn 1998-99, 280.

they collected stones or wooden pieces to construct their machines. Some siege towers were built of bricks from abandoned quarters.[74] From the top of these towers, they were able to shoot stones and arrows into the city. The siege and bombardment started on January 29th.[75]

By the 4th of February, the Mongols concentrated on a single point and managed to cut a breach in the southeastern corner, near the so-called Persian tower (burj ‘ajamī), thus establishing a crucial foothold for Hülegü’s army.[76] By the next day, they controlled a stretch of the defense wall between the Persian tower and the Bāb Tillism.[77] At this point, the caliph became willing to negotiate and sent his *wazīr* and the Nestorian Patriarch, but Hülegü refused them an audience. The time for diplomacy had passed for Hülegü.

Six days later, on the 10th of February, the city was in Hülegü’s Hands. He promised to spare the God's erudite, the sheikhs, the descendants of Ali (the sayyids), the merchants, and all of those who had not borne arms against him.[78] As might be expected, this promise was not to be kept entirely. Hülegü received the Caliph with kindness and asked him to order his soldiers to lay down their arms. But when they did so, they were divided into groups and butchered by the Mongols. The city itself had been given to the troops for looting, but before entering the city, the Mongols tore down large sections of the walls and filled the moat. On the 13th of February, they started a seven-day-long orgy of massacre, looting, arson and rape, as described by al-Waṣṣāf:

“They swept through the city like hungry falcons attacking a flight of doves, or like raging wolves attacking sheep, with loose reins and shameless faces, murdering and spreading fear [...].”[79]

The number of people murdered remains unclear, but it must have been huge. The sources speak of something between 200.000 and 2 million[80], which

[74] Ibid.

[75] The Chinese specialists on siege warfare were best equipped and knowledgeable about the “high-tech” of the Middle Ages. One of the most important devices they used was called “Trebouchet” or “Mangonel” in Europe. For further information about Mongol military techniques, see: Thomas Allsen, “The Circulation of Military Technology in the Mongolian Empire. Warfare in Inner Asian history (500-1800),” *Handbook of Oriental Studies. Section 8: Central Asia* 6 (2002) and May 2007.

[76] Hammer-Purgstall 1974, 150 and al-Dīn 1998-99, 282.

[77] Also known and often mentioned in texts as the Racecourse-Gate. It is the gate neighboring the Persian tower.

[78] al-Dīn 1998-99, 282 and Spuler 1968, 47.

[79] Quoted in: Bertold Spuler, History of the Mongols Based on eastern and Western Accounts of the thirteenth and fourteenth centuries (New York, 1972), 29.

[80] For instance, (Pseudo-) Ibn Fuwaṭī speaks in his report of 800.000 victims “ *ʿaddat al-qutlā bi-Baġdād zālat ʿan ṯamān miʾat alf nafs!*” Such a number would exceeded Bagdad’s estimated population of that time Ibn al-Fuwaṭī 1922, 331.

is surely a bit exaggerated since Baghdad never had so many inhabitants.[81] We must keep in mind that we cannot take such a "body count" at face value, and I agree with Morgan when he says that we should not regard the numbers in those chronicles as statistical information but rather "as an evidence of the state of mind created by the character of the Mongol invasion."[82] The Mongol troops treated the Christians and the Shiites more favorably than they did the Sunnis and even gave the Nestorian patriarch a residence of the Caliph, which deepened the distrust on the part of the Muslims. According to May, the Christians became a target for Muslims who wanted to avenge the destruction of the city and to punish the Christians for their collaboration.[83]

4. The fate of the Caliph

This part of the Mongol conquest of Baghdad is ideal for showing the different narratives. As mentioned before, we have different versions and different traditions, handed down in different cultural contexts. As a matter of fact, it is not very useful to try to reconstruct "the truth" because, lacking conclusive evidence, we can only find out 'a' truth among others. Of more interest could be the ways in which the various narratives have been spread and the traditions in which they have been told. Apparently, the Caliph survived the first phase of the Mongol conquest of Baghdad. After Hülegü's troops were able to enter the city, the Caliph was most likely brought to the conqueror. It seems that Hülegü initially treated the Caliph with great kindness. Hülegü inspected the Caliph's palace and treasures, and walked through the vast complex of the palaces.

From that point on, several different accounts of the last days of the Caliph exist. Actually, there are three main stories which have been handed down to us. The first one tells us that the Caliph was starved to death amidst the gold plates of his treasury. Because the Caliph loved his treasures more than anything, so the story goes, Hülegü put him in a tower without food and water and left him to die surrounded by nothing but his treasures. This version of his death has probably been inspired by a dialogue between Hülegü and the Caliph as written down by Rashīd al-Dīn:

[81] Actually, it is almost impossible to estimate the amount of people who were in Baghdad when the pillage took place. We have to consider that large numbers of refugees from the hinterland had headed for Baghdad to escape the approaching Mongol troops and to take shelter there. Baghdad still had an impressive fortification and seemed to offer a safe refuge. Besides the city of Baghdad, there were not many other places of refuge for the fleeing rural population.

[82] Morgan 2007, 68.

[83] May 2007, 133.

"He (Hülegü) set a golden tray before the Caliph and said: "Eat!" "It's not edible, " said the Caliph. "Then why didst thou keep it," asked the King, "and not give it to thy soldiers? And why didst thou not make these iron doors into arrow-heads and come to the bank of the river so that I might not have been able to cross it?" "Such, " replied the Caliph, "was God's will." "What will befall thee, " said the King, "is also God's will."[84]

Although it is quite unlikely that the Caliph was starved to death in a tower, this conversation between the two could have a basis in reality. It is of great interest that Marco Polo, the famous Venetian traveler (ca. 1254-1324), mentions precisely this version in his travel record "Il Milione". Most likely, therefore, he heard of this story somewhere on his way to the east and spread this eastern narrative in the west through his book. When he tells about this incident, the caliph's neglect of his troops seems to carry a heavy moral weight for him.[85]

Another narrative tradition has mainly been handed down through Georgian sources. They tell us that Hülegü himself executed the Caliph with the sword.

The last version, and the one likely to be nearest to the truth, comes from the Muslim tradition, which in turn could derive from Mongol traditions. Because the Mongols had superstitious scruples about shedding the blood of their own princes[86], they were afraid of shedding any royal blood. The likely consequence was the use of a more sophisticated method in bringing a person of such high standing to his death. Therefore, it is not surprising to read the stories of some ancient Muslim historians which describe the Mongols rolling up the Caliph in a carpet and then killing him by having the carpet kicked or trampled[87], likely by a horse. This method was used to avoid the shedding of blood on earth, which was superstitiously believed to cause some heavenly punishments like floods or earthquakes. The historiographer Ibn al-Fuwaṭī, who was a witness to the incidents in 1258 in Baghdad, reports in his chronicle a similar story. The Sultan (i.e. Hülegü) ordered to kill the caliph on Wednesday 14., in the month ṣafar. In order to avoid shedding blood, they put him into a

[84] al-Dīn 1998-99, 159.

[85] Cf. Elise Guignard, trans., *Marco Polo die Wunder der Welt. Il Milione* (Frankfurt a. M.: Insel Verlag, 2003), 36.

[86] al-Dīn 1998-99, 150.

[87] John Andrew Boyle, "*The Death of the Last Caliph. a Contemporary Muslim Account*," Journal of Semitic Studies 6 (1961), 150.

sack and kicked him until he died. Afterwards, he was buried and all traces of his grave were erased.[88]

When we analyze earlier Mongol rituals and traditions, we see that not shedding blood was a central aspect of killing close relatives of the Khān and noble enemies in accordance with the ancient religious beliefs of Mongol and Turkish tribes.[89] So it had to be more or less a "bloodless death", which was not literally the case with the caliph, but those who killed him at least saw to it that no blood was mixed with earth. A similar fate was met by Jamuqa, the blood brother of Chingiz Khān.[90] Since such a custom or notion is not common in the Middle East, it could be the genuinely "Mongol" element in this account of the caliph's death that lends it the greatest historical credibility.

Résumé

In spite of all those records mentioned above, we cannot verify that the Mongols completely destroyed Baghdad. We read, for instance, in (Pseudo-) Ibn al-Fuwaṭī's chronicle about the devastation and sacking of the city. His report has a very dark and depressing note. But some pages later, we read about reconstruction and reorganization of the city, which points to a new beginning and to efforts to make it function again.[91] Even though numerous sources have come down to us, there is no Master Narrative on which we can rely. Hence, we should rather speak of different traditions and/or different narratives, as the records of the death of the last caliph have shown us. In fact, Hülegü even ordered to have some of the buildings repaired and placed some officials, such as the Shiite *wazīr* of the Caliph, in new positions. Their newly given task was to clean the city and to reopen the Bazaars. In 1340, a military leader of the Il-khāns even chose Baghdad as his place of residence and founded a branch dynasty there, the Jalāyirids. Besides, Tabriz Baghdad was the most important city in the empire of the Il-khāns, and as such it started to attract scholars again. To be sure, some records of travelers exist which describe Baghdad as being in a terrible condition. However, it is important to note that those records are not

88 "*fa-ʿamara al-sulṭān yaqtulahu fa-qatala yawm al-ʾarbʿāʿ rābiʿ ʿašr ṣafar wa lam yahraq dammahu bal jaʿala fī ġirāra wa rafasa ḥattā māt, wa dafana wa ʿafiya aṯar qabrihi*, […]" (Pseudo-) Ibn al-Fuwaṭī 1922, 327.

89 Cf. Igor de Rachewitz, trans., The secret History of the Mongols. A Mongolian Epic Chronicle of the Thirteenth Century (Leiden: Brill, 2006), Vol.2, 753.

90 Ibid., 753.

91 I agree with Gilli-Elewy that the destruction of Baghdad could not have been of an apocalyptic scale since life seems to have gone on in Baghdad immediately after the conquest. Gilli-Elewy 2000, 33.

contemporary. Al-Maqrīzī wrote after his visit to Baghdad 1437 that it could not be called a city anymore and that it was in ruins; neither a market nor a mosque was operating, and most of its palm trees and irrigation channels had been destroyed.[92]

The Mongol conquest of Iraq meant, first of all, its separation from the Arabic tradition. Together with the eastern part of Syria, Iraq came to constitute the only Arabic region of the new Il-khanid empire, which can be seen as a Persian empire.[93] The center of the Islamic World was now the Cairo of the Mamluks, and the Euphrates in Syria became the new natural border between the two empires. Looked at historically and economically, therefore, the Mongols simultaneously severed/detached and integrated Baghdad and Iraq and had a great influence on the future development of this region.

Unfortunately, it is nearly impossible to determine how strong the Mongol impact on Baghdad was in 1258. In Baghdad, i.e. Mesopotamia, there is a prevalence of mud brick architecture which is not as solid and lasting as stone architecture. We must keep in mind that only the representative buildings were built of fired adobes[94], the majority of urban structures being vernacular houses made of sun dried mud bricks which were easy and cheap to produce.[95] After a catastrophic incident such as a war, fire, flood etc., it is much easier to build new structures than to repair the old ones, which explains why not much has survived of the medieval city and only a few buildings which date back to before 1258, such as the Mustanṣiriyya and the Bāb al-Wasṭanī, have been preserved. The aforementioned Bāb Tillism was destroyed in an accidental explosion in World War I in 1917. Another problem, of course, is the very strong urbanization which took place in Baghdad during the last century. Numerous old structures were destroyed in the process of gentrification which created new urban spaces. The famous round city of the Caliph al-Mansur was already in ruins when the Mongols arrived. After the Mongols conquered the city, it was sacked twice in 1393 and in 1401 by Tamerlane. Those two instances of destruction must have been as terrible as the Mongol sacking if not even more devastating.

If we wanted to shed light on this matter, only some thorough new surveys could be of help. The cadasters, as far as they exist, should be consulted and

92 Duri 1960, 894.

93 Cf. Gilli Elewy 2000, 3

94 Cf. as a parallel Example: Murhaf al-Khalaf, "Die abbasidische Stadtmauer von ar-Raqqa/ ar Rafiqa," *Damaszener Mitteilungen* 2 (1985) and John Warren, "The date of the Baghdad Gate at Raqqa," *Art and Archaeology Research Papers* 13 (1978).

95 If such a structure is not regularly maintained, it only takes a few years for it to fall apart and become no longer recognizable. Still can still be seen in rural areas of Mesopotamia, where people still use this traditional building technique.

studied anew, taking into account the changes of the last decades as well as the information contained in the Ottoman documents on the city. Perhaps in the next years, some changes will occur in the situation in Iraq, offering us a chance to investigate this matter further, by means which include excavation works in the district of old Baghdad. Until then, we must mainly rely on the written sources and the few traces that were left behind in our attempts to try to understand the events of February 1258.

III. Historicizing Extraordinary Violence

JUDITH FRÖHLICH (University of Zurich)

Between Local History and National Myth: The Mongol Invasions in Japan*

1. Introduction

The Mongols invaded Japan twice, in 1274 and 1281. Although both expeditions failed, the Japanese warrior government, the so-called Kamakura Bakufu (1185-1333), anticipated a third invasion. Already after the first invasion, the regent of the Bakufu, Hōjō Tokimune (1251-1284), had a defence wall erected around Hakata Bay in the north of Kyushu. In the subsequent decades, the Bakufu held the warriors of Kyushu in a constant state of preparedness and also deployed a large number of warriors from eastern Japan in Kyushu. The Mongols did not make another attempt to invade Japan. Many people, however, especially those living in northern Kyushu and the Islands of Iki and Tsushima where the battles had taken place, kept alive the memory of the Mongol invasions and their warrior ancestors who had bravely repelled the foreign invaders, over the centuries.[1]

The Mongol invasions first attracted scholarly interest during the eighteenth century. Under the influence of *kokugaku*, nativist school, a school of philological and philosophical thought, scholars gathered the historical records of Japan's past and, in this context, turned to the Mongol invasions. In 1758, Tsuda Genkan (1734-1815), a physician in Hakata – in the present-day city of Fukuoka – in northern Kyushu, published his *Sankō mōko nyūkō ki*, "Reference Work on the Mongol Invasions," an early erudite source edition.[2] Thereafter,

* Special thanks go to Thomas Conlan, Haruta Naoki, Hattori Hideo, Monica Juneja, Miyazaki Katsunori, Saeki Koji, Ethan Segal and Akira Takenaka for their valuable advice and support. The following institutions and individuals granted me the permission to reproduce illustrations (in the order of the illustrations): The Sannomaru Shozokan, Museum of the Imperial Collections in Tokyo, Mr. Nakamura Reisaburō, resident of Maebaru, Fukuoka prefecture, the Library of the Historiographical Institute of the University of Tokyo, The Kyushu University Museum and the Yūshūkan, Museum of the Yasukuni Shrine in Tokyo.

1 The standard reference work on the Mongol invasions and their historicisation in the later epochs is: Kawazoe Shōji, *Mōko shūrai kenkyū shiron* (Chūseishi sensho 1) (Tokyo: Oyamakaku Shuppan, 1977).

2 There are several copies of the *Sankō mōko nyūkō ki* that have been preserved: one from 1843 at Tokyo University, one copy from 1854 that was handed down in the Uto Hosokawa family,

scholarly dedication to the historical event experienced three waves: A first wave is discernible in the mid-nineteenth century, as the awareness of the Mongol invasions, which up to then had represented the greatest external threat to the Japanese archipelago, grew in response to the pressure of Western imperial powers. A second wave extended from the eve of the first Sino-Japanese War of 1894-95 to the Russo-Japanese War of 1904-05. A third wave of scholarly interest arose between the Manchurian Crisis in 1931 and the end of World War II. Clearly, scholarly interest in the Mongol invasions intensified when Japan felt threatened by foreign powers.[3]

The Mongol invasions might thus appear to have been "nation-defining events in Japanese history"[4] which added a "new dimension," as the title of the workshop implies, to political, social and cultural spheres in Japan. In the thirteenth and fourteenth centuries, according to this view, the Mongol invasions would have enhanced the notion of the native and the foreign among the Japanese people. During the rise of nationalism in the nineteenth century, they would then have been transformed into a metaphor of Japan's divine nature and superiority over other countries.

This article, however, suggests quite the opposite, namely that the Mongol invasions were akin to other battles fought within Japan in their social, cultural or historical significance. Throughout the centuries, the Mongol invasions were but a part of the local history of northern Kyushu, shaping the identity of warrior families and commoners there. Even at the end of the nineteenth century, i.e. at the height of Japan's nation-building process, when local actors in northern Kyushu alluded to the Mongol invasions in historical and patriotic discourses, they propagated ideas that were quite different from those supported by the national leaders. It was not until after the Russo-Japanese War, when intellectuals and politicians in Tokyo increasingly promulgated a propaganda of national defence, that they defined the Mongol invasions as events of national significance, attributing to them an exceptional place in Japanese history.

and one copy handed down in the Higaki family, both at the Historical Records Section of Kyushu University (*Kyūshū bunka shi kenkyū jō*), and one copy at the Fukuoka Prefecture Library. According to the *Kokusho sō mokuroku* (Tokyo: Iwanami Shoten, 1963), vol. 3, 776, a further copy is at the Kyushu University library, but its whereabouts seem unclear. Finally, a version with the title *Sankō mōko shūrai ki* is at the Ashishobō Bookstore.

3 Kawazoe 1977, 1; Saeki Kōji, *Mongoru shūrai no shōgeki* (Tokyo: Chūō Kōronsha, 2003), 248-49.

4 Wikipedia, "The Mongol Invasions of Japan," http://en.wikipedia.org/wiki/Mongol_invasions_of_Japan

2. The Illustrated Story of Mongol Invasions and other War Tales

The Mongol invasions had far-reaching effects on Japanese medieval society. The enormous military effort and the subsequent social and economic changes eventually led to the fall of the Kamakura Bakufu.[5] Still, according to the predominantly Marxist Japanese historiography, people in thirteenth-century Japan did not realise that they were facing foreign invaders. As Kawane Yoshiyasu, an adherent of this view, has argued:

> Having had almost no experience of foreign invasions in Japan, warriors as well as the common people had difficulty in distinguishing between civil war and a national war of defence.[6]

The fact that the warriors deployed to repel the Mongols asked the Bakufu for land as a reward for their military deeds, as was custom following civil wars, underscores the argument that they had lacked the notion of fighting for a common "national" cause. Of course, the Bakufu could not comply with the demand since there were no spoils of war. This stood in contrast to other battles after which the victorious lord confiscated the land of the defeated adversary and distributed it among his retainers.

There are indeed parallels between warrior conduct during the Mongol invasions and other battles, or more importantly, between the contemporary descriptions and illustrations of warrior conduct. During the battle of Gosannen, fought in the far northeast of Japan in the years 1083 to 1087, Minamoto no Yoshiie (Hachiman Tarō) asked the Imperial court for the confirmation of his victory against Kiyohara no Takehira and Kiyohara no Iehira. The text of the "Illustrated Story of the Battle of Gosannen" (*Gosannen kassen ekotoba*), written in the mid-fourteenth century, indicates that the court council determined that the battle against the Kiyohara clan had been a private war of Yoshiie and that the court would therefore not grant rewards to him. Upon hearing the outcome of his appeal, Yoshiie "threw the enemy's head away on the road and made his way to the capital [Kyoto] futilely" (*kubi wo michi ni sutete, mun-*

[5] On the impact of the Mongol invasions in Japan, see Thomas D. Conlan, "Part Three: In Little Need of Divine Intervention," in *In Little Need of Divine Intervention: Takezaki Suenaga's Scroll of the Mongol Invasions of Japan* (Ithaca: Cornell University, 2001), 254-275; William W. Farris, *Heavenly Warriors: The Evolution of Japan's Military, 500-1300* (Cambridge: Harvard University Press, 1992), 328-334; Ishii Susumu, "The Decline of the Kamakura Bakufu," *in The Cambridge History of Medieval Japan*, ed. Kozo Yamamura (Cambridge: Cambridge University Press, 1990), 128-174.

[6] Kawane Yoshiyasu, "The Formalisation of Testimonials of Valour in Medieval Japan," in *Pragmatic Literacy, East and West 1200-1330*, ed. Richard Britnell (Woodbridge: The Boydell Press, 1997), 247-259, here: footnote 20 on page 252.

ashiku miyako he noborinikeri).[7] According to the description of this fourteenth-century illustrated story, the reason for collecting the enemies' heads was the prospect of obtaining rewards.

The "Illustrated Story of the Mongol Invasions" (*Mōko shūrai ekotoba*), the most important contemporary illustration of the Mongol invasions, depicts a very similar scene. According to its epilogue, Takezaki Suenaga, a warrior from the Higo province in central Kyushu (the present-day Kumamoto prefecture) commissioned the account, consisting of two scrolls, in 1293 to demonstrate his exploits during the Mongol invasions. Illustration 21 of scroll 2 shows Takezaki recounting his military exploits to the military governor (*shugo*) of Higo province, Adachi Morimune, while a scribe takes the minutes. To the left of Takezaki can be seen two heads of Mongols that illustrate his account.[8] The "Illustrated Story of the Mongol Invasions" in its overall design and its description of events clearly fits into the genre of war tales (*gunki monogatari*) from the thirteenth and fourteenth centuries. People equated the Mongol invasions with other battles in Japan.

The above episode from the "Illustrated Story of the Mongol Invasions" suggests that warriors expected rewards after the Mongol invasions. Whether the demand for rewards really proves, as some historians assume, that the warriors did not realise that they were fighting against foreign invaders remains open to debate. In analysing Japanese warfare of the time, the military historian Stephen Turnbull has stated that, precisely because the issuing of challenges and the seeking out of a worthy opponent were the norm, "surely no samurai would have been stupid as to think that the Mongols spoke Japanese."[9] For him, it is obvious that the Japanese had the notion of fighting against foreigners. But the foreign 'other' and the native 'self' are not obvious concepts when applied to pre-modern Japan.

Bruce Batten has pointed out that borders were not confined to the coasts of the Japanese archipelago but also ran along socio-cultural lines between Eastern and Western Japan.[10] In the thirteenth century, court aristocrats in the capital Kyoto characterized warriors from Eastern Japan as "barbarians" (*ebisu*), comparing them with foreign ethnicities at the periphery of the Chi-

[7] Komatsu Shimemi, ed., *Gosannen kassen ekotoba* (Nihon no emaki, vol. 14) (Chuō Kōronsha, 1988), 106.

[8] Komatsu Shimemi, ed., *Mōko shūrai ekotoba* (Nihon no emaki, vol. 13) (Chuō Kōronsha, 1988), 114-115. For a reproduction of the scene, see figure 2 in Julika Singer's contribution to this book.

[9] Steffen Turnbull, *The Samurai Swordsman: Master of War* (North Clarendon: Tuttle Publishing, 2008), 37.

[10] Bruce Loyd Batten, *To the ends of Japan: Premodern Frontiers, Boundaries and Interactions* (Hawaii University Press, 2003).

nese Empire.[11] The foreign 'other' in medieval Japan was thus not only perceived on the basis of geographic and ethnic distinctions towards the outside but also constructed along group differences within Japan.

The Japanese use various terms to designate the Mongol invasions. *Mōko shūrai* literally means "Mongol invasion" while *Genkō* can be translated as the "Yuan invasion", Yuan dynasty (1271-1368) being the name of the Chinese dynasty founded by the Mongols. These terms might suggest that the Japanese were aware of the 'foreignness' of those invasions. But while the term *shūrai*, "invasion," is used from the Heian period (794-1185) onwards, usually in connection with "rebel invasion" (*zokuto shūrai*), *Mōko shūrai* is only attested in four documents of the Kamakura period (1185-1333), and its use is restricted to the years 1275 and 1281.[12] Neither the term *Genkō* nor the term *Mukurikokuri no oni*, "demons from Mongolia and Koryŏ (Korean dynasty, 918-1392), appear in documents of the thirteenth or early fourteenth centuries.

Thomas Conlan has observed that, although contemporaries such as Takezaki Suenaga viewed the Mongols as "rebels" or "foreign pirates," the representation of the Mongols as barbarians, almost surreal beings, did not become a phenomenon until the eighteenth century – at a time when the Japanese only rarely engaged in direct exchange with the outside world.[13] Furthermore, Ethan Segal has argued that internal economic growth and the spread of popular religious movements and literary narratives may have contributed more to the emergence of proto-nationalism during the thirteenth and fourteenth centuries than the direct encounter with the Mongols.[14] It would seem that the Mongol invasions neither caused great changes in the conceptualisation of the 'foreign' nor promoted the rise of a collective identity in the medieval period.

[11] Saeki Shin'ichi, "Figures du samuraï dans l'histoire japonaise depuis Le Dit des Heiké jusqu' au Bushidô," transl. Pierre-François Souyri, *Annales HSS* 63:4 (2008): 875-894, here: 878-879.

[12] *Kamakura ibun*, nr. 12078, 14278, 14422, 14400. Thomas Conlan and Fabian Drixler brought my attention to these various terms.

[13] Thomas D. Conlan, "Myth, Memory and The Mongol Invasions of Japan," in *Reinventing the Past: Archaism and Antiquarianism in East Asian Art and Visual Culture*, ed. Katherine Tsiang Mino and Hans B. Thomsen (Chicago: The Center for the Art of East Asia, University of Chicago and Art Media Resources, Inc., forthcoming).

[14] Ethan Segal, "Changing Medieval Identity and the Mongol Invasions" (paper presented at the Asian Studies Conference Japan, Tokyo, Japan, summer 2000).

3. Remembering the Mongol Invasions in the Eighteenth and Early Nineteenth Centuries

A first sign of the rising awareness of the Mongol invasions that appeared among intellectuals and leading warrior families during the eighteenth and early nineteenth centuries was the heightened interest shown in the "Illustrated Story of the Mongol Invasions" of the thirteenth century. The scholar Arai Hakuseki (1657-1725) drew attention to the existence of the illustrated story in 1709. The signs of usage suggest that, thereafter, the scrolls were subjected to intensive study. Various scholars rearranged the sequences, modified the illustrations and added inscriptions over the course of time. Moreover, the many copies that came into circulation from the late eighteenth century onwards underscore the unparalleled interest in the scrolls. Forty-six copies are known to have been produced during the years 1795 to 1916, including excerpts showing texts or image sequences. When, at the end of the Bunsei era (1818-1830), the missing second text-image sequence reappeared in the house of the Ōyano family, which owned the scroll, the exciting discovery was immediately incorporated into subsequent copies. Obviously, people went to great lengths to reconstruct the scrolls and the events they showed.[15]

There are various reasons for the reinvigorated interest in the "Illustrated Story of the Mongol Invasions." First, intellectuals, in particular the adherents of *kokugaku*, explored historical events and exchanged information on source materials. In this context, scholars made and passed around copies of the scrolls. Second, the warrior families of northern Kyushu were keen on acquiring copies of the scrolls because the scrolls described the merits not only of the protagonist Takezaki Suenaga but also of other famous warriors. Illustration 12 of scroll 2 shows Takezaki Suenaga and his companions riding along the defence wall erected on the coast of northern Kyushu. His lord Kikuchi Takefusa and other retainers watch the parade (figure 1). The warriors are immediately recognizable by having their names inscribed next to them. It is no coincidence that copies of the scrolls came into circulation especially in the area of Higo, the homeland of the descendants of the warriors depicted in the scrolls. Finally, the scrolls were a model for artists who painted scenes of the past. The scrolls depicted in great detail the weapons and armours of the Mongols and Japanese warriors as well as the scenic background, including buildings, the pine forests, shores and the defence wall at Hakata Bay.

15 For a very interesting overview of the biography of the scrolls on the Mongol Invasions, see Conlan (forthcoming); Horimoto Kazushige, "Mōko shūrai ekotoba no genjō seiritsu katei nitsuite," *Fukuokashi hakubutsukan kenkyū kiyō* 8 (1998): 15-57, for the discovery at the Ōyano family's house: 20.

The intensive study of the "Illustrated Story of the Mongol Invasions" was certainly not related to a growing awareness of the outside world but, on the contrary, mirrored the self-absorption of the ruling class at that time. The eighteenth and early nineteenth centuries were characterised by deep-seated social and economic changes. The shifting socio-economic structures, in turn, called into question the old hierarchical order. In these times of intellectual and political turmoil, the ruling classes looked back to their own past. Intellectuals developed new ethnographical and historical approaches, and the warriors, who had given up warfare and evolved into bureaucrats, were increasingly interested in their belligerent ancestors. The attention directed to the scroll was thus typical of a general interest in Japan's past.[16]

Not only intellectuals and influential warrior families concerned themselves with the accounts of the bygone times. Lower classes of society, too, rediscovered their ancestors in old documents. In the Enkyō period (1744-48), the Nakamura family, peasants living on the shore of Hakata Bay in northern Kyushu, commissioned a painting of their forebear Nakamura Tsuzuku (figure 2). The hanging scroll was undoubtedly based on a thirteenth century report of Tsuzuku on his warrior band during the defence against the Mongols.[17] The scroll – nowadays displayed at Obon, the Japanese ancestors' festival – firmly established the forebear, who had fought against the Mongols, in the memory of the Nakamura family.

The commemorative actions of the Nakamura family were a part of a general trend. Wealthy peasants in other regions of Japan recollected glorious battles and local military heroes, too. In the Kobe region, a peasant and merchant family organised a celebration of the five-hundredth anniversary of the death of Kusunoki Masashige (1294-1336) on the banks of the Minatogawa – Kusunoki was known for his loyalty to and death for the Emperor Go-Daigo in 1336. The family claimed that one of their ancestors had been one of his foot soldiers.[18] In other words, ruling classes and commoners alike were establishing links to historical figures in order to help define their identity in the pre-

[16] On the intellectual atmosphere in the eighteenth century, see Harry Harootunian, *Things Seen and Unseen: Discourse and Ideology in Tokugawa Nativism* (Chicago: University of Chicago Press, 1988). On the warriors of that time, see Karl Friday, "Bushido or Bull? A Medieval Historian's Perspective on the Imperial Army and the Japanese Warrior Tradition," *The History Teacher* 27:3 (1994): 339-349.

[17] The scroll is still in the possession of the Nakamura family. On the date and artist of the scroll, Yukihiro Kii no kami, see Ogino Masatarō, "Ito Matsuuratō to Genkō to no kankei," *Chikushi shidan* 4 (1915): 30-36, here: 31. The thirteenth-century report on Tsuzuku's warrior band is published in Masaki Kisaburō and Shinjō Tsunezō, eds., *Chikuzen no kuni Ito no shō shiryō* (Kyūshū shōen shiryō sōsho 4) (Tokyo: Takeuchi Rizō, 1963), no. 68.

[18] The celebration is mentioned in Kobe City, ed., *Kōbeshi shi* (Tokyo: Meicho, 1972), oral communication by Dani Botsman.

sent. The point was not simply whether one's ancestors had fought against foreign invaders or during civil wars but whether they had distinguished themselves by brave conduct.

In the 1820s, Okumura Gyokuran (1761-1828), who descended from a soy sauce brewer family in Hakata, created the *Chikuzen meisho zue*, "Collected Illustrations of Famous Sites in Chikuzen," a guide to the region of present-day Fukuoka prefecture. Illustrated guides to famous sites, especially in the capital region, formed a highly popular genre in the early nineteenth century, providing people with detailed geographical and historical information of specific places. These guides certainly inspired Okumura when he designed his "Collected Illustrations of Famous Sites in Chikuzen." Chapter 2 featured an illustrated account of the Mongol invasions.[19] Obviously, the Mongol invasions were deemed a part of the local history of northern Kyushu.

4. The Mongol Invasions as Metaphors of Anti-Foreignism in the 1860s

The increasing appearance of foreign ships off the shores of Japan and accounts of Qing-China's defeat in the Opium War of 1839-41 let Western powers appear to be an immediate threat. In 1853, the American commodore Matthew C. Perry compelled the opening of Japanese ports to foreign trade. In the same period, nearly a century after Tsuda had published his source edition on the Mongol invasions, the *Sankō mōko nyūkō ki*, new editions of his work appeared, indicating a renewed interest in the Mongol invasions. A copy from 1843 and another from 1854 have been preserved until today.[20] The scholarly interest in the Mongol invasions in the mid-nineteenth century was probably triggered by the growing concern about the West.

The 1860s saw the emergence of anti-foreign movements, known by the slogan of that time "Revere the Emperor, expel the barbarians" (*sōnnō jōi*). In particular, the warriors from the Chōshū Domain, the present-day Yamaguchi prefecture, translated the slogan into practice by attacking foreign ships in the Kanmon Straits between the islands of Honshu and Kyushu in June and July 1863. The attacks, which violated the conciliatory policy that the Tokugawa Bakufu (1603-1868) officially pursued towards the West since it had been forced to conclude the so-called 'Unequal Treaties' with the latter in the 1850s, escalated into several naval battles. Great Britain, France, the Netherlands and the United States eventually emerged as victors in 1864. Between the summers of 1863 and 1864, i.e. at the height of the *sonnō jōi*-movement, several artists

[19] A copy of the *Chikuzen meishozue* is at the Kyushu University Museum.

[20] See note 2.

created satirical prints of the naval battles fought by the Chōshū warriors against Western powers. A common pattern was to disguise these battles in the historical garb of the Mongol invasions.

In September 1863 (the eighth month of the third year of Bunkyu), the artist Kawanabe Kyōsai (1831-1889) designed two woodblock prints of the Mongol invasions: one with the title "Repelling of the Mongol Villain Ships" (*Mōko zokusen taiji no zu*) and the other called "Sketch on the Repelling of the Mongols" (*Mōko taiji no ryakki*).[21] The first print shows a red fireball, its radiating thunderbolts whirling Mongol warriors and wrecks through the air while towering waves crush and swallow the rest of the enemy fleet (figure 3). On the horizon, burning ships add to the dramatic setting. The fireball that anticipated the *hi no maru* flag with sixteen rays, used by Japan's armed forces later on, points here to the legendary salvation of the Japanese archipelago from the foreign invaders. The priest Nichiren (1222-1282), who is said to have predicted the Mongol invasions, supposedly used the mandala, magical circle-shaped symbols, to conjure up "divine winds" (*kamikaze*). Legend has it that the divine winds materialised as red clouds and saved Japan from the Mongol fleets. The fireball probably alludes to the mandala of Nichiren or to the divine winds. Other prints, like the second one by Kawanabe, clearly refer to the mandala of Nichiren.

The print shows banners in the upper-left-hand corner that are inscribed with red and white mandala and incantations, so-called mantra (figure 4). Behind the banners poses Nichiren in a scarlet dress. Devotees draped in white surround him and chant prayers. In the foreground, Japanese warriors atrociously execute Mongol prisoners by flaying, shooting, or blinding them. A white curtain divides the warriors from the priests. The *mitsu-uroko* (literally: three scales), the crest of the Hōjō family which is imprinted on the curtain, points to Hōjō Tokimune, the leader of the Japanese defence against the Mongols. By arranging the print into a front and a back scene separated by a width of curtain, Kawanabe clearly alluded to Takezaki's parade at the defence wall, depicted in the "Illustrated Story of the Mongol invasions." The artist, by inserting the Hōjō family's crest and shaping his composition according to the thirteenth-century model, established an unmistakable historical link.

In contrast, the barrel to the left of the wall makes the image highly topical, alluding to the ongoing naval battles between the Chōshū warriors and Western

[21] On the two prints, see Fujita Noboru, "Watashi no motteiru Kyōsai 59: Kawanabe Kyōsai hitsu Mōko taiji no ryakki." *Kawanabe Kyōsai Kenkyū shi* 85 (2004): 29-32. On the *Moko zokusen taiji no zu*, see also Timothy Clark, *Demon of Painting: The Art of Kawanabe Kyosai* (London: The British Museum Press, 1993), no. 74.1; Kawanabe Kyōsai Kinen Bijutsukan (The Kawanabe Kyōsai Memorial Museum), ed., *Kawanabe Kyōsai to Edo Tōkyō* (Warabi: Kawanabe Kyōsai Kinen Bijutsukan, 1994), no. 32.

powers. By choosing the Mongol invasions that stood for Japan's perseverance against foreign influence as a metaphor for the contemporary conflicts with the West, Kawanabe and other artists conveyed a clear political message without having to be explicit. They criticised Western aggression and, even more, the conciliatory policy of the Tokugawa Bakufu towards the West. The woodblock prints obviously reflected political concerns and people's anxieties about the opening of the country. The prints indicate that the clashes in 1863 and 1864 attracted countrywide attention and that there was a sense of solidarity with the insurgent warriors. The prints thus anticipated a sense of national unity.

Following the Meiji restoration in 1868, the central government promoted a national historiography and other *lieux de mémoire*, "sites of memory", in the form of monuments, rituals and the illustrated banknotes of the newly created national currency.[22] As shown by Julika Singer in her contribution to this book, the Mongol invasions featured in officially approved history textbooks from 1872 onwards and were used as design motifs on the reverse side of the one-yen paper bill of the Japanese National Bank in 1873 (figure 8 of Julika Singer's contribution to this book). In 1891 Yamada An'ei (1852-1922) edited the *Fukutekihen*, the most extensive source edition on the Mongol invasions until today, under the supervision of Shigeno Yasutsugu (1827-1910), vice director of the House of Historical Compilation (*shūshikan*) from 1881 and director of the Provisional Bureau of Historical Compilation (*rinji shūshikyoku*) from 1886, both preceding institutions of the Historiographical Institute of the University of Tokyo.[23]

Nevertheless, the Mongol invasions were only one of many historical topics to be interpreted within a national framework. Moreover, the influence of local actors in northern Kyushu is obvious with respect to the preparation of the standard reference work on the Mongol invasions, the *Fukutekihen*. A chief promoter of the *Fukutekihen* was Yuchi Takeo (1847-1913), who originated from Kumamoto – the birthplace of the thirteenth century warrior Takezaki Suenaga who commissioned the "Illustrated Story of the Mongol Invasions." Yuchi was in regular correspondence with Yamada An'ei, the compiler of the *Fukutekihen*, and eagerly provided the source material that he collected in Kyushu. Moreover, he wrote the epilogue of the *Fukutekihen*.[24] The making of

22 For an assessment of Pierre Nora's term of *lieux de mémoire*, see Monica Juneja "Architectural Memory between Representation and Practive: Rethinking Pierre Nora's *Les lieux de mémoire*, in *Revisiting Sites of Memory: New Perspectives on the British Empire*, ed. Hagen Schulze and Indra Sengupta (London: German Historical Insitute, forthcoming).

23 Yamada An'ei, *Fukutekihen* (Yoshikawa Hanshichi, 1891). On the founding of the Historiographical Institute, see Margaret Mehl, *History and the State in Nineteenth-Century Japan* (London: MacMillan, 1998).

24 Kawazoe1977, 116-119.

the *Fukutekihen* shows that, although bureaucrats in Tokyo included the Mongol invasions in history textbooks, primary source editions and national banknotes, the Mongol invasions remained a subject of the local historiography of northern Kyushu up to the late nineteenth century.

5. From Warriors to the Way of the Warrior: Reinterpretations of the Mongol Invasions in the late Nineteenth Century

Yuchi Takeo founded the "movement for the establishment of a monument for the Mongol invasions" (*Genkō kinenhi kensetsu undō*) in 1888. Pamphlets indicate that Yuchi originally planned to set up an equestrian statue of Hōjō Tokimune, who had organised the defence against the Mongols, on the peninsula of Shika off Fukuoka.[25] Reasons for his commitment to the monument were apparently threefold. First, in 1886 clashes between sailors from Qing-China and members of the Nagasaki police resulted in heavy casualties on both sides. Yuchi, who was a police captain in the neighbouring Fukuoka prefecture at that time, was deeply shaken by the incident that reflected the tense atmosphere in the years before the Sino-Japanese War of 1894-95. In the same year, a cholera epidemic broke out that reminded Yuchi of the suffering of the population during the Mongol invasions. Finally, in 1887, negotiations to revise the unequal treaties between Japan and Western powers failed, thus fuelling anti-western sentiments. Yuchi's movement was hence a product of the Zeitgeist.[26]

In 1894, Yuchi met the artist Yada Isshō (1858-1913) in Kumamoto during one of his campaigns to promote the monument to the Mongol invasions. Yada, who had been trained in Western painting in the United States, had just moved to Kumamoto from Tokyo to paint the first Kyushu panorama. In his panoramas – a new medium that experienced a boom at the end of the nineteenth century throughout Europe, the United States and Japan –, Yada clearly sympathised with the government of the newly restored Meiji Emperor. [27] Following his encounter with Yuchi, Yada moved to Fukuoka to support Yuchi's project. The artist was enthusiastic about the idea of a monument to the Mongol invasions and became involved in the campaign by contributing the pictorial illustrations. Yuchi had originally used painted glass slides during his talks. Since the latter could only be used in the dark, Yuchi readily accepted Yada's

[25] Kawazoe1977, note 18 of chapter 2; Nishimoto Masanobu, ed., *Yomigaeru Meiji kaiga: shūfuku sareta Yada Isshō "Mōko shūrai ezu"* (Fukuoka: Fukuoka Prefecture Art Museum 2005), 75, no. 12.

[26] Kawazoe 1977, 117-118; Nakamura Kuji, *Yuchi Takeo* (Tokyo: Maki Shobō, 1943), 31-32.

[27] Nagasawa Saburō, "Yada Isshō to Kyūshū harigakan kankei shiryō." *De arute* 2 (1986), 79-84.

large-format oil paintings. In 1896, i.e. the year after the Sino-Japanese War, Yada completed a first series on the Mongol invasions, consisting of fourteen paintings. Yada displayed his compositions during one of Yuchi's campaigns in various locations in Kyushu. He not only appeared together with his paintings but also commented on them, as contemporary newspaper articles reveal.[28]

In the subsequent decades, the campaign was extended to other parts of Japan, including major cities as well as rural regions up to the Tōhoku region and Hokkaidō in the northeast of Japan.[29] This multimedia event, combining paintings in a new Western style with speeches by the organisers, deeply impressed the visitors. The writer Kikuchi Kan (1888-1948) notes in his autobiography:

> When we were small, there was a person who showed oil paintings of the Mongol invasions all around the country and preached about the importance of national defence. These oil paintings showed the cruelty of the Mongols so powerfully that, even after forty years, I can still see them before my eyes.[30]

Yada's paintings were impressive and unique not only due to the use of oil on canvas but also with respect to the composition of the scenes. The artist represented persons, horses, vehicles, banners and natural forces in transitory moments in a manner reminiscent of photographic snapshots. Apart from the artistic precision, Yada's art reflected a meticulous study of the historical material provided by the leaders of the "movement for the establishment of a monument for the Mongol invasions." In the eleventh of the fourteen paintings of 1896, Yada showed the renewed attack of the Mongols in 1281 (figure 5). By depicting the defence wall at Hakata Bay as well as the gunpowder used by the Mongols, he included elements described by contemporary sources such as the "Illustrated Story of the Mongol invasions." Yada also based his compositions on earlier artistic works originating from northern Kyushu such as the *Chikuzen meisho zue* by Okumura Gyokuran from the beginning of the nineteenth century (figure 6).

Moreover, Yada's paintings were based thematically on illustrations previously used for Yuchi's campaigns, such as those included in the *Genkō hangeki gokoku bidan*, "Beautiful Tales of National Defence through Counter-

[28] *Fukuoka Shinpō*, May 30, 1896 (Meiji 29); Nishimoto 2005, 69, 77, no. 20-22.

[29] A newspaper article portrays Yuchi's campaign on the island of Hokkaido: *Yomiuri Shinbun,* November 19, 1892 (Meiji 25). On Yuchi's campaign in Aomori in the northeast of Japan, see Ōta Kōki, "'Genkō gakan' to dai panorama ga: shikai wo tōshite no gokoku undō," in *Matsuuratō kenkyū*, ed. Matsuuratō kenkyū rengōkai (Sasebo: Geibundō, 1980), vol. 22, 4-23.

[30] Kikuchi Kan, "*Hanashi no kuzukago*, Article of July 1943 (Shōwa 18)," in *Kikuchi Kan: Bungaku zenshū*, ed. Yamamoto Yūzō (Tokyo: Bungeishunjū Shinsha 1960), 539.

attacks against the Mongol Invasions," first edited by Yuchi in 1891.[31] As the fifth of six illustrations the *Genkō hangeki gokoku bidan* shows Kōno Michiari "aboard a light boat about to attack the enemy ships" (figure 7). Yada included the same scene into his large-format series (figure 8). And yet, Yada's paintings followed a scheme different from earlier models. Although the *Genkō hangeki gokoku bidan,* like Yada's paintings, had a pedagogic function of reminding the readers of the history of Japan and of the exploits of their ancestors, its illustrations were still reminiscent of the earlier simplistic, ethnographic approaches to the Mongol invasions. There was not yet an overt ideological message or a glorification of heroes to be found. In contrast, Yada's paintings carried an unmistakable ideological message, namely loyalty to the nation and willingness to make sacrifices for it.

In the fourth painting in the series of 1896, Yada represented the death of Sō Sukekuni (1207-1274), vice military governor of Tsushima (figure 9). The scene captures the moment as three assailants in the background kill the wounded Sukekuni. Sukekuni turns into an exemplary historical figure, reminding those viewing the scene of their military duties in the present. By promoting loyalty to the nation and devotion beyond death, Yada propagated the new ideology of *bushidō*, literally "the way of the warrior," which Karl Friday summarises as follows:

> Modern *bushidō* is closely bound up with the notion of a Japanese "national essence," and with those of the *kokutai*, or Japanese national structure, and the cult of the emperor. [...] Warrior values were held to be the essence of Japanese-ness itself, unifying traits of character common to all classes. The abolition of the samurai class thus marked not the end of *bushidō*, but the point of its spread to the whole of the Japanese population.[32]

Yada's work was closely aligned with the objectives of the Meiji government. Still, the reception of his paintings was restricted mainly to the area of northern Kyushu. Of the four known series on the Mongol invasions painted by Yada, three have been kept in northern Kyushu: one series from 1909 at the Honbutsu Temple in Fukuoka, another one from the same year at the Iki Shrine on Iki Island and an undated series at the Archive of the Mongol Invasions (*Genkō shiryōkan*) in Fukuoka. Only his first series from 1896 reached nationwide fame by being transferred to the Yūshūkan, the Museum of the Yasukuni Shrine in Tokyo. But this did not happen until 1912. For the most part, Yada's

31 Shizan Koji and Chūshū Koji, *Genkō hangeki gokoku bidan*, ed. Yuchi Takeo (Seikodō, 1891).

32 Friday 1994, 342. The most recent publication on the development of the warrior and the way of the warrior is Saeki 2008.

oeuvre did not enter a national arena because his paintings referred to a local commemorative tradition and were embedded in a local political movement. The fate of Yada's paintings is symptomatic of the limited success of the "movement for the establishment of a monument to the Mongol invasions."

The participants of the movement all had ties to the area of northern Kyushu, like the leader Yuchi, who originated from Kumamoto, or Yada, who stayed in Fukuoka until his death in 1913. In addition, despite Yuchi's endeavour to raise funds throughout Japan, responses to the movement were mainly restricted to the area of northern Kyushu. Yuchi did not manage to erect his monument until 1904, at the height of the Russo-Japanese War, i.e. nearly two decades after he had founded his movement. Moreover, he only managed to do so with the decisive support of Sano Zenrei, a priest from the Honbutsu Temple in Fukuoka. Instead of the originally planned statue of Hōjō Tokimune, two statues were inaugurated in the Higashi Park in Fukuoka: one of the Retired Emperor Kameyama (1249-1305) and one of the priest Nichiren. According to legend, both fended off the Mongols by praying. Obviously, Yuchi's original plan to build a statue of the regent of the Bakufu was short-sighted at a time when the central elite was promoting the cult of the Meiji Emperor.[33]

Yuchi's ideas appealed to the population of Kyushu but clearly failed to gain nation-wide acclaim. While Yuchi, who came from northern Kyushu, committed himself to the historiography of the Mongol invasions, members of the local elite in other parts of Japan brought attention to wars fought in their home regions. For instance, in Aizu (in today's Fukushima prefecture) in the northeast of Japan, local politicians and historians worked to transform the tragic story of the White Tiger Brigade, a group of young samurai boys who had committed mass suicide during the civil war of 1868, into a myth of national sacrifice at the end of the nineteenth century.[34] Yuchi was just one of many local actors throughout Japan who endeavoured to elevate events of local historical importance to national myths.

6. Conclusion

In 1916, Yamada Nakaba published a book in English with the title *Ghenkō: The Mongol Invasion of Japan*. The illustrations at the end of the book, repro-

[33] On the completion of the monument, see Kinoshita Toshihiro, Nakamuta Yoshiaki and Tanaka Kazuyuki, *Fukuokashi Higashi kōen Nichiren shōnin dōzō* (Fukuoka: Nishi Nihon Shinbunsha, 1986).

[34] Shimoda, Hiraku, "Making the Poster Boys of Aizu: The Unlikely Apotheosis of the White Tiger Brigade" (paper presented at the 123rd Annual Meeting of the American Historical Association, Jauary 2009).

duced without source reference, are drawn from the posters announcing the transfer of Yada's series from 1896 to the Yūshūkan. Yamada wrote in his introduction:

> "Ghenko," as the Japanese call "the Mongol Invasion" [...] is, in my opinion, one of the most important facts, which should be known by our friends who take interest in the evolution of the Japanese power. For Japan is not a nation which became a world power simply because of the victories won in the Chino-Japanese and Russo-Japanese Wars, but because of the superior spirit that has existed in the heart of the nation from earliest times.[35]

Two decades after Yada had composed his first paintings of the Mongol invasions, the warriors fighting against the Mongols had become central figures for the Japanese national identity.

In 1943, the chapter on the Mongol invasions in the new officially accredited history textbook was titled "Divine Winds" (*kamikaze*) for the first time. The textbook thereby made clear that the Mongols had been defeated because Japan was under the protection of the Gods. By referring to the "divine winds" that had allegedly protected Japan from the foreign invaders, the textbook authors used a metaphor that woodblock print artists had appropriated exactly eight decades earlier to hint at the weakness of the government of that time. This time, the divine winds were a symbol supporting the national policy. The textbook's chapter on the Mongol invasions closed with the following words:

> When we now visit the East [Higashi] Park in Fukuoka and seek out the statue of the retired Emperor Kameyama, looking out to the East China Sea in the distance, we think of the events of 650 years ago as if they were those of today and are deeply moved.[36]

While the textbook established a direct link between the events of the thirteenth century and the present, it did not indicate that the statue of the retired Emperor Kameyama had been the fruit of a local nineteenth-century movement. National historiography had absorbed local memory. Whereas Yada's paintings and the monument for which they had been painted entered national historiography, the "Illustrated Story of the Mongol Invasions" experienced a different fate.

35 Nakaba Yamada, *Ghenkō: The Mongol Invasion of Japan* (London: Smith, Elder & Co., 1916), vi.

36 Kaigo Tokiomi and Naka Arata, eds., *Nihon kyōkasho taikei* (Tokyo: Kōdansha), vol. 20, 286, cit. and trans. in: John Caiger, "The Aims and Content of School Courses in Japanese History, 1872-1945," in *Japan's Modern Century* (A Special Issue of *Monumenta Nipponica*), ed. Edmund Skrzypczak (Tokyo: Sophia University with Charles E, Tuttle Co 1968), 79.

In 1890, i.e. four years before the beginning of the first Sino-Japanese war, the Ōyano family, warriors in Kyushu and owners of the "Illustrated Story," donated the scroll to the Imperial collection. The physical locking up of the scroll stood metaphorically for the end of the traditional illustrations of the warriors who had fought against the Mongols and also for the end of the earlier interpretations of their battles: A symbolic and aesthetic ideology had replaced the earlier historical and ethnographical interest. While in the early nineteenth century warriors of the thirteenth century had acted as identity-generating figures of families in northern Kyushu, by the early twentieth century the celebrated warriors who had fought against the Mongols had vanished into the nameless masses of the Japanese population. They stood for essential moral values valid for all classes of society – in a word, for a specific Japanese identity. The Mongol invasions had entered a truly national historiography and, in this context, evolved into the metaphor of national defence.

And yet, until the early twentieth century, the Mongol invasions were much more closely related to the local memory of the people in northern Kyushu than to an all-embracing national identity. The "movement for the establishment of a monument to the Mongol invasions" came into being in Kyushu, where collective memory had kept the Mongol invasions alive over the centuries, and was nowhere as successful as there. Although the Mongol invasions would seem to have been suited to the construction of national myths like no other event in (pre-modern) Japanese history, their significance as an epoch-making event, opening up a new dimension by establishing a common identity, was confined to northern Kyushu for a surprisingly long time. The Mongol invasions were just one of many historical events to be commemorated at the national level. Moreover, it seems that, beside a doubtlessly nationalist historiography of the Mongol invasions that began after the Russo-Japanese War and reached its peak during the Pacific War (1937-1945), a local historiographical tradition rooted in northern Kyushu still survives in a certain sense, as even nowadays most historians concerned with the Mongol invasions come from Kyushu.[37]

[37] A collection of primary source materials by Kyushu historians is Kawazoe Shōji, Shinjō Tsunezō and Yamaguchi Takamasa, eds. *Shiseki genkō bōrui kankei hennen shiryō* (Fukuoka: Fukuokashi kyōiku i'inkai, 1967). Secondary references are Kawazoe 1977; Saeki 2003.

Figure 1

"Illustrated Story of the Mongol Invasions" (*Mōko shūrai ekotoba*), sheet 7 of scroll 2: "Takezaki Suenaga and his companions ride along the defence wall, while his lord Kikuchi Takefusa and other retainers watch the parade," colours on paper, around 1293, The Museum of the Imperial Collections, Tokyo.

Figure 2

Yukihiro Kii no Kami, „Nakamura Tsuzuku, leading his warrior band in Imazu," colours on paper, around 1744-48, Nakamura Reisaburō Archive, Fukuoka.

Figure 3

Kawanabe Kyōsai (1831-1889), “Repelling of the Mongol Villain Ships” (*Mōko zokusen taiji no zu*). Triptych, Signature: „Seisei Kyōsai“, colour print (*nishiki-e*), 1863 (Bunkyū 3). Library of the Historiographical Institute, University of Tokyo.

Figure 4

Kawanabe Kyōsai (1831-1889), "Sketch on the Repelling of the Mongols" (*Mōko taiji no ryakki*). Diptych, Signature: „Chikamaro", colour print (*nishiki-e*), 1863 (Bunkyū 3). Library of the Historiographical Institute, University of Tokyo.

Figure 5

Yada Isshō (1858-1913): *The Mongol Invasions*, picture 11: "The Repeated Attack of the Mongols at Hakata Bay", oil on canvas, 1896, Yūshūkan, Yasukuni Shrine, Tokyo.

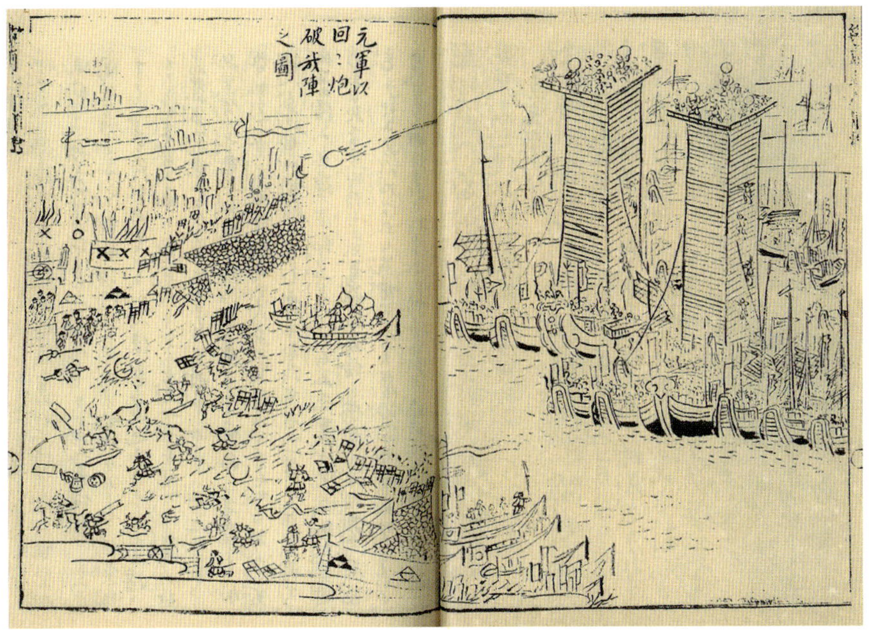

Figure 6

Okumura Gyokuran (1761-1828): *Chikuzen meisho zue*, volume 2: „The Yuan army is catapulting our camp from all sides," print, around 1804-1829 (Bunsei and Bunka eras). The Kyushu University Museum, Fukuoka.

Figure 7

Yuchi Takeo, ed. *Genkō hangeki gokoku bidan*, illustration 5: „Kōno Rokurō aboard a light boat about to attack the enemy ships," print, 1891.

Figure 8

Yada Isshō (1858-1913): *The Mongol Invasions*, picture 12: "Defying the Great Warships of the Mongols", oil on canvas, 1896, Yūshūkan, Yasukuni Shrine, Tokyo.

Figure 9

Yada Isshō (1858-1913): *The Mongol Invasions*, picture 4: "The Death of Sō Sukekuni (1207-1274), Vice Military Governor of Tsushima", oil on canvas, 1896, Yūshūkan, Yasukuni Shrine, Tokyo.

JULE NOWOITNICK (Berlin)

Heroic Violence, Violent Heroes. Transcultural Representations of Violence in Recent Western Historical Novels

Historical novels that are set in the past of their readers' own cultural space can presuppose a certain amount of background knowledge on their part.[1] This does not quite apply to Western historical novels about a non-Western figure, as is the case in the novels on Chinggis Khaan treated in this article. The average Western reader will have a vague idea of medieval Mongolia in general and Chinggis Khaan in particular, but only a bare minimum of factual knowledge. This increases both the authors' creative freedom in dealing with the genre's "Hiatus von Fiktion und Historie" ("hiatus of fiction and history"),[2] as their readers cannot judge the historical authenticity of their work, and the demand for a detailed description of not only historical but also cultural facts, as their readers might not be able to follow the plot without such knowledge.

In the case of the novels analyzed in this article, the authors therefore have to impart not only the culture and history, but also the understanding of violence in medieval Mongolia. For, even though Chinggis Khaan is increasingly acknowledged as an extraordinary military tactician and a visionary statesman,[3] the horrifying acts of violence committed under his command during the Mongolian invasions, especially in the Western Wars, are still most present in the Western collective memory. A closer look at Chinggis Khaan's biography reveals that violence not only was a major factor in medieval Mongolian society in general, characterized as it was by clan feuds and power struggles, but also played a central role in Chinggis Khaan's life in particular.

1 See Franz K. Stanzel, "Historie, historischer Roman, historiographische Metafiktion," *Sprachkunst* 26 (1995) H.1: 113-123. Here 119.

2 Hans Vilmar Geppert, *Der ‚andere' historische Roman: Theorie und Strukturen einer diskontinuierlichen Gattung* (Tübingen: Niemeyer, 1976), 34.

3 Nicholas Kristof's understanding of Chinggis Khaan can be seen as typical of this new perspective: "He may have killed people by the millions, but he was also a great nationalist and one of the most brilliant commanders in history." (Nicholas Kristof, "Where Genghis Khan Is In," *The New York Times Magazine* (May 27, 1990), 23.)

Interestingly, *The Secret History of the Mongols*[4] shows Chinggis Khaan, born Temüjin in 1162, as a victim and perpetrator of violence as well as its observer: When he is approximately nine years old, his father is murdered by the Tatar tribe,[5] leaving Temüjin and his family fighting for survival on their own. Against this backdrop, Temüjin kills his half-brother Bekhter, who would not stop stealing booty and undermining Temüjin's role as clan chief.[6] Soon after, he is abducted and tortured by the Tayicut,[7] once again switching his role to that of a victim. In his adult life, he almost exclusively appears as a perpetrator – directly and indirectly – of violence, as he brings the violence of war upon the steppes and eventually upon the world beyond as well. But even though the sheer brutality of the Western wars is indisputable, it is important to note that these wars were not primarily meant to be conquests, but rather, retribution for the murder of Mongolian messengers by the Khwaresm Shah. Another side to Chinggis Khaan is shown when his blood brother Jamukha, who by this point has been his sworn and vicious enemy for years, is brought before him as prisoner; Chinggis Khaan offers him not only his life but a place at his side.[8] In conclusion, *The Secret History of the Mongols* presents a very pragmatic view of violence based on a morality very different from its modern Western counterpart. Temüjin's fratricide is not praised, but it is seen as legitimate, as it is necessary to keep the hierarchy of power intact. This indicates that the differentiation between legitimate and illegitimate violence is not based upon the character of violence itself but on its necessity.

This article aims to investigate how recent historical novels on Chinggis Khaan – exemplified by Pamela Sargent's *Ruler of the Sky* (1993), Homeric's *The Blue Wolf* (1998), Galsan Tschinag's *Die neun Träume des Dschingis Khan* (2007) – reconcile all these different roles Chinggis Khaan embodies regarding violence, how they convey this violence, how they mediate between medieval Mongolian reality and modern Western ethics, and how they handle the literary conventions of the historical novel.

*****

4 *The Secret History of the Mongols*, which narrates the Mongols' mythical ancestry, Chinggis Khaan's life and times and closes with the reign of his son Ögöödei, is the only original Mongolian source to have come upon us from the Middle Ages and is therefore one of the main sources for academic research as well as for literary writing on medieval Mongolia and Chinggis Khaan.

5 Igor de Rachewiltz, trans., *The Secret History of the Mongols: A Mongolian Epic Chronicle of the Thirteenth Century* (Leiden: Brill, 2004), § 67f.

6 *The Secret History of the Mongols*, § 76-78.

7 *The Secret History of the Mongols*, § 79-87.

8 *The Secret History of the Mongols*, § 200f.

According to Wilhelm Heitmeyer and John Hagan, a clear-cut definition of the phenomenon violence is neither possible nor desirable due to its constantly shifting nature. Therefore, there can only be a very basic common understanding of violence as an "*over-stepping of boundaries*," which "causes injury and sometimes death and results in many different forms of destruction."[9] Not only do concepts of violence change with the times, but there is an "*ambiguity* of violence itself,"[10] indicating that the positive or negative interpretation of a particular act of violence depends on the personal, historical, political as well as cultural perspective.[11] In contrast to Jürgen Nieraad, who bases his two-fold typology of literary representation of violence – "critical and censuring presentations of violence or apologies for violence" – on "the basic opposition between negatively and positively connoted violence," formed through the civilizational discourse of the 19th century,[12] Heitmeyer's and Hagan's concept of ambiguity compensates for shifting interpretations of the same act of violence. Thus, an act of violence is not ascribed an inherent ethical value; a value judgment depends on the perspective of the observer.

As is the case in Nieraad's article, most research on literary representation of violence as well as research on historical novels tends to take a monocultural perspective, focusing on Western representations of Western violence or Western history. Seeing that today's societies are more and more shaped by the effects of globalization, it seems important to broaden this perspective. The need for such a step has, among others, been vocalized by Herbert Uerlings, who stresses the fact that "interkulturelles Erzählen" ("intercultural narration") has played a vital role in the development of the historical novel in the 20th century since it allowed a reflection upon the Self and the Other and, through it, offered a way out of the 'crisis of representation.'[13] Touching upon this, Klaus Scherpe introduces a number of interesting insights in his examination of the challenges that the complex of Otherness (Fremde) and violence constitutes for representation in (post-)colonial literature. His findings indicate that

9 Wilhelm Heitmeyer and John Hagan, "Violence: The Difficulties of a Systematic International Review," in *International Handbook of Violence Research*, ed. Wilhelm Heitmeyer and John Hagan (Dordrecht: Kluwer Academic Publishers, 2003), 3-11. Here 4.

10 Heitmeyer/Hagan, "Violence," 4.

11 Heitmeyer/Hagan, "Violence," 5.

12 Jürgen Nieraad, "Violence and the Glorification of Violence in the Literature of the Twentieth Century," in *International Handbook of Violence Research*, ed. by Wilhelm Heitmeyer and John Hagan (Dordrecht: Kluwer Academic Publishers, 2003), 1023-1039. Here 1027.

13 Herbert Uerlings, "Die Erneuerung des historischen Romans durch interkulturelles Erzählen. Zur Entwicklung der Gattung bei Alfred Döblin, Uwe Timm, Hans Christoph Buch und anderen," in *Travellers in Time and Space / Reisende durch Raum und Zeit. The German Historical Novel / Der deutschsprachige historische Roman*, ed. by Osman Durrani and Julian Preece (Amsterdam and New York: Rodopi, 2001), 129-154. Here 129.

the volatile mélange of violence and Otherness is not tacitly compensated for but instead explicitly focused upon in a literary criticism of representation, drawing attention to the aspects of trespassing.[14]

Like Uerlings, however, Scherpe focuses on literary texts depicting a direct encounter between a representative of the Western culture and the Other, for which Uerlings applies the term 'intercultural.' The novels analyzed in this article forego such a mediating character in their representation of the Mongolian Other and its violence. Instead, as will be shown in the analyses, the authors write medieval Mongolia *into* Western understandings of ethics and violence. This seems to match with the term 'transcultural' as Wolfgang Welsch coined it, who observes that cultures have assumed a new and intricately entangled form today which "*passes through* classical cultural boundaries."[15] Even though the newness that Welsch stresses here seems questionable – and Welsch himself relativizes this later in the same article[16] – the basic process certainly applies here.

Examining this transcultural form of representing the violence of the Other in popular, commercially successful historical novels on Chinggis Khaan is not only prompted by Chinggis Khaan's strong biographical link to violence. Additionally, the genre of the historical novel lends itself to such an undertaking since, as Simon Edwards points out, it is strongly characterized by a "universal concern with violence as it plays itself out in different national and cultural traditions, different patterns of political and social development."[17] At the same time, if one follows Nieraad, the genre's dependence on conventions and its strong orientation towards the reader would almost certainly preclude the development of "characteristic new forms" in the description of violence.[18] By examining novels from various national literatures, this article aims to take a first step towards finding out whether such a 'universal concern' is indeed mirrored by universal narrative approaches and tactics and to what extent these are dependent on literary and social conventions in representing violence.

14 Klaus R. Scherpe, "Die Gewalt des Fremden. Über Repräsentation," in *Der schöne Schein der Kunst und seine Schatten*, ed. by Hans-Richard Brittnacher and Fabian Störmer (Bielefeld: Aisthesis Verlag, 2000), 366-379. Here 375.

15 Wolfgang Welsch, "Transculturality – the Puzzling Form of Cultures Today," in *Spaces of Culture: City, Nation, World*, ed. by Mike Featherstone and Scott Lash (London: Sage, 1999), 194-213. Here 197. – Thus I here propose an expansion of the common understanding of transcultural literature as being written by authors with a transcultural biography, e.g. migrants.

16 Welsch, "Transculturality," 199f.

17 Simon Edwards, "The Geography of Violence: Historical Fiction and the National Question," *Novel* 34.2 (Spring 2001): 293-308. Here 295.

18 Nieraad, "Violence and the Glorification of Violence in the Literature of the Twentieth Century," 1027.

In the novels analyzed here, it is the titular hero, Chinggis Khaan, who embodies the epicenter of violence. Interestingly, according to Hinrik Schünemann, the figure of the hero is also the epicenter of genre expectations and thus the central factor in a novel's success. A mythical hero who represents the values and virtues of his readers' culture thus provides a model on how to balance individual wants and social needs while achieving greatness not only for oneself but also for the society at large.[19] In Western literature, this hero is characterized by a unique name that he has made for himself.[20] He is a doer, a leader and a visionary, and he does not bow to social norms but follows his own social ideals.[21] He is characterized by professionalism, adaptability and mobility.[22] While Schünemann's last-mentioned mark of the hero – a lack of sexual motivation[23] – seems debatable, overall, his template of the Western hero certainly indicates a central challenge for the novels analyzed here: Whereas Chinggis Khaan is historically and culturally bound to the Mongolian 'myth,' the novels' readerships are bound to their own, Western 'myth' of the hero. It falls to the authors to mediate between these spheres.

*****

Pamela Sargent's novel *Ruler of the Sky*, which spans the entire life of Chinggis Khaan (Genghis Khan),[24] is narrated from the point of view of the women in his life. This not only limits the readers' insight into the figure of Chinggis Khaan but also has distinct consequences for the representation of violence in the novel. The text focuses on the female perspective towards violence, e.g. on the experience of rape and forced marriage, and on the indirect repercussions of the violence of war on women, e.g. losing the men of the family. In contrast, there are almost no descriptions of the violence of battle.

In describing the lives of its female protagonists, the novel is very much characterized by an awareness of cultural differences between the Western and the Mongolian understanding of violence without devaluating the ramifications of violence. The portrayal of the young Chinggis Khaan generally follows the

19 Hinrik Schünemann, *Mythos und Profit. Zur Vermittlung sozialer Interaktionsmodelle über fiktionale Informationsdienstleistungen am Beispiel des amerikanischen Beststeller-Romans* (Würzburg: Königskausen & Neumann, 2000), 277.

20 Schünemann, *Mythos und Profit*, 166.

21 Schünemann, *Mythos und Profit*, 277-287.

22 Schünemann, *Mythos und Profit*, 343.

23 Schünemann, *Mythos und Profit*, 325.

24 To avoid confusion by adopting the novels' different transcriptions (indicated in brackets), this article will stay within its own transcription of the Mongolian names, which is based upon the modern academic convention. Exceptions are, of course, direct quotes.

same lines. It presents the horrifying consequences of his violence but does not criticize the medieval Mongolian way of life as such, of which violence is an intrinsic part. Instead, expression is given to the importance of cultural perspective by conveying not only historical but also cultural knowledge.

The depiction of Temüjin (Temujin) killing his half-brother Bekhter (Bekter) is a perfect example for this approach, while it also shows its apparent limitations. Fratricide is one of the basic taboos of Western society. The text does not transform this act of violence into one of self-defense, nor does it give another 'excuse' which would absolve Temüjin of all guilt. Rather, it conveys the pressure of a teenager having to fulfill the role of clan chief and the truly existential danger Bekhter's behavior presents to the family. While this is certainly within medieval Mongolian reasoning, *Ruler of the Sky* adds one more motivation for the deed by introducing a homoerotic element to the relationship between Temüjin and his blood brother Jamukha. Even though Temüjin does not really seem to share that aspect of the love between them, Bekhter manages to not only infuriate him with his constant stealing and bullying but also to frighten him by needling him about his relationship to Jamukha. Interestingly, this added motivation works both within Mongolian thinking, where homosexuality is a taboo, as within the Western perception, where it introduces a more personal and thus perhaps more comprehensible reason. Still, despite his fury and fear, Temüjin gives Bekhter one last chance to change his ways before making the decision to kill him.

This moment of decision-making is presented as a rite of passage: The boy who enlists his brother Khasar to murder their half-brother and who plans this murder as one would plan a hunt is every part the master tactician, the efficient leader who will rise to power in the steppes. As no female character participates in the actual murder, the role of narrator is now filled by Khasar. His perspective is very much influenced by inner turmoil, as he has his own reasons to want Bekhter dead and at the same time shies away from the act. His consequent inability to judge how cold and collected Temüjin truly is, and to what extent this perception of his mirrors his own need for a strong leader, is directly conveyed to the reader.

> They stripped the body, left it on the hill, and herded the horses back to the forest. Temujin was silent. Khasar could not tell if his brother was rejoicing over his deed or already regretted it.[25]

This ambiguity in the face of the harsh reality of fratricide allows the reader to still believe in Temüjin's heroic qualities. The text encourages this interpretation by not establishing violence as the central factor in his successful rise to

25 Pamela Sargent, *Ruler of the Sky* (London: Chatto & Windus, 1993), 139.

power. This, again, is in part due to the story being almost exclusively narrated from the perspective of women who do not actively take part in battles, so that the reader is rarely directly confronted with this aspect of Temüjin's life.

Instead, the focus lies on Temüjin's qualities as a doer, a leader and a visionary – in short, on his qualities as a mythical hero as Schünemann defines them. His intelligence, his generosity and his close connection to Tengri, the God of Heaven, are decisive factors in his rise to power. The most important factor, though, is his charisma, which is exuded mostly through his eyes that captivated his first wife Börte (Bortai) when they were both children:

> Temujin seemed unlike the other boys she knew. [...] There were also his eyes, as wary and observant as a cat's, pale eyes unlike any she had ever seen.[26]

As the reader is almost exclusively told about this charisma through the eyes of women, of whom almost all end up becoming intimate with him – willingly or not –, there is always a clearly erotic connotation to these descriptions and thus to the character of Chinggis Khaan.

Another notable dimension of this sexual aspect is the fact that Sargent does not gloss over his violent acts of rape. However, though the horror of the women suffering through these acts is vividly described, these rapes always lead in the end to genuine passion or at least a stalemate, in which the woman in question no longer appears as a victim of violence. A reason for this shift in the characters' perception of rape seems to be that it allows the readers to continue to view Chinggis Khaan as a hero, as can be seen in the following example of Temüjin's first night with his main wife Börte. After their 'first time,' which essentially amounts to marital rape that Börte suffers through as a wifely duty, Temüjin explains himself:

> "Others tell me that a man must seize his woman, that otherwise she'll think he's a weakling and mock him in secret, and when I saw you, I couldn't hold myself back. But I –" His throat moved as he swallowed. "I wanted it to be more."[27]

In contrast to Schünemann's asexual hero, this passage clearly speaks to a more romantic version of a Western hero.[28] Upon closer inspection, though, it becomes apparent that the 'more' need not necessarily be love even if this may be the case in Temüjin's relationship with Börte and with some of his other wives. The main motivation appears, rather, to be his ambition for power – the need to prove to himself that he can conquer any woman, just as he can con-

26 Sargent, *Ruler of the Sky*, 56.

27 Sargent, *Ruler of the Sky*, 197.

28 The role Pamela Sargent's own gender identity plays for this portrayal would certainly be of great interest but cannot be further examined here due to spacial constrains.

quer any land. In this sense, violence is simply a means of realizing those ambitions, which the young Chinggis Khaan uses as pragmatically as he uses his intelligence.

Still, the novel's depiction of the young Chinggis Khaan is, for the most part, characterized by an approach sensitive to the matter of culturally and historically different perspectives towards violence. In contrast, the portrayal of the old Chinggis Khaan, who appears to be simply cold and cruel where his younger self had been heroically charismatic, seems to be almost exclusively dominated by a Western view. On the level of the text, it is the death of his blood brother Jamukha that marks the turning point. On a meta-level, it is apparent that this switch coincides with Chinggis Khaan's move beyond the steppes, which marks a crucial increase of violence both in terms of quality and quantity.

This change on the part of Chinggis Khaan is intensified through the gendered understanding of war and violence in the novel. The increase of male violence, which is centered on Chinggis Khaan, is contrasted to a mounting female desire for peace, which can be observed in the development of his mother Öelün (Ho'elun). In the beginning of the novel, her understanding of violence is very practical. She admonishes her first husband for failing to protect her, as he "'should have gone after [the enemy] [...] and put an arrow into his back'",[29] thus giving him no chance to come after them. After Temüjin's and Khasar's murder of Bekhter, though, which leaves her horrified, Öelün has to struggle to "'be as wise and practical as [Temujin].'"[30] A decade later – when Temüjin goes into battle after battle –, she wishes: "Let it end, she thought fiercely, knowing such a prayer was futile, that more wars would inevitably be fought."[31] Possibly because such a far-reaching evolution of character would appear unrealistic, this process culminates in another female character, Chinggis Khaan's wife Khulan, yearning for a different world. Instead of only wishing for an end to the violence, Khulan wishes for an alternative, for men finding other ways of occupying themselves. Promptly, the males label her wish "'a foolish thought'", as: "'There's nothing else. It's a man's work to make war [...].'"[32]

The strongest outward indication of the changes in Chinggis Khaan is the changed characterization of his eyes. Whereas their cat-like intensity had been positive for Börte, the first impression they make on Ch'i-kuo – a Chinese princess given to Chinggis Khaan against her will as a political gift and a guar-

[29] Sargent, *Ruler of the Sky*, 4.

[30] See Sargent, *Ruler of the Sky*, 143.

[31] Sargent, *Ruler of the Sky*, 243.

[32] Sargent, *Ruler of the Sky*, 459.

antee for peace – causes her to feel horror not only toward Chinggis Khaan but also toward the Mongolian people as a whole, who appear very barbaric to her.

> She had not expected to see such eyes. His had the folds of his people and hers, but they were pale eyes [...]. A demon's eyes, she thought, eyes from which nothing could be hidden, terrifying eyes she might see in her worst dreams.[33]

As the mature Chinggis Khaan grows colder and more distant towards the people around him, his attitude towards violence shifts accordingly. Chinggis Khaan recognizes the potential of terror for warfare and uses it towards his goal of ruling the world. He revels in it:

> "We are few," he said, "and our enemies are numerous. We could defeat them only by making them too fearful to resist. But I must admit that I took more joy in their deaths than I might have. To think that they might be nothing, that only a void awaited them – I could be happy believing that."[34]

In this vicious self-absorption, the old Chinggis Khaan no longer embodies a hero. If one follows Schünemann's definition of the term, he actually shifts towards the anti-hero by distinctly deviating from the ideal of the hero.[35] But this role shift is not completed, since an excuse for Chinggis Khaan's change is provided that allows keeping his moral integrity intact on the textual level.

Violence is no longer simply a means to an end but constitutes both a means and an end. The moment of violence is the only way for Chinggis Khaan to still feel alive and connected to reality, whereas the spoils have already ceased to bring him satisfaction:

> The void inside Temujin seemed to increase the more he won; he toyed with his spoils as if uncertain of what to do with them. Khulan did not know what caused the hollowness in his soul, but realized at last that he wanted his enemies to share his emptiness.[36]

This twisted utilization of violence to deal with the 'hollowness,' brought on by a steadily mounting fear of his own death and his inability to truly connect with others, is also recognized by Yisui, another of his wives: "He was a dying man, whose pain fuelled his rage; that was how she explained it to herself."[37]

Aside from making others share in his fear of death, Chinggis Khaan also tries to conquer it by attaining immortality. While this quest is supported by

33 Sargent, *Ruler of the Sky*, 530.
34 Sargent, *Ruler of the Sky*, 607.
35 Schünemann, *Mythos und Profit*, 182f.
36 Sargent, *Ruler of the Sky*, 583.
37 Sargent, *Ruler of the Sky*, 659.

historical sources, in *Ruler of the Sky* it is transformed into an obsession that steadily and increasingly corrodes his persona. By thus putting one of humanity's primal fears and his obsessive, necessarily futile attempts to deal with it at the center of the seemingly inhuman violence of the Western wars, the text humanizes the character of Chinggis Khaan. This allows a description of the violence and his role in it without turning him into a monster. He is responsible for it in the sense that he gave the orders, but he cannot really be held morally responsible if he is of an unsound mind. Chinggis Khaan remains in the role of the hero and can be redeemed in the end. Thus, his legacy would not be reduced to the memory of the deaths he brought to the world, as Khulan predicted.[38] Instead:

> His descendants might lose the world, but they would leave their mark upon it. [...] His realm would link the east and the west for a time, connecting lands long divided and unknown to one another, and something new would grow from them.[39]

In conclusion, the two approaches towards representing violence as featured in Sargent's *Ruler of the Sky* seem to be a direct consequence of the two different levels of violence found in the biography of Chinggis Khaan. The violence of the young Chinggis Khaan is conveyed to a Western readership by explaining medieval Mongolia and the role it ascribed to violence. In contrast, the violence connected to the old Chinggis Khaan – that is, the horrors of the wars beyond the steppes – can apparently only be rendered comprehensible by excusing Chinggis Khaan, by making him not fully responsible, as the violence itself is no longer excusable from a modern Western point of view. As 'realistic' historical novel,[40] *Ruler of the Sky* does not edit away the violence of the Western wars to make them less horrifying. Thus, in order to not alienate Chinggis Khaan from his readership, relating cultural perspective seemingly has to take a back seat next to the demands of portraying a mythical hero. But while Chinggis Khaan's unsound state of mind excuses him to an extent, it does also lead to his turning into a flat, one-dimensional character. This is furthered by the fact that the female narrators limit the insight into not only Chinggis Khaan himself but also his (male) world. In the last parts of the novel, so many new female characters are introduced that Chinggis Khaan becomes a minor character in his own story.

*****

[38] Sargent, *Ruler of the Sky*, 607.

[39] Sargent, *Ruler of the Sky*, 680.

[40] For a typology of the historical novel, see Ansgar Nünning, *Von historischer Fiktion zu historiographischer Metafiktion.* 2 Vols. (Trier: WVT Wissenschaftlicher Verlag Trier, 1995).

In Homeric's novel *The Blue Wolf*, too, Chinggis Khaan is not the narrator; instead, this role is embodied by his first comrade-in-arms, Boorchi (Bo'urchu). Just as the female point of view in *Ruler of the Sky* influences the novel's perspective on violence, the male point of view in *The Blue Wolf* has immediate consequences, as it allows the description of the violence of war. The way the text revels in this opportunity and its erotically charged language evokes what Edwards aptly describes as "'pornography of representation' that continues both to shock and excite us [...]."[41]

> I [Bo'urchu – JN] felt strange pleasure hewing into Merkid flesh. [...] If my blade became embedded, hitting but not slicing through the bone, my shoulder shuddered in protest. But when the thrust was true I felt pure elation – the body fell away, split in two, trembling, convulsing, gurgling, sometimes even with the sound of a death rattle as its spirit flew into my arm as fast as the wind.[42]

This 'blood lust' is excused and thus legitimized by a form of warrior code that is best characterized in a scene of Chinggis Khaan leading his men on a practice hunt in weather so cold that horses and men freeze to death:

> He had no pity for those who gave up, the sniveller, the weakling, the doubter, the paralysed. [...] And yet, to the man who struggled to the limit of his strength, who met pain with pain, wounds with wounds, he would give even his own coat lined with wolf's fur, which warded off the most bitter cold.[43]

In contrast to *Ruler of the Sky*, which is in large parts characterized by acknowledging the matter of (trans-)cultural perspective, *The Blue Wolf* ascribes to the Mongols, and especially to Boorchi, a code of conduct and honor that seems less a reflection of medieval Mongolia than of a modern Western interpretation drawing on the exotistic stereotype of the 'noble savage.'

But while the text does not differentiate between levels of violence, it does differentiate between legitimate and illegitimate forms of violence, placing the violence of war into the former category. It is excused not only by the above-mentioned warrior code, but also by modern Western understandings of violence or as Johan Galtung puts it:

41 Edwards, "The Geography of Violence," 299.

42 Homeric, *The Blue Wolf* (London, Orion Books, 2002), 99f. Original edition: Le Loup Mongol. Paris: Edition Grasset & Fasquelle, 1998)

43 Homeric, *The Blue Wolf*, 140.

> One way cultural violence works is by changing the moral color of an act from red/wrong to green/right or at least to yellow/acceptable: an example being 'murder on behalf of the country as right, on behalf of oneself wrong'.[44]

The length to which this value of war violence is embedded in Western society is mirrored by the fact that it is a vital part of the biography of Western heroes. In contrast, rape is presented as an illegitimate form of violence in Homeric's novel. Again, this reflects not so much medieval Mongolian ethics but modern Western concepts of the inviolability of human rights.

This distinction between socially accepted violence for the greater good and socially shunned violence for individual greed also marks the distinction between Boorchi, who figures not only as the narrator but as the 'true' hero of the novel, and Chinggis Khaan, its titular hero. Both of them possess the qualities of a mythical hero according to Schünemann. Their prowess and professionalism are never in doubt, nor are their roles as doers, visionaries and leaders, with Chinggis Khaan clearly being characterized as superior.

What sets Chinggis Khaan apart, above all, is his charisma, which again is mostly expressed through his eyes:

> Squatting around the fire, the shepherds described Temüjin's eyes – they were those of a big cat or a wolf, but greater still and more terrifying; undoubtly the mark of Tenggeri. Moreover, didn't the events of Temüjin's life, from his birth holding a clot of blood in his fist to the recovery of his wife, bear witness to Heaven's favour?[45]

The wolf-motif which the shepherds perceive as evidence of the divine marking of Chinggis Khaan, alludes to the mythical ancestors of the Mongols: a fallow doe and a blue-grey wolf.[46] And like the wolf in Chinggis Khaan with whom already the title identifies him shines through his eyes, Chinggis Khaan shines through the eyes of the wolf which Boorchi repeatedly sees in his mind's eyes and whose eyes bore into him like "two incandescent knife blades."[47] These mythical elements give rise to an almost animalistic quality in Chinggis Khaan, which is complemented by a seemingly telepathic ability to read people's minds and by an extraordinary way of interacting with women and horses:

> I was about to ask him how he had found the key to the black horse's heart, when he turned and said, with a radiant smile, "It's a secret, Bo'urchu. I cannot tell you

[44] Galtung, "Cultural Violence," *Journal of Peace Research* 27 (1990): 291-305. Here 292.
[45] Homeric, *The Blue Wolf*, 110f.
[46] See *The Secret History of the Mongols*, § 1.
[47] Homeric, *The Blue Wolf*, 17.

because only women and horses benefit from its charms. It is Temüjin Khan's caress!"[48]

But these qualities seem more appliqued than being a part of Chinggis Khaan's character. Attention is called to them so explicitly and abruptly that they do not quite fuse with the rest of his character traits. As a consequence, Chinggis Khaan appears cold and flat. This is partly due to the fact that the text either winnows out those episodes in the sources that would have given him a more rounded, more 'human' character or edits them in a way which again focuses on violence. For example, in *The Secret History of the Mongols*, his father asks his future father-in-law to muzzle his dogs because Temüjin is afraid of them.[49] In *The Blue Wolf* his father makes the same request[50] and though it is left in doubt whether or not Temüjin is actually afraid of dogs, he states full of conviction that "[he] would have buried [his] knife in their guts," had they not been muzzled, because he loathes dogs for being cowards.[51]

Furthermore, Chinggis Khaan appears almost incapable of forming emotional bonds. Instead of being torn over the fate of Jamukha (Jamuka), Chinggis Khaan only hesitates to kill him because he fears the consequences of breaking the basic sacredness of their bond as blood brothers.[52] And there is no doubt as to Temüjin's judgment of the Fratricide he commited: "I felt then as if a thorn had been pulled from my foot."[53] His whole being is focused on what Jamukha calls the "three treasures which make him strong which he'd never share with anyone":[54] his first wife Börte, power, and horses. As can be seen, however, when Chinggis Khaan starts a war over his kidnapped wife, his love to her is at least strongly interwoven with, if not reducible to, possessiveness. This clearly is the case with his horses, whose worth is mostly defined by his enjoyment of conquering them and conquering with them.

Power, therefore, is clearly the focal point of his 'treasures' and violence the preferred method of attaining and preserving it, which he is not shy to use even upon members of his own family if they question his standing.[55] Fitting seamlessly into this understanding of violence, Chinggis Khaan does not only see the rape of women as his right, because: "'[a]s the warhorse must obey his

48 Homeric, *The Blue Wolf*, 177.
49 *The Secret History of the Mongols*, § 66.
50 Homeric, *The Blue Wolf*, 11.
51 Homeric, *The Blue Wolf*, 13.
52 Homeric, *The Blue Wolf*, 250.
53 Homeric, *The Blue Wolf*, 65.
54 Homeric, *The Blue Wolf*, 251.
55 See for example Temüjin's reaction to Suchigil publically questioning the righteousness of his murder of her son Bekhter (Homeric, *The Blue Wolf*, 54f).

warrior, so the woman must yield.'"[56] He also understands and enjoys its psychological effect on the husbands of these women:

> "The most exciting thing is not the men we kill or the herds we take, but the women we make pregnant. Humiliating our enemies like that is the greatest pleasure battle can give a man."[57]

So while Chinggis Khaan possesses all the abilities of a hero, his cavalier attitude towards rape is seemingly the most important reason, coupled with his coldness and flatness of character, why he is not fully identified as the hero. He does not strive for betterment of the whole society but only for fulfilling his own personal ambitions of grandeur.

In sharp contrast, Boorchi – after forcing himself to rape his first wife to make her submit to his will, which horrifyingly backfires[58] – is no longer able to commit rape even when he tries to "be like the wolf", to be like Chinggis Khaan.[59] The figure of Boorchi adheres to modern Western restrictions on violence and to the heroic concept of fighting not primarily for his own ambitions but for the greater good, unlike the animalistic Chinggis Khaan. Boorchi comes close to violating these limitations, though, when he brutally tortures Jamukha to death after the latter had humiliated him by robbing him of his wife.[60] Even though he clearly is driven only by personal motives in this instance that lead to his ignoring a direct order of Chinggis Khaan, it does not really endanger his role as hero, as it proves his passion in war and in love, which puts him into the tradition of the kind of romantic hero, that also Pamela Sargent's Temüjin is established at.

Upon closer inspection, it is apparent that Boorchi strives for the same three treasures that constitute the objectives of Chinggis Khaan's ambition. But whereas Chinggis Khaan wants to possess his wife and his horses and wants power for himself, Boorchi truly loves his wife and his horse, to which he has an almost symbiotic relationship.[61] And though he strives for power, he wants it for the sake of his khaan so that it may reflect on the Mongol peoples. In this respect, Boorchi clearly possesses not only the skills and the charisma but also the inner motivation of a hero. As already mentioned, Chinggis Khaan's superiority to him is never directly questioned on the level of the text, but on the deeper level of the readers' perception, Boorchi's role as true hero not only sets him apart but puts him above Chinggis Khaan.

[56] Homeric, *The Blue Wolf*, 77.
[57] Homeric, *The Blue Wolf*, 316f.
[58] Homeric, *The Blue Wolf*, 76.
[59] Homeric, *The Blue Wolf*, 154.
[60] Homeric, *The Blue Wolf*, 258.
[61] See e.g. Homeric, *The Blue Wolf*, 122.

Again, it is through the representation of violence that the text hints at this aspect, as Boorchi continuously surpasses Chinggis Khaan on the battle field. A perfect example is the first time they ride together to recapture Temüjin's stolen horses, when Temüjin is almost over-powered by an enemy.

> He stumbled again but managed to brace himself and knock Temüjin off balance, who rolled over him. I had more luck. I grabbed his topknot, wrenched back his skull and slit his throat. Inflamed now, I cut off his head and laughed at the sight of his face in the first light. His bulging eyes wore a look of dumb amazement.[62]

Chinggis Khaan is without a doubt the one in charge, the one who makes the tactical decisions, the one in power. But it is Boorchi who outdoes him not only in matters of the heart but also in the heat of the battle, shining as the true hero.

A very important factor in Homeric's portrayal of *The Blue Wolf* and in his introduction of Boorchi as the hero, most likely is the fact that the historical sources only contain limited information on Boorchi. This allows an almost complete freedom in depicting him and thus shaping him into the perfect hero. On the other hand, however, it forces the author to create and re-write episodes in the sources in order to be able to give a clear-cut picture of his protagonist in the first place. The above-quoted scene gives an example for such a re-writing. Not only does *The Blue Wolf* give a more detailed account than *The Secret History of the Mongols,* mostly benefiting the characterization of Boorchi, but it also brutalizes the version in the sources, where the two young men manage to recapture the horses without any blood being shed.[63]

In conclusion, Homeric utilizes the element of violence as one of his main devices in characterizing and distinguishing his two central characters. To this end, the text employs a two-fold approach to the representation of violence, building upon a differentiation not based on levels of violence but values ascribed to it. In comparison to Sargent's novel, *The Blue Wolf* seems to relate the matter of cultural perspective more limitedly – e.g. in descriptions of daily routine – and not in relation to the representation of violence: The warrior code, which is presented as authentically Mongolian on the level of the text, turns out upon closer inspection to be a modern Western notion of the concept, marked by exotistic images. Consequently, the violence of the battle field is almost excessive, as it is justified on the textual level by the warrior code and on the interpretative level by modern Western ethics.

*****

[62] Homeric, *The Blue Wolf*, 8.

[63] *The Secret History of the Mongols*, § 90f.

Galsan Tschinag's *Die neun Träume des Dschingis Khan* focuses on the last days of Chinggis Khaan (Dschingis Khan) and reveals his life in flashbacks and feverish dreams. This shifting of time frames is mirrored in a shifting of narrative perspectives. The novel is narrated from the point of view of the dying Chinggis Khaan. While most of the text is mediated through the third person, often in the form of the impersonal "man," sometimes it switches to the first person in order to quicken the pace and to draw the reader ever closer into the story.

This novel, too, differentiates sharply between the young and the old Chinggis Khaan. The old and dying Chinggis Khaan remembers his vibrant young self with a degree of detachment that seems to suggest almost a personality split. Interestingly, this split is clearly marked by two different approaches towards violence on the textual level.

The young Chinggis Khaan embraces violence not only as a part of medieval Mongolian life but as a legitimate and intrinsic part of his destiny. Still, his rise to power in the steppes is not based primarily on his being vicious and cruel. The main factors, rather, are his intelligence, his vision, his passion and his perfectionism. As is the case in the other two novels, all of these qualities resonate with Schünemann's template of a hero. An example for this heroic quality is the episode of his horses being stolen. He does not win them back by brute force, as *The Blue Wolf* describes it, but by outsmarting his opponents. Pretending to be a shaman, he walks up to the men guarding the horses and uses the trust instilled by his assumed identity to send them away on various errands. He does use force to subdue the last remaining man but only knocks him unconscious before racing away with his horses.[64] While this scene showcases Chinggis Khaan's intelligence in battle, his reaction afterwards demonstrates his perfectionism, as he cannot stop thinking about a possibly even better way to have dealt with the situation and how he would have reacted, had the circumstances been different.[65]

But while his success may not be primarily based on violence, violence constitutes the basis of his pride and of his belief in himself. Chinggis Khaan is convinced that he is destined to be khaan and that to fulfill that destiny means utilizing violence:

> "Heißt es von euerm Khan nicht, dass er mit einem schafknöchelgroßen Blutgerinsel in der Hand ins Leben getreten sei? Er musste damit wohl eine aus dem Urgrund der Lebensquelle mitgebrachte Erkenntnis zeigen und sein künftiges Werk

64 Galsan Tschinag, *Die neun Träume des Dschingis Khan* (Main and Leipzig: Insel, 2007), 129-132.

65 Tschinag, *Die neun Träume des Dschingis Khan*, 136f.

> schon ankündigen wollen: Ohne Blut geht nichts mehr zwischen Himmel und Erde. Des einen Tod ist des anderen Leben."[66]

Against this backdrop, his unscrupulous use of violence can be read as testing heaven's favor, which is how the old Chinggis Khaan judges his younger self. An example is Temüjin's (Temüdschin) murder of his brother Bekhter (Bekter). The description of the deed itself keeps close to the sources both in content and in style of writing.[67] In hindsight, though, the young Chinggis Khaan is actually proud of having killed "nicht nur Aberschwärme neben Aberschwärmen von Menschen fremder Länder und Stämme, sondern auch meinen eigenen Bruder" without ever having been punished for it by heaven.[68]

In his feeling of superiority, Chinggis Khaan is fascinated by violence and its effect on others.

> [...] die Schneide des Schwertes verschwand genau dort, wo sie sollte: drei Fingerbreit unterhalb des Ohrläppchens, denn das war die einzig mögliche Stelle, gelegen zwischen Kieferknochen und Halsband, ein fingerbreiter, freier Streifen nur, wenn der Kopf mit einem Hieb abgeschlagen werden sollte. [...] Dennoch gab es, so sauber der Hieb auch ausgeführt war, einen kleinen Zwischenfall: Während der Kopf von den Schultern rutschte, kam ein Blutstrahl heraufgeschossen und traf Dschingis Khan mitten ins Gesicht. [...] ihm hätte es nichts ausgemacht, bis zum Ende der Abschlachtung des verhassten Tatarenpacks gerade mit dem blutüberströmten Gesicht dem grausig-lustigen Schauspiel zuzuschauen.[69]

The amount of detail in this depiction of violence certainly equals that of Homeric's description, for instance, of Boorchi's and Temüjin's attack on the Sovereigns. Yet, the description of the Tatar king being beheaded does not

66 Tschinag, *Die neun Träume des Dschingis Khan*, 43. ["'Isn't your khan supposed to have entered life with a blood clot the size of a sheep's ankle-bone in his hand? He must have wanted to demonstrate an insight that he had brought with him from the depths of the spring of life and herald his future work: Nothing gets done anymore between heaven and earth without blood being spilled. One man's death is another man's life.'"] – All translations of quotes in this article by JN unless otherwise noted.

67 Tschinag, *Die neun Träume des Dschingis Khan*, 110f.

68 Tschinag, *Die neun Träume des Dschingis Khan*, 151. ["not only masses and masses of people of foreign countries and clans, but also my own brother"]

69 Tschinag, *Die neun Träume des Dschingis Khan*, 42. ["[…] Because the blade of his sword vanished at the exact spot where it was supposed to: three fingers' breadth beneath the earlobe, as this was the only possible spot, located between the jawbone und neckband, a stripe of only a finger's breadth, if the head was to be chopped off with a single stroke. [...] But there was, as clear as the hit was executed, a little accident: While the head slid off the shoulders, a stream of blood gushed forth, hitting Chinggis Khaan directly in the face. [...] it would have been fine for him to watch the gruesome-funny spectacle till the end of the slaughtering of the hated Tatars, precisely with his face streaming with blood."]

give rise to 'pornography of representation,' as it evokes neither blood lust nor sensualized excitement. Instead, the pragmatic and clinical attitude seems to demonstrate a certain detachment on the part of the characters. Violence is a spectacle to "Ahh" about,[70] and in Chinggis Khaan's case, to be almost amused by as well. This almost cynical approach to violence allows the modern reader to keep a comfortable distance from the bloodiness while, at the same time, it implies a clearly critical judgment on the nonchalant Chinggis Khaan.

In sharp contrast to this detached, arrogant Chinggis Khaan, the old Chinggis Khaan's approach to violence is marked by humbleness and, above all, horror over his own past deeds. The resulting deep chasm between the young and the old counterparts becomes apparent in the very modern, very psychological evaluation of his own motivation. Whereas the young Chinggis Khaan valued defeats in battle for making him stronger, the old Chinggis Khaan values them as lessons in humbleness and moderation.[71] Whereas his young self was absolutely convinced of his divine right to be khaan and of the legitimacy of the violence he committed, the old Chinggis Khaan rues his excuses, which he now acknowledges as "Schutzwall vor dem eigenen schlechten Gewissen, ohne den es wohl kein Khanleben gibt."[72] The old Chinggis Khaan, who, interestingly enough, never really questions that destiny, is grateful for his status as khaan. For, if he had not become khaan and thus well cared for, he would have surely died a lonely and cold death a long time ago on some battlefield fighting for some lord.[73]

The decisive moment which initiates this change in Chinggis Khaan is his first encounter with his servant Oldoi, the "Findling" ("foundling"), who is an original character created by Tschinag.[74] They meet amidst the violence of the Western wars, which Oldoi brings to a halt by not running in panic and despair like the other inhabitants of the city. Instead,

> Er saß – richtiger gesagt: er ruhte – ein wenig abseits auf gekreuzten Beinen, mit einem breiten, seligen Lächeln auf dem Gesicht. Seine ganze Gestalt fiel auf: ein Zwerg, nicht größer als ein zwölfjähriges Kind, mit dem Gesicht eines Erwachsenen aber.[75]

70 Tschinag, *Die neun Träume des Dschingis Khan*, 42.

71 Tschinag, *Die neun Träume des Dschingis Khan*, 49f.

72 Tschinag, *Die neun Träume des Dschingis Khan*, 152. ["protective barrier against one's own guilty conscience, without which there would probably be no life as khaan."]

73 Tschinag, *Die neun Träume des Dschingis Khan*, 16ff.

74 Tschinag, *Die neun Träume des Dschingis Khan*, 27.

75 Tschinag, *Die neun Träume des Dschingis Khan*, 24. ["He was sitting – or more precisely: he was resting – a bit aloof on crossed legs, with a broad, blissful smile on his face. His whole

It is certainly of no coincidence that this first image of Oldoi strongly evokes commonly known imagery of Buddha, as he fulfills a role combining a jester and a wise man for Chinggis Khaan. Most importantly, he challenges his new master to reflect upon his decisions and actions. In that first encounter, Oldoi remarks on how lonely Chinggis Khaan's position as khaan really is, as he has no relatives anymore after they have been reduced to his subjects. At this point, Chinggis Khaan does not yet understand Oldoi's message.

It is only on his deathbed that this lesson slowly takes hold of him and he fully realizes the consequences of his reign, which are tied closely to his (ab-) use of the power and the violence at his command:

> Furcht einflößen, das war einer seiner Hauptvorsätze. Ob Völker oder Stämme, Führer oder Geführte, Khatune oder Dienerinnen … Wenn es sein musste, einen Teil des Volksstammes auslöschen, damit der andere Teil nicht in die Versuchung käme, ungehorsam zu werden [...].[76]

As successful as his psychological warfare was, he now recognizes that the price he paid for it was, indeed, loneliness: Through his enthusiastic use of his preferred tool, he even alienated his closest comrades and friends, who by now are so wary of him that they are unable to relax around him.[77] He recognizes his perhaps too swift rise to power, his hubris and most of all "[das] Meer von Blut, der Berg von Leichen, die Wüste von Asche"[78] he left in his wake as having been the true reasons for his fall – both for the literal fall from the horse and for the metaphorical one from the grace of his own false belief in heaven's favor, the grace of his ignorance. Under the guidance of Oldoi, who at this stage appears to be almost a mythical guiding spirit, Chinggis Khaan finally sentences himself to death, as he finds himself – or rather his younger self – guilty of so many and so horrible crimes that this seems to be the only possible atonement: "Der Preis seiner großartigen Siege ist Menschenschinderei, Zerstörung und Mord gewesen!"[79]

figure caught attention: a dwarf, no taller than a 12-year-old child, but with the face of an adult."]

76 Tschinag, *Die neun Träume des Dschingis Khan*, 228. ["Inspiring fear was one of his main objectives. Whether they were peoples or tribes, leaders or followers, the khan's wives or servants ... If need be, annihilate a part of a people so the other part would not be tempted to disobey..."]

77 Tschinag, *Die neun Träume des Dschingis Khan*, 216-222.

78 Tschinag, *Die neun Träume des Dschingis Khan*, 83. ["[the] ocean of blood, the mountain of bodies, the desert of ashes."]

79 Tschinag, *Die neun Träume des Dschingis Khan*, 230. ["The price of his splendid victories has been slave-driving, destruction and murder!"]

In conclusion, *Die neun Träume des Dschingis Khan*, too, presents two different perspectives on violence on the textual level. But as the episodes featuring the young Chinggis Khaan are mediated through the judgment of the old Chinggis Khaan, the latter's torment, and finally his decision to atone by sentencing himself to death, are so dominant that the critical voice of the old Chinggis Khaan is the only one to reach the reader on a meta-level. The extent as well as the seemingly almost pathological, obsessive quality of Chinggis Khaan's self-criticism is magnified by the fact that there is no distinction between either levels or forms of violence. When Galtung reminds his readers that "the mega-versions of the pale words used above for violence should also be contemplated,"[80] this is undoubtedly problematic in its ideological connotations. But it also very aptly stresses the fact that we emotionally and ethically differentiate between – to put it more pragmatically – different quantities of violence. Tschinag's Chinggis Khaan does not do that. He feels as guilty for the egoistic murder of his brother and for letting Jamukha die, as it was more convenient than finding a way to keep him alive,[81] as he does for the violence on and related to the battlefield that led to the deaths of thousands.

In comparison to Sargent's *Ruler of the Sky* and Homeric's *The Blue Wolf,* Tschinag's novel actually appears the most 'Westernized.' This finding is all the more interesting, as Tschinag is Tuvan and grew up in Mongolia, though he has spent a considerable part of his life in Germany and writes in German. He therefore combines an intimate knowledge of the Mongolian way of life and the Mongolian understanding of Chinggis Khaan with a clear understanding of Western ethics and literary norms. He does utilize his insights in order to convey medieval Mongolian reality to a modern readership, but as it seems, only insofar as it does not jeopardize Western acceptance and genre norms, which the violence of Chinggis Khaan has the potential of doing. It cannot be explained or excused but only atoned for.

This results in a portrayal of two extreme, almost antithetical personas of Chinggis Khaan: The young Chinggis Khaan at times seems as extreme in his arrogance and nonchalance as the old one is in the length to which he goes in his self-loathing and his desire to atone. The dominance of the old Chinggis Khaan on the textual and the meta-level results in a disqualification of the young Temüjin, negating not only the 'bad' – his approach to violence – but also the 'good' – his passion, his capacity for love, etc. It would be interesting to examine further how Tschinag's own transcultural biography and his at times ostensible play with genre norms factor into this tendency toward extremeness. In any case, even if one allows for an element of meta-fictional

[80] Galtung, "Cultural Violence," 292.

[81] Tschinag, *Die neun Träume des Dschingis Khan*, 153-159.

irony, the resulting portrait seems to tell Chinggis Khaan's "wahre, menschliche Geschichte"[82] less than a modern Western interpretation of such an undertaking.

*****

All three novels represent the Mongolian Other and its violence in a way which could be – with the possible exception of Tschinag – called 'otherness simulated for the own,' in a spin of agency compared to Welsch's postulation of transculturality turning authenticity into "ownness simulated for others."[83] Regardless of the agency, it is the 'simulation' which is the key term and which coincides with Scherpe's understanding of representation. But while the novels focused on here do not seem to consciously expose this simulation, the instances in which the illusion of an authentic representation of the Other are breaking down, do highlight the points where the violence of the represented Other can no longer be reconciled with the demands of genre convention interwoven with the expectations of their intended readership and, of course, with the authors' national, cultural and individual identities.[84]

The convention most important in these novels seems to be the shaping of the hero in the Western understanding of the term and the values and ethics associated with this narrative and social role. It is this basic conception which seems to necessitate the introduction of certain limits to violence, which the novels put to practice by introducing a clear distinction between legitimate and illegitimate violence. Contrary to Nieraad's thesis that popular literature would be less creative than 'high' literature due to the pressure exerted by norm expectations, however, these novels utilize this differentiation between two forms of violence creatively as a tool for characterization.

Thus, Sargent differentiates between the legitimate violence of the charismatic young Chinggis Khaan and the illegitimate violence of the unstable old Chinggis Khaan, affirming a critical approach towards violence that is illegitimate in its quality and quantity. Homeric contrasts Boorchi, who stays within

82 Tschinag, *Die neun Träume des Dschingis Khan*, 244. ["true, human story"]

83 Wolfgang Welsch, "Transculturality – the Puzzling Form of Cultures Today," 198. – For authenticity still being an important category of literary practice and theory, see Virginia Richter, "Authenticity – Why We Still Need It Although It Doesn't Exist," in *Transcultural English Studies. Theories, Fictions, Realities*, ed. by Frank Schulze-Engler and Sissy Helff (Amsterdam and New York: Rodopi, 2009), 59-74.

84 I have touched upon the latter aspect with regard to Galsan Tschinag. And although the spacial constraints of an article do not allow me to elaborate on this issue, it would be most interesting to further examine the impact of the authors' respective gender, ethnic, etc. identities.

the realm of the hero by staying within the realm of the legitimate violence of war, with Chinggis Khaan, whose perpetration of illegitimate violence coupled with a one-dimensionality of character disqualifies him as hero. By establishing Boorchi as the narrator, it is his critical point of view which is conveyed to the readership. Tschinag presents an apologetic viewpoint through the young Chinggis Khaan but negates it by the comments and the judgment of the old Chinggis Khaan, whose critical understanding of all forms of violence leaves only one possibility of atonement – his own death sentence.

While the novels thus differ in the extent to which they allow (trans-)cultural perspectiveness to shape the interpretation of violence, in their concrete ensemble of characters and the definition of legitimate and illegitimate violence, my findings clearly point to a number of structural parallels between the novels: On the fictional level of the text, they differentiate between legitimate and illegitimate violence – be it by level, value attribution or perspective – which they ascribe to two different personas. They present both an apologetic and a critical approach, but only affirm the critical one on a meta-level.

Thus, it seems that, instead of Nieraad's dichotomy of 'either – or,' literary representations of violence can also encompass an 'as well as,' mirroring the shifting nature of violence itself. The fact that all the novels analyzed here in the end present a critical view of violence further indicates that not all popular literature

> [...] continues to employ violence episodically or thematically in an unproblematic and reader-friendly manner within the context of fictional constructs of meaning and narrative conventions [...].[85]

The broad commercial success of these novels furthermore indicates that their shifting, critical representation of Chinggis Khaan and the violence associated with him mirror Western culture's general understanding of violence. And while nationality might indeed lose its attraction and power as a frame of identity, as concepts of transculturality suggest, there is obviously still a notion of the Own and the Other, connected by notions of authenticity and perhaps by what Scherpe, following Thomas Mann, calls modern Western societies' "'Durchbruchsbegierde' zur zivilisatorisch verlorenen 'Ganzheit' von Kultur, als 'Kultur' aktiviertes Helden- und politisches Kämpfertum."[86]

[85] Nieraad, "Violence and the Glorification of Violence in the Literature of the Twentieth Century," 1027.

[86] Scherpe, "Die Gewalt des Fremden," 367. ["desire to break through to the 'unity' of culture that has been lost to civilization, to the heroism and political combativeness activated as 'culture'."]

JULIKA SINGER (Heidelberg)

The visual representation of violence as political strategy – The illustration of the Mongol invasions of Japan in Meiji-period Japanese textbooks

This paper analyses the depictions of the Mongol invasions in Japanese history textbooks for elementary schools dating from the Meiji-period (1868-1912), i.e. the age of the emergence of the modern Japanese nation-state. It will be shown that there was a close relationship between the textbook depictions of the invasions and the various visual representations of the same events in official, government-related contexts. A special focus of the paper will be on the visual display and the political exploitation of the invasions' violence.

The pictorial representation of historical events – appropriately called history painting – grew to become one of the most esteemed painting genres in 19th century in the West as well as in Japan[1]. History painting involves more than mere reconstruction of historical events; in fact, it strongly mirrors contemporary values by symbolically linking history with topics such as nation, state and religion. And within the genre of history painting, the depiction of national myths is of particular importance, regardless of whether they are based on historical facts or purely invented. Especially in times of national crisis, they seem to have served individual and collective needs of stability, continuity and identification with a strong community. Such myths can only be effective with the help of the media and within a certain institutional environment. Being omnipresent without their precise origins necessarily being known contributes to the potency of national myths. This ubiquity, primarily a visual one, is achieved by popular institutions such as festivals or public rituals and by an advertisement-like repetition of visual images through various means of

1 An excellent introduction to and overview of Japanese history painting is offered by Yamanashi Toshio: *Egakareta rekishi: Nihon kindai to 'rekishiga' no kiba* (Tōkyō: Brücke, 2005) and by the exhibition catalogue with a similar title *Egakareta rekishi: Kindai Nihon bijutsu ni miru densetsu to shinwa – The Images of History in Japanese Modern Art*, ed. Prefectural Museum of Modern Art, Hyōgo; Prefectural Museum of Modern Art, Kanagawa (Tōkyō: Inshōsha, 1993).

communication such as books, paintings, magazines, etc. [2] Thus, in late 19th-century Japan, the repelling of the Mongol invasions, which represented an essential Japanese national myth, also found its representation in a broad variety of visual media and art genres ranging from the "high arts" made by and for elite artistic circles and popular woodblock prints to more function-oriented visual materials such as votive picture tablets (*ema*), postcards, bank notes as well as illustrations in school textbooks. In the myth-building process, textbook illustrations play a pivotal role as an official instrument of transmission, as they familiarize children with images of a myth from an early age on. Moreover, moral and didactic messages regarded as universal are transmitted to the public and hence used as an influential political instrument. As such, illustrations in school textbooks – which show rather close iconographical parallels to history painting – are a most revealing source in investigating the official political and ideological stances of a particular period, as they provide an insight into the contemporary educational goals, political values and conceptions of man. These depictions of the Mongol invasions are also illuminating with respect to the relations between Japan and Asia. As the ways in which Asian countries are portrayed in Japanese history textbooks have been central to the still-ongoing controversies about Japanese history textbooks since the end of World War II[3], these early illustrations of the Mongol invasions might also shed some light on an early phase of the developments that are relevant to this debate.

In any case, from the early Meiji-period onwards, strengthening of Confucian morality and virtue that were to provide a firm basis for the imperial authority clearly became the 'leitmotiv' of the school textbooks. This is, of course, the case with the illustrations as well. Their didactic and moralizing aims are manifested in the official education principle, the *Kyōgaku seishi* ("The Imperial Will on the Principles of Education") of 1879, in which the advisor and lecturer of the imperial household Motoda Nagazane (1818-1891) states:

> *It is necessary to engrave the holy duty of loyalty and filial piety in the minds of the young from the beginning of their school attendance and to admonish them by dis-*

2 Stefan Germer, "Retrovision: Die rückblickende Erfindung der Nationen durch die Kunst", in *Mythen der Nationen: Ein europäisches Panorama*, ed. Monika Flacke (München/Berlin: Koehler & Amelang Verlagsgesellschaft mbH/Deutsches Historisches Museum, 1998), 33-52.

3 On the controversies over Japanese history textbooks with a focus on the Japanese consciousness on their colonial past see: Sven Saaler, *Politics, Memory and Public Opinion. The History Textbook Controversy and Japanese Society* (München: Iudicium, 2005).
Ienaga Saburō, *Japan's Past, Japan's Future: one Historian's Odyssey* (Boston: Rowman & Littlefield, 2001).

playing images and illustrations of loyal followers of the emperor, children full of piety and faithful wives.[4]

Hence, illustrations in textbooks were to serve as instruments for inculcating young citizens with patriotic sentiments towards the Japanese emperor from an early age. From this educational perspective, the representation of the Mongol invasions in modern Japanese textbooks is of particular interest since the traumatic encounter of the 13th century was retrospectively viewed as a prototype of foreign threat and as such suitable to be applied to the ideological shaping of national subjects. In this context, the victorious outcome of the Japanese battle against the Mongols was used to underpin a notion of invincibility and a strong feeling of national consciousness among the members of the young Japanese nation-state. As is widely known, this interpretation was most fatally utilized in World War II, when thousands of young pilots plunging into US-warships with their airplanes were declared to be like the divine winds (*kamikaze*) that had once protected Japan from the Mongols.

But back to the textbooks: Around fifty illustrations of the Mongol invasions that appeared in official elementary school textbooks since the beginning of textbook production in 1872 up to the Second World War have heretofore been compiled.[5] Among them, an interesting development – a shifting preference for specific motifs – took place during the first decades of the Meiji-period that will be the subject matter of the following case study. In this period, nearly all textbooks contained merely one or occasionally two illustrations per chapter, hence the specimens of iconography deliberately chosen to represent a particular topic are quite revealing.

Methodologically, one can classify the image types into different iconographic categories and identify a process in the particular interpretation and display of the experienced violence. In the following, I will structure the material into three thematic types: The "revenge and punishment scenes", the "victorious battle scenes" and thirdly the "divine winds scenes".

The first category, "revenge and punishment", is characterized by an explicit display of violent acts as seen in figure 1.[6] This illustration is taken from the

4 Motoda Nagazane, "Kyōgaku seishi", *Kindai Nihon shisō taikei 30 – Meiji shisō shū I*, ed. Matsumoto Sannosuke (Echima shobō: Tōkyō, 1976), 263. [Translated by the author]

5 See *Nihon kyōkasho taikei kindai-hen*, 18-20, ed. Kaigo Muneomi (Tōkyō: Iwanami shoten, 1962-63); Noguchi Shūichi, „Mōko shūrai ni kakawaru sashie ni tsuite", *Niijima gakuen joshi tanki daigaku kiyō*. 22 (2002): 113-137. This study encompasses forty-eight illustrations from 1872 to 1944.

6 All textbooks, together with their illustrations mentioned in this text, can be found at the Tōyō bunko, the Oriental Library in Tōkyō, which has a particularly comprehensive collection of historical textbooks.

Shiryaku (Concise of History)[7], the earliest schoolbook on history from the Meiji-period, compiled by the Ministry of Education (*Monbushō*) in 1872. This illustration of the Mongol invasions shows a rather gory decapitation scene. On the upper left, one can recognize the 13th-century warrior Takezaki Suenaga presenting two head trophies to his commander Adachi Morimune, who sits on the right-hand side surrounded by a writer and two followers in the lower part. The warrior Takezaki Suenaga of the Higo province (today's Kumamoto prefecture) is famous for being an eyewitness of the invasions and having commissioned the earliest illustrated hand scrolls on the Mongol invasions in 1297, the *Mōko shūrai ekotoba*, the "Illuminated records of the Mongol invasions".[8] A comparison between the textbook scene and 13th-century hand scroll *Mōko shūrai ekotoba* and a 19th-century woodblock[9] print reveals that this image type is heavily indebted to classical models (figure 2 and 3)[10].

However, the connotation of the depiction has been greatly changed by having been taken out of its original narrative context and made to stand alone as being representative of the whole incident. Accordingly, the title in the cartouche says in a generalizing manner '*Batsu Genkō*' or "punishment of the Mongol invaders". This title distorts the meaning of the original scene in a subtle but substantial way. There, Suenaga is primarily demanding rewards for his service to the Kamakura military government to gain a confirmation of his status as a military retainer. In his late 13th-century scrolls, Suenaga himself pragmatically states: "The way of the bow and arrow is to do what is worthy of reward. Charge!"[11]. This is definitely not what the textbook illustration is suggesting: Here, the scene gains a new dimension pointing to a conflict and clash between two hostile nations. By the way, the none too informative text does not comment on the depicted scene but only briefly mentions the storm that arose during the battles, going on to dwell upon the sequence of the emperors and commanders of the time.[12] It is the titled image that carries a drastic nationalist notion of power and hierarchy which was part of the identity policy of the Meiji government.

7 *Shiryaku*, Ministry for Education and Culture (Monbushō) (ed.), Tōkyō: 1872.

8 Thomas Conlan's recent publication *In Little Need of Divine Intervention – Takezaki Suenaga's Scrolls of the Mongol Invasions of Japan* (New York, Ithaca: Cornell University East Asia Program, 2001) offers a full translation of the text into English together with important primary documents of the invasions as well as an interpretive essay.

9 The woodblock print is a part of the so called *Tankaku sōsho* version of the compilation *Fukuteki*-hen published in 1891 by Yamada An'ei.

10 All images appearing in this paper are reproduced with the kind permission of their owners.

11 Thomas Conlan, *In Little Need of Divine Intervention* (New York, Ithaca: Cornell University East Asia Program, 2001), 64.

12 *Nihon kyōkasho taikei – kindai-hen, vol. 18, rekishi 1*, ed. Kaigo Muneomi (Tōkyō: Kōdansha, 1963), 14.

It is quite conspicuous that an explicit display of violence as seen in the previous example is confined to the early years of the Meiji-period until around the Sino-Japanese war of 1894/95, in which Japan, striving to be treated on equal terms with the Western powers, emerged as a dominant power in East Asia. Popular motifs were the revenge scenes as well as the punishment of the Korean messengers, as can be observed in the *Teikoku shōshi* (Short History of the Empire) and the *Kōtō shōgaku kokushi* (National History for Higher Elementary School) in figures 4 and 5 – two scenes of a similarly violent and demonstrative display of asymmetric power. It is questionable, however, whether the captives could be recognized by readers as Koreans since the images are not labeled. The Korean captives submissively kneel in front of the regent Hōjō Tokimune (1251-1284)[13] and his retinue immediately before their execution – a scene referring to classical topoi that remains popular until about 1893 but completely vanishes thereafter.

This may also be due to the fact that the emphasis shifted towards more glorious scenes, i.e. motifs such as victorious battles and depictions of the divine winds which began to spread in the late 1880s. Until the end of WWII, this thematic group, the "victorious battle scenes", remained a popular type throughout the years.

One representative example of this kind of textbook is the *Shōgakkō yō rekishi* (History for elementary school) published by Tsuji Keisuke in 1887 and authorized by the government in the same year. This textbook is noteworthy in that it shows a strong emphasis on loyalty towards the emperor: The name of the emperor Meiji is written in large characters on the cover and frontispiece. Likewise, the text stresses imperial authority, mentioning Emperor Kameyama (1249-1305)[14] being deeply concerned about the invasions and dedicating a votive letter to the Great Shrine of Ise to pray for the welfare of the country. In particular, it calls attention to the praiseworthy merits of warriors known for their bravery, such as Sō Sukekuni[15] and the regent Hōjō Tokimune. While the early Meiji textbooks were scarcely informative and did not show any tendencies to elevate the Imperial house, this changed during the late 80s, and a strong emphasis on loyalty and bravery towards the Emperor or the country

[13] Hōjō Tokimune (1251-1284) was the eighth regent of the Kamakura military government, the *bakufu*, and is known for his merits in strengthening the national defense against the Mongols.

[14] Kameyama Tennō (1249-1305) is another high-ranking figure that is customarily associated with the defense against the Mongol invasions. He is said to have called on the wind gods of his ancestral shrine in Ise – successfully – to protect the Japanese islands.

[15] Sō Sukekuni (1207-1274) was the head of the Sō clan, a family that served for the governors of Dazaifu and the Tsushima island. He died during the first Mongol invasion in 1274, when the island Tsushima was almost completely devastated, and has since been worshipped as a tragic hero.

became evident in all kinds of textbooks. They were thus meant to serve as a means of shaping the minds of future soldiers who were expected to defend Japan as their ancestors did.

The illustration of the Mongol invasions in the *Shōgakkō yō rekishi* (History for Elementary School) reflects this attitude, as it displays the dramatic turmoil of a battle at the seashore with some heroic victorious Japanese warriors on horseback in the center driving back the Mongol troops into the sea (figure 6). Some of the latter are already about to drown while others are falling from their horses; to sum it up, their imminent defeat is obvious. In the background, furthermore, a Mongolian ship is tilting over dangerously against the backdrop of a gloomily gathering thunderstorm.

A formal analysis brings some remarkable features to light. With respect to iconography, one can recognize that the illustration combines different stages of the narrative plot of the invasions, mixing them together in one single scene (the victorious land battle, the storm, and the naval battle between the Japanese and the Mongolian ships are simultaneously shown). This rather arbitrary combination gives the illustration an iconic character that lets it stand as a symbol for the whole incident. In addition, the image style reflects a certain hybridity – a peculiar mixture of western and eastern elements – by using a composition known from Western battle depictions and by showing the Mongolian warriors in armor reminiscent of Roman warriors with protectors for arms and legs and round shields. The classical depiction of the Mongols as known from the Takezaki Suenaga's scrolls (figure 7), in contrast, show the invaders merely wearing battledresses made of softer cloth simply held together by a thin belt and a head gear with long sides and upper parts made of fur.

This iconography as well as the Western style of depiction must have been familiar to the contemporary school pupils, as it was borrowed from the reverse side of the one-yen paper bill issued in 1873 by the National Bank of Japan (figure 8, lower part). Despite the different image genres and techniques of image production, one can clearly make out close parallels with respect to the figure types. Also, the composition with the sloping coastline on the right hand side and the capsizing ship in the upper right, individual motifs such as a Mongolian warrior shooting backwards and the Japanese warrior at the center on a white horse are quite alike. This one-yen paper bill was valid for a quite long period – from 1873, i.e. the early Meiji-period, until 1899. As such, it must have been a most familiar scene for the contemporary Japanese. The design of the banknotes originally derives from the Western-influenced history painter and printer Ishii Teiko (1848-1897), who is famous for having developed the Western technique of lithography in Japan. By the way, in the early Meiji period, the final stages of banknote designing using a copper etching technique was carried out in the United States, so that the striking similarity to contemporary US bills is not surprising. Although Teiko's original design of the motif that was sent to the US became lost, there still exists a lithography dating from 1874 which is close to the motif on the bill (figure 9). Following the typical iconography of Western battle scenes as had been common in European paintings since the 17th century (for comparison, see figure 10: Delacroix's "Battle of Taillebourg" of 1843), the composition and iconography of Teiko's invasion scene show a distinctive emphasis on a centrally positioned figure on a white horse that is rearing up, contrasted with the enemies falling to the ground below. And even if the painting by Delacroix had not served as the model in this particular case, there would surely have been other Western paintings of battle scenes known to the Japanese contemporaries. The fact is that, in spite of a long Japanese tradition of pictorial representation of battles, Western-style images were favored for the official representation of the Mongol invasions in state-authorized textbooks as well as on national banknotes. As might be surmised, this was not just the case with the depictions of the Mongol invasions but the general trend in early Meiji-Japan with respect to officially endorsed art until the 80s and early 90s of the 19th century.

A closer analysis of the banknote's immanent iconographical context gives further insights into its symbolic loading: There is a meaning that is deliberately conveyed by the combination of the different subjects shown on the back and front of the bill.

On the back side, one can see an approaching ship with warriors on the left-hand side, and on the other side, there is a warrior with a ferocious facial expression leaning on a large bow (figure 8, upper part). There are different opinions concerning the identity of this archer. While some suggest that he is the famous archer Minamoto no Tametomo[16], information from the Bank of

[16] See, for example, Uemura Takashi, *Shihei shōzō no rekishi* (Tōkyō: Tōkyō bijutsu sensho, 1989), 56-57.
Minamoto no Tametomo (1139-1170) was a warrior fighting on the side of Emperor Sutoku (1119-1164) in the late-Heian Hōgen rebellion (1156). He was known for his incredible skills with bow and arrow. However, after being defeated by his brother Minamoto no Yoshitomo (1123-1160) and the later shōgun of the new military government, Taira no Kiyomori (1118-1181), he was exiled to Izu island, where he is said to have committed the first recorded ritual suicide.
The figure appearing on the paper bill from 1873 is also quite possibly Minamoto no Tametomo. In this case, the image would be a symbol for the loyality and dedication towards the emperor and a statement of disapproval of the earlier military government, the *bakufu*, which first came into existence in the Kamakura-period (1185-1333) with Taira no Kiyomori as its first shōgun. This interpretation would also fit the political slogan *sonnō jōi* ("worship the emperor and expel the barbarians") which became extremely popular in the 1850s and 1860s.

Japan and some Meiji-period documents[17] indicate that he is Kamitsukeno Tamichi, an ancient figure from one of Japan's oldest existing semi-mythological historical records, the *Nihon shoki* ("Japanese Chronicles") dating from 720. In this text, Kamitsukeno Tamichi, a historical figure who was later to become a Shintô deity, is characterized as a high-ranking commander of Emperor Nintoku in the 4th century who gained merits in battles against the Korean kingdom of Silla but later lost his life while defeating the so-called Emishi, the "barbarians" who inhabited the northern parts of the Japanese islands.[18]

This delicate combination of the Mongol invasions with the tragic commander Kamitsuke no Kimi evokes the image of a doubly belligerent Japanese nation: Well-fortified against foreign invaders on the one hand, and prepared to fight against internal trouble makers with rigor on the other.

This image, created as a kind of omnipresent admonition to the Japanese nation (since the one-yen paper-bill was the most numerously printed banknote), can also be understood as a symbolic metaphor for a young and not yet stable nation that had to deal with the external threat of foreign (Western) powers as well as with the internal uprisings of the discontented former warrior-class, which had been deprived of their privileges beginning in 1869 and whose last rebellion culminated in the so called Seinan war[19], a civil war, in 1877.

The remembrance of victorious historical battles against foreigners within and outside of Japan, even if they had taken place many centuries ago, seems to have been used as a stabilizing and comforting spiritual prop by the young Meiji-state.

Besides such scenes of victorious battles and the aforementioned punishment scenes, there is a third pictorial type that was often used to represent the Mongol invasions: the depiction of the divine winds. This motif particularly gained enormous popularity around the time of the Sino-Japanese War of 1894/95; during these years, it was stunningly predominant. The textbook illustration seen in figure 11 shows a dramatic typhoon scene influenced by the traditional Japanese painting style, as can be recognized by the bold diagonal brush strokes suggesting the ravaging tempest and some decorative clouds on

[17] *Hōki bunrui taizen – shihei-hen* 2, 1894; Institute for Monetary and Economic Studies – Bank of Japan: http://www.imes.boj.or.jp/cm/htmls/feature_gra2-10.htm (accessed July 2009)

[18] Aston, William George, *Nihongi – Chronicles of Japan* from *the Earliest Times to A.D. 697*, (Tōkyō: Tuttle Classics of Japanese Literature, 2005), 296-297. The original article was published in *Transactions and Proceedings of The Japan Society London, Supplement I, Volume I*, (London: Kegan Paul, Trench, Trübner & Co., 1896).

[19] The Seinan war of 1877, also called the Satsuma rebellion, was a revolt by former warriors from the province of Satsuma (today's Kagoshima) against the Meiji government. It lasted more than half a year and was the last and most serious uprising against the newly established government.

the bottom typical for Japanese paintings. It was published in the *Kōtō shōgaku shinrekishi* (New History for Higher Elementary School) in 1893 and executed by the popular history painter Matsumoto Fūko (1840-1923)[20]. The prominence of his name is revealed by the artist's seal on the bottom right. It is likely that there was a Japanese style painting that served as a model for the illustration since Fūko actually painted this special scene in various formats (one famous example is the hanging scroll *Mōko shūrai-zu* from 1900 which is in a private collection[21]). They basically go back to the almost identical depiction of the Mongol invasion on a hanging scroll by Kikuchi Yôsai (1788-1878) which is dated to 1862 (figure 12). The textbook illustration seems to be a close-up of the scene shown in the hanging scroll painting. This portrayal of the fateful moment of the Mongolian fleet's sinking is set against an elaborate and almost romantic scenery of nature with an ominously darkening sky and a rough sea, suggesting a turbulent storm and tempestuous forces of nature. The execution in wet ink washes and light color emphasizes the atmospheric impact of the scene. In the lower part, one can recognize some tiny figures of the Japanese warriors watching the dramatic scene safely sheltered under some pine trees. There is no display of a heroic battle, no individually recognizable human character and not the slightest trace of man-made violence. It is obviously nature that dominates the small human beings; in short, this is the depiction of the divine winds, the *kamikaze*.

As an artist and the head of a painting school, Matsumoto Fūko was involved in a great number of educational textbook designs, beginning with his illustrations of the *Yōgaku kōyō* (The Essentials of Learning) that was published in 1881 and written by the above-mentioned educator of the imperial household, Motoda Nagazane. In the following years, Matsumoto Fūko was actively engaged in the illustration of numerous schoolbooks and became an influential textbook illustrator. As such, he deserves a closer examination.

But first, the trends in the politics of art in his time should be briefly described. During the late 1880s and beginning 1890s, the officially patronized imagery underwent a great stylistic change. As we have seen in the former textbook illustration, in the first decades of Meiji-period, the Western-style painting was officially fostered, as anything of Western origin was eagerly

[20] Matsumoto Fūko (1840-1923) was one of the most prominent illustrators of the early Meiji period. He participated in the production of official textbooks, magazines and newspapers. Besides, he was one of the leading figures of the newly emerging *Nihonga* circles in Tōkyō and fostered the development of history painting, a genre to which he was introduced by his mentor Kikuchi Yōsai (1788-1878).

[21] A color plate can be found in *Egakareta rekishi: Kindai Nihon bijutsu ni miru densetsu to shinwa – The Images of History in Japanese Modern Art*, ed. Prefectural Museum of Modern Art, Hyōgo; Prefectural Museum of Modern Art, Kanagawa (Tōkyō: Inshōsha, 1993), 139.

emulated. However, in the following decades, there was a clear shift towards more traditional modes of pictorial depiction. This reflects a re-assessment of the "original" Japanese culture and arts as was enthusiastically propagated by influential cultural reformers such as Ernest Fenollosa (1853-1908) and Okakura Kakuzō (1862-1913) (alias Okakura Tenshin, who is known in the West for his famous *The Book of Tea*).[22]

Evidently, this development was not just confined to cultural matters. In 1890, the eminent Imperial Rescript on Education (*kyōiku chokugo*) proclaimed new moral guidelines for the educational system that was based on a Tennō-centered patriotism and at the same time admonished the Japanese subjects not to carry Westernization too far. Fittingly in this political atmosphere, Okakura Kakuzō became one of the principal founders and head of the influential Tōkyō bijutsu gakkō (Tōkyō Academy of Fine Arts) in 1891. As such, he was directly involved in the development of the educational system and its driving forces, and one of his favored artists was the above-mentioned painter Matsumoto Fūko. Fūko himself was an early pioneer in the development of the modern Japanese-style painting called *Nihonga* – a neo-traditionalist painting genre which still enjoys vitality today and is formally defined by the use of traditional techniques and materials such as ink and mineral color on silk or paper. The painting formats also refer back to traditional ones such as hanging scrolls, hand scrolls or folded picture screens. Through the establishment of departments within official exhibitions and art academies exclusively for *Nihonga* and for western-style painting (the so-called *Yōga*) since the 1890s, the *Nihonga* genre was deliberately juxtaposed to the western-style painting, and an officially endorsed dichotomy between "national" and "foreign" paintings emerged.[23] Therefore, the preference for traditional Japanese-style illustrations

[22] Interestingly enough, important stimuli for a revival of the Japanese artistic and cultural traditions came from outside of Japan. In his pioneering speech *Bijutsu shinsetsu* ("The True Theories on the Arts"), the American philosopher Ernest F. Fenollosa (1853-1908) first mentioned the concept of *Nihonga*, the indigenous Japanese-style painting, and encouraged the Japanese to foster and promote their aesthetic heritage. Always aware of the marketability of the Japanese arts, which had already gained a high reputation through the world fairs and the European Japonism, he initiated a movement for the preservation and an innovative revival of the Japanese arts – a project which his disciple Okakura Kakuzō (1862-1913) was to carry on and shape distinctively. For further information, see Doris Croissant, "Fenollosas ‚Wahre Theorie der Kunst‘ und ihre Wirkung in der Meiji-Zeit (1868-1912)". *Saeculum – Jahrbuch für Universalgeschichte*, 38/1 (1987).

[23] It has to be noted that this dichotomy, which continues to even characterize contemporary painting, can of course never be an absolute one since artistic currents cannot be tied to an arbitrary art-political concept and there have always been stylistic overlaps and vivid mutual influence.

in schoolbooks can bee seen as a clear political statement and a part of the identity-formation policy of an increasingly self-confident nation state.

Incidentally, Matsumoto Fûko's teacher Kikuchi Yōsai (1788-1878) created several paintings with this topic.[24] Since Kikuchi Yōsai was one of the most eminent history painters at the close of the Edo-period, his disciple Fūko's textbook illustration is a citation of a renowned traditional painting that dates back to pre-modern times. During the 1890s, Yōsai's hanging scrolls were published in journals and widely known[25], and it probably inspired his disciple Matsumoto Fūko to do similar paintings such as the six-paneled folding screen seen in figure 13.

Here, on the folding screen, the *kamikaze* scene gains a more narrative thrust than that on the hanging scrolls due to its horizontal format. On the folding screen, in comparison, the human figures are much more emphasized and the storm-tossed Mongolian ships are more dramatically in motion. However, the most significant difference compared to the hanging scroll is the screen's formation as a pair, meaning that it has a counterpart – a common practice for folding screens. This second painting which forms the right half of the screen pair also represents a historical scene of a belligerent encounter with an Asian country. It depicts a scene from the first attempt by Toyotomi Hideyoshi, the famous military ruler and one of the unifiers of Japan, to invade Korea in 1593 (figure 14) and shows the victorious battle at Byokchekwan, where Hideyoshi's army under the command of Kobayakawa Takakage triumphed over a Chinese force. It was one of the few victorious episodes in Toyotomi Hideyoshi's megalomanical attempt to conquer not only Korea but also China in late 16th century.

This screen pair was shown at the 4th National Industrial Exhibition (*Naikoku kangyō hakurankai*) in 1895 and was enthusiastically praised[26], as it was regarded as symbolizing Japan's Zeitgeist shortly after its victory over China. This screen pair is elaborately composed: On each side, the Japanese warriors are shown in the foreground, and the respective alien enemy seems to almost disappear into the misty background. Thus, it is not only in formal respects that the two parts of the screen mutually correspond with each other. Taken together, they give expression to a historical interpretation that was popular at

24 There is an even earlier and very close portrait of the divine winds dating to 1847 by Kikuchi Yōsai. See *Dschingis Khan und seine Erben*, exhibition catalogue of Kunst- und Ausstellungshalle der Bundesrepublik Deutschland (München: Hirmer Verlag, 2005), 331.

25 One can find Meiji-period reviews, for example, in the art-journal *Kokka* (No. 107) from 1898 or in Fujioka Sakutarō's book on the history of pre-modern painting *Kinse kaiga shi* from 1903.

26 He won the third art prize (*myōgi shō*) at the 4th National Industrial Exhibition's competition.

the time and which one can also find in the writings of Okakura Kakuzō.[27] The earliest written references to his theories concerning the Mongol invasions can be found on the first pages of his book, Japanese Art History (*Nihon bijutsu shi*), based on the lectures which he held in 1890-1893 at the Tōkyō bijutsu gakkō (Tōkyō Academy of Fine Arts). After this, he left a great number of comments on the Mongol invasions in his English-language books *The Ideals of the East* (1903) and *The Awakening of Japan* (1904), repeatedly establishing a rather questionable causal relationship between the 13th-century invasions and later belligerent encounters with other countries:

> *A long time ago, our ancestors subdued the Three Kingdoms [of Korea] and defeated the mighty armies of the Mongols. Though we ourselves did not live through those times, the colonization of the Three Kingdoms and the incident involving the Mongols became as historical events, a part of our thought.*[28]

> *Their [the Mongol's] belligerent attitude continued for nearly forty years; and though, thanks to our insular position and the prowess of our warriors, we were able successfully to repel their attacks, remembrance of their aggression was not to be effaced, and even led to retaliatory steps on our part. The memory of our ancient friendship with the courts of the Tang and Sung dynasties was lost. One of the latent causes of our late war with the Celestial Empire [China] may be found in the mutual suspicion with which the two nations have now regarded each other for many centuries.*[29]

> *The attempted Mongol invasion of the thirteenth century kindled in us a feeling of animosity toward the Koreans who led the Chinese vanguard. Our only act of retaliation, however, consisted in the unique expedition of the Taiko Hideyoshi, who, in the sixteenth century, led an army into Korea to measure swords with those whom he considered as his hereditary enemies.*[30]

These comments on the Mongol invasion imply that Toyotomi Hideyoshi's invasion attempts at the end of the 16th century had been an act of revenge against Korea and China for the earlier Mongol invasions – a futile retaliatory strike which was finally brought to fruition three hundred years later in 1895 with the victory in the Sino-Japanese war. Matsumoto Fūko's pair of folding screens that were publicly celebrated just after the Japanese victory in that war reflects this view of history.

[27] Kawazoe Shōji, "Okakura Tenshin no Mōko shūrai kan", *Nihon rekishi*, 524 (1992).

[28] Okakura Kakuzō, "Nihon bijutsu shi", *Kindai Nihon shisō taikei, 7: Okakura Tenshin shū* , ed. Umehara Takeshi (Tōkyō: Echima shobō, 1976), 195. [English translation by the author]

[29] Okakura Kakuzō, *The Awakening of the Japan* (New York: The Century Co., 1905), 12-13.

[30] Ibd., 205.

Okakura Kakuzō's writings also touch upon the relationship between the West and Japan as he compares the fateful arrival of the American warships under the command of Commodore Perry in 1853 that initiated the opening of the country to the onslaught of the Mongolian fleet in the 13th century (that he here calls "Tartar armada").

> *The appearance of American war-ships in the bay of Yedo [Edo] was a mighty shock. Hitherto the alarms of foreign attack had meant but little to the country at large, for it was a long cry to Hakodate or Nagasaki; but now within a day's march of the city of Yedo lay the black hulks of a formidable fleet whose admiral refused to retire until a treaty was signed. Recollection of the Tartar armada flashed through the minds of our grandfathers. Was the samurai to be intimidated in his own waters? Was not the divine land always prepared to repel an invasion?*
>
> *What right had a foreign nation to impose a commerce which we did not want, a friendship which we did not ask? To arms! Jhoi! Jhoi! Away with the barbarians! The alarm-bells clanged throughout the country. Foam-covered riders rushed through every castle gate, spreading the momentous news. Spears were torn from their racks and ancient armor was eagerly dragged from dust-covered caskets. Night and day could be heard the clanging of steel on anvils forging the accoutrements of war. The old prince of Mito was summoned from his hermitage to take command, and his cannon lined the principal points of defense. Buddhists wore away their rosaries in invoking Kartikiya, the war-god, and Shinto priests fasted while they called on the sea and the tempest to destroy the invader.*[31]

In this account of the dramatic late Bakumatsu events, Kakuzō gives expression to the widespread belief in Japan's invincibility due to its divine protection. As already mentioned, the mythic-religious belief in the *kamikaze* – the divine winds that once had purportedly saved Japan from the Mongols – was the most popular topic in late 19th century's textbook illustrations. Accordingly, Matsumoto Fūko's *kamikaze* imagery is no singular phenomenon. While, in the previously discussed textbooks, the typhoons accompanying the invasions play a subordinate role and are, in addition, not referred to as being of divine origin, this assessment changes in a striking manner. Beginning in the late 1880s and 1890s, this mythical aspect of the invasions narrative suddenly becomes noticeably predominant: In the brief period between 1889 and 1894, an astonishing majority (15 of 23 illustrations found) of schoolbooks chooses the kamikaze-scene to illustrate the Mongol invasions. The illustrations seen in figures 15 a–d offer some examples of this phenomenon.

The schoolbook texts of this time aim to strengthen the patriotic consciousness by claiming that Japan was the only country which had been able to resist

[31] Ibd., 110-112.

the Mongols[32], stressing the importance of a strong military and a united populace to defend the nation against its enemies, praising the heroic bravery of the Japanese warrior, etc. The crucial difference from the previous decades, however, is the predominant stress on the supernatural and religious aspect of Japan's victory. The texts of this period emphasize the role of the Imperial house even more than that of the warriors or the military leader Hōjō Tokimune, especially focusing on the supposed merits of Emperor Kameyama, who had prayed for divine intervention.[33]

However, in the following decades, the kamikaze scenes fade away, not to reappear until the ultra-nationalist era of the 1930's. As the state's demand for soldiers committed to self-sacrifice grew, the representation of the Mongol invasions likewise changed to blunt war propaganda with an explicit stress on the national and religious aspects of the divine protection of Japan, the land of the gods.

This case study has offered just a small insight into a larger project that has yet to be finished. However, as images are a source of construction of our images of reality, and as they consequently shape our self-perception and influence the ways we perceive our environment, it is of great importance to look more closely at just such marginalized visual materials as historical textbook illustrations.

As the foregoing analysis was able to show, the Meiji-period textbook illustrations of the Mongol invasions reflect the historical situation at the time of their production in many ways. It is not only the chosen styles and models of the illustrations but also the choice of specific motifs which reflect the political background and the corresponding identity-formation policies of a particular period. As such, the "revenge-and-punishment scenes" with an explicit display of violent power against foreigners were favored in the early years of the Meiji-period when Japan had not yet established itself amongst the imperialist industrial nations and had itself to fear imperialist infringement from Western powers. Its vanishing popularity may well be due to the fact that Japan itself went on to become an imperialist power that was no longer in need of this kind of demonstrative and violent display of power.

Instead, there was a shift towards more glorious scenes such as the victorious battle scenes – a topic that could also be found on the one-yen paper bill

[32] This claim is not quite accurate since several other countries, as for example Vietnam, Java and the empire of the Mamelukes, were also able to resist the medieval Mongol invasion attempts.

[33] Noguchi Shūichi, "Meiji-ki ikō reikishi kyōkasho ni okeru Mōko shūrai shōkō", *Kyōai gakuen Maebashi kokusai daigaku ronshū*, 2 (2002), 97.

and was to remain popular throughout the whole Taishō (1912-1926) and early Shōwa (1926-1989) period. Here, the heroic merits of brave warriors were emphasized, and the focus lay on the strengthening of the national military capabilities precisely in accordance with the official slogan *fukoku kyōhei* (enrich the country and strengthen the army).[34]

Later on, the motifs in the late 80s and 90s of the 19th century shows a great inclination towards the divine-winds imagery; it was taken up precisely at the time of military aggression, this time on the part of the Japanese against the great Asian neighbor China. In these depictions of the *kamikaze*, human strength appears to be insignificant in the face of the almighty celestial power.

Hence, in conclusion, one can state that the representation of power and violence in 19th-century history textbooks was progressively sublimated; here, the very apt German expression "Gewalt" in the sense of concrete physical violence turned into an immaterial "Gewalt" coupled with the notion of supernatural power and might. Of course, this may have partly had to do with the nature of the images – gory scenes such as those in the early-Meiji textbooks might have been found inappropriate for elementary school pupils. It is, however, conspicuous that the mythological-religious interpretation of the Japanese victory over the Mongols came to flourish just in the years when Japan itself was turning to aggression. The pictorial 'euphemism' that conveyed the notion of a divinely ordained Japanese invincibility, so it can be surmised, helped elevate patriotic feelings far more than any display of naked violence could ever have done. Incidentally, during the relatively liberal era following the Meiji-period, namely the Taishō-period (1912-1926), the medieval events were in most cases conveyed in a more objective and scholarly manner, with maps, photographs and portraits of important figures serving as illustrative materials, and the texts generally refrained from stressing mythological-religious features. It can thus be observed in retrospect that the enthusiasm for the *kamikaze* theme during the Sino-Japanese War foreshadowed the disastrous culmination of its exploitation in World War II.

34 The words '*fukoku kyōhei*", derived from a concept which had had its origins in China of the Warring States (c. 403-221 BCE), became the central slogan and national rallying cry of Meiji Japan since the 1870s. *Fukoku kyōhei* entailed the formulation of far-reaching policies to transform Japanese society in an all-out effort to catch up with the West.

Fig. 1: *Shiryaku* (Concise of History), woodblock-printed book, 1872; Tōyō bunko, Tōkyō

Fig. 2: Detail of the *Mōko shūrai ekotoba* (Scrolls of the Mongol Invasions), handscroll with ink and colors on paper, second scroll 40,2 × 2111,8 cm, 1297; Sannomaru Shōzōkan, Tōkyō

Fig. 3: *Tankaku sōsho* version of the compilation *Fukuteki-hen* published in 1891 by Yamada An'ei; Tōyō bunko, Tōkyō

Fig. 4: *Teikoku shōshi* (Short History of the Empire), woodblock-printed book, 1888; Tōyō bunko, Tōkyō

Fig. 5: *Kōtō shōgaku kokushi* (National History for Higher Elementary School), woodblock-printed book, 1887; Tōyō bunko, Tōkyō

Fig. 6: *Shōgaku kōyō rekishi* (History for Elementary School), woodblock-printed book, 1887; Tōyō bunko, Tōkyō

Fig. 7: Detail of the *Mōko shūrai ekotoba* (Scrolls of the Mongol Invasions), handscroll with ink and colors on paper, first scroll, 40,3 × 2450,6 cm, 1297, Sannomaru Shōzōkan, Tōkyō

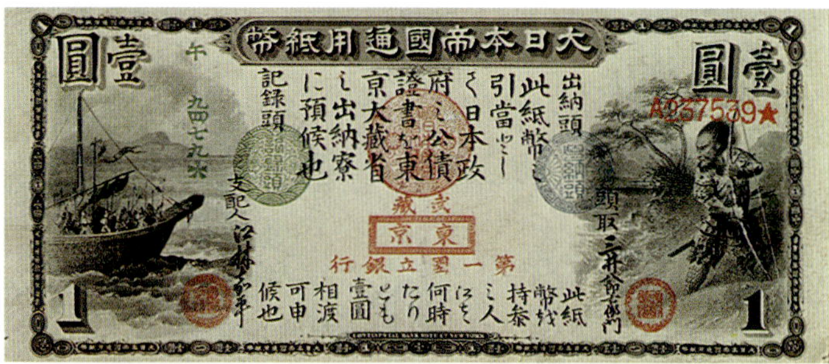

Fig. 8: One yen paper bill, 1873; Bank of Japan, Tōkyō

Fig. 9: Ishii Teiko: *Kōan yo'nen ōgenpei ochikkai zu* (The Elimination of the Mongols at the Sea of Echizen in the Year Kōan 4), lithography, 26,2 × 38,9 cm, 1874; City Museum, Kōbe

Fig. 10: Eugène Delacroix: *Battle of Taillebourg*, oil on canvas, 485 × 555 cm, 1847; Musée du Louvre, Paris

Fig. 11: Matsumoto Fûko: Illustration of the *Kōtō shōgakkō shinrekishi* (New History for the Higher Elementary School), woodblock-printed book, 1893; Tōyō bunko, Tōkyō

Fig. 12: Kikuchi Yōsai: *Mōko shūrai* (The Mongol invasion), hanging scroll, ink and light color on silk, 161,2 × 83,2 cm, 1862; Prefectural Museum, Shizuoka

Fig. 13: Matsumoto Fūko: *Mōko shūrai zu* (The Mongol invasion), 1895, six-paneled folding screen, colors and ink on silk, 162,7 × 365,6 cm; Seikadō Bunko Art Museum, Tōkyō

Fig. 14: Matsumoto Fūko: *Hekiteikan zu* (Battle of Byokchekwan), six-paneled folding screen, colors and ink on silk, 162,7 × 365,6 cm, 1895; Seikadō Bunko Art Museum, Tōkyō

Fig. 15a: *Shogaku shidan* (Talk on History for First Learners), woodblock-printed book, 1893; Tōyō bunko, Tōkyō

Fig. 15b: *Nihon shō rekishi shoho* (First Steps in a Short Japanese History), woodblock-printed book, 1893; Tōyō bunko, Tōkyō

Fig. 15c: *Kōtō shōgaku Nihon rekishi* (Japanese History for Higher Elementary School), woodblock-printed book, 1894; Tōyō bunko, Tōkyō

Fig. 15d: *Shintai Nihon rekishi shoho* (New First Steps in Japanese History), woodblock-printed book, 1894; Tōyō bunko, Tōkyō

Personenregister

Ortsregister